TO TAYLOR — Hoping this
does not create a fear of
flying —
Bill Hubert

PILOT HERE OR PILE IT THERE

A Memoir

Flight-Fright-Plight-Delight

Lt. Col. William E. Hubert, USAF (Ret.)

Bloomington, IN   authorHOUSE®   Milton Keynes, UK

AuthorHouse™
1663 Liberty Drive, Suite 200
Bloomington, IN 47403
www.authorhouse.com
Phone: 1-800-839-8640

AuthorHouse™ UK Ltd.
500 Avebury Boulevard
Central Milton Keynes, MK9 2BE
www.authorhouse.co.uk
Phone: 08001974150

First published by AuthorHouse 12/18/2006

ISBN: 978-1-4259-5689-9 (sc)

Printed in the United States of America
Bloomington, Indiana

This book is printed on acid-free paper.

IN APPRECIATION

To Marilyn Danzig whose experience in publishing,
and unlimited patience combined with her computer
expertise made this publication possible.

To Doctor John Anderson whose
encouragement and editing assistance
encouraged me to attempt to have my story published.

PILOT HERE OR PILE IT THERE

CONTENTS

CHAPTER ONE

IN THE BEGINNING

I have thought about attempting to write this manuscript for many years but could never actually get started. Now I believe is the right time, so here I go. Initially, I have no commercial purpose in making my numerous experiences in aviation available to the general public. I reason that if any of my immediate family, friends or descendants are interested in my career, they may find some of my experiences a little unusual, particularly when comparing my flying career to aviation as they see it today. My thoughts concerning publishing my work may change later as I see how my story progresses.

As I start writing, I have my 4 ½ year old Great Grandson in mind who I have encouraged to become a pilot long before he knew what an airplane was. I remember on his third birthday I sent him a small check to add to his college fund and asked on the card if he had selected a university to attend. I added that I strongly recommend the Air Force Academy. I hope that someday he may get some pleasure out of reading my story. Perhaps when he is a General in the Air Force!

I will now attempt to explain why and how I was motivated into making aviation my career and the unanticipated reasons I became involved in so many aspects of the business. I also had several unusual, challenging or what I considered interesting, experiences that I will attempt to relate, keeping them as engaging as possible.

During my tenure as a pilot I was privileged to observe many upgrades in aviation technology such as communications, basic equipment instrumentation, engine performance, airframe designs to improve structural strength and efficiency and most importantly, the emphasis placed on "safety."

When I started flying, "Pilotage," (using visual check points) was the primary means of navigation and radio ranges, (beams projected from a low frequency radio station,) were available for instrument flying. Airways were depicted by having light beacons properly spaced along a designated route which were primarily used as a navigation aid during night flight. Mountain peaks above a certain altitude were identified by bright red lights. Cockpit instruments consisted of needle/ball, airspeed, a magnetic compass and sometimes a rate of climb indicator. Old pilots will tell you of the many complications and limitations encountered while using this equipment. The needle indicates wings level or degree of "bank," which is controlled by applying side pressure to the stick or turning the wheel on the control column in the direction you intend to turn. Applying pressure to the right or left rudder pedal in the direction you intend to turn establishes "turn," which is indicated by the ball in the needle/ball instrument. If the ball was centered during a turn as indicated by the needle, you were making a coordinated turn. Climbs and descents are controlled by applying "back" pressure or "forward" pressure to the stick or wheel. I have described the effects when using these controls because I will be referring to them at times during this story.

In the early days of flying "coordination" was emphasized and we continuously were told that if you lacked coordination, you would never become a pilot. "Coordination" was normally thought of as the proper pressure simultaneously applied to the stick and rudder avoiding a "slip" or "skid" while maneuvering the plane. Very quickly you find that coordinated use of the stick or wheel and rudders becomes automatic and almost everything pertaining to flying requires some form of coordination. Examples are communicating to controllers on the ground, spacing between aircraft and making good an expected time of arrival (ETA) over designated check points. There are more, but these illustrate what some additional forms of coordination are. The form that I became very exposed to was the coordination between crew members on military aircraft. In my mind this was the most important aspect in evaluating a crew's performance and can very well single out one particular crew member's weakness in not supporting the rest of the crew. Now that you are ready to go "solo," I will continue on with my story and you will understand the importance of "coordination," as its many aspects were obvious throughout my civilian and military career.

From what I have heard and read, civilian and military pilots today are operating very complex systems and I must admit that I know very little about them. As I understand it, electronics have taken over the controls in most of these aircraft, so to prevent exposing my very limited knowledge of "flying," as it is today, I will not carry this story beyond my days in a cockpit except for this thought: Electronics controlling an airplane in almost every phase of flight, including emergencies such as loss of an engine on take-off, must take a lot of the satisfaction a pilot experiences when performing maneuvers requiring his piloting skill. I may be wrong, but this is my personal opinion!

My interest in flying began when I first realized that my Uncle Pete was the "crazy" pilot that frequently buzzed our home in Elmhurst, IL. He owned a biplane which he maintained at Elmhurst Airport and was known to be an excellent mechanic and pilot, spending his time repairing planes and "hopping" passengers. My Dad took me to the airport when I was about five years old for a ride with Uncle Pete. At the time his plane was grounded, needing repairs, so he arranged for us to be taken up by his good friend, Ed Brazilton. Ed was very well known in Elmhurst, his name already being familiar to me. My Dad and I were strapped into the back seat and we took off. I was in awe, but calm, until my Dad insisted that I st and up to look out the side window. This terrified me because I thought I would fall through the floor or the floor, with my added weight, would fall out of the airplane

Once convinced I would not fall out I was really thrilled and amazed but in wonder as to what kept the plane airborne. I might mention at this time, that not very long after that flight, Ed Brazilton was killed while flying in an airliner (DC-3) shortly after taking off from an airport in Chicago. This is still very vivid in my mind, because the accident took place just North of Elmhurst and my Dad took me out to the wreckage which was widely scattered. However, this did not dampen my growing enthusiasm to becoming a pilot someday. After much pestering and insistence from me, my Dad again took me to the airport. This time my Uncle Pete took us up in his open cockpit biplane. I quickly learned why he was known as "crazy Pete Hubert." Take off and climb out were uneventful, but after attaining some altitude, I realized why Uncle Pete made sure we were securely strapped into the back seat. I had no idea what was happening, but remember seeing sky, then ground and at times some of both. I later realized he was "wringing" the plane out, (performing acrobatics). Then I remember we were suddenly in a dive which I thought, with my *limited* experience, was a pretty steep angle to strike the ground if we were intending to land. When I saw a picnic grounds with lots of people gathered around I felt relieved. We flew very low over the picnic area then zoomed up and circled around to land on an adjacent farm field. It seemed to me that everyone at the picnic knew my Uncle and Dad and immediately invited them to the beer keg tent. I won't comment further on that, but it does bring back an old Pilot's proverb: "Eight hours between bottle and throttle!" We finally took off again and landed back at Elmhurst Airport. Of course, I immediately thought, "Boy, this is the life!"

With an introduction to flying like that, I was convinced I wanted to be a pilot. Within a year after that flight, Uncle Pete was test hopping a bi-plane and according to him, he had put the plane through all kinds of stressful maneuvers, but to be completely satisfied as to it being airworthy, he decided to put it into a spin. This was a quick way to descend down to traffic pattern altitude. Upon reaching traffic pattern altitude which is usually between 800 and 500 feet he was unable to recover from the spin. Parachutes were fairly new at this time but fortunately Uncle Pete was wearing one. Somehow he managed to get out of the spinning plane and we were told that his chute opened just prior to his body striking the ground. His only injury was a large gash in his leg which he said was caused by striking the vertical stabilizer. As fortune would have it, an organization had recently been formed called the "caterpillar" club. The prerequisite for becoming a member was limited to those having saved their lives by successfully bailing out of a disabled airplane. As I recall, we were told that Uncle Pete qualified to become the third member of that prestigious club. This had to be about 1930 as I was staying with my Grand Mother, Uncle Pete's Mother at the time, because my Mother was having my sister, Joanie, who you will become acquainted with later. I also remember Uncle Pete taking me for rides on his motorcycle during this time which you can be sure, now that you have "met" him, were very exciting.

I had other motivating factors whetting my appetite to be a pilot such as my idol and mentor, Jim Cronin, joining the Army Air Corps and becoming a fighter pilot. He was flying the awesome P-38 fighter and assigned to the famous Eddie Rickenbaker, "Hat in the ring," squadron operating out of North Africa. Up to this part of Jim's career it was a very envious assignment. Much more about Jim as my story continues.

I was a senior in high school in December, 1941, when America entered World War II and with the "draft" in effect, knew that immediately after turning eighteen I would be inducted into military service. I most certainly did not want to end up in a front line trench! I was too small, weighing 114 lbs. and just 5' 61/2 inches tall, to engage in hand to hand combat. This has to do with knowing your limitations which I will mention again later. If for no other reason, my size alone would have been an influencing factor in my decision to join the Army Air Corps.

Prior to World War II Uncle Pete left Elmhurst with a friend, Ted Baker, who intended to start an airline- National Airlines- on the Albert Whitted Airport, in St. Petersburg, Florida . This was extremely significant to me as it had a lot to do with my future aviation career. As I understand it, Uncle Pete was chief mechanic, pilot and wore other hats which can be expected with a starting up airline. Sometime later, National moved down to Miami because of limited facilities provided at Albert Whitted Airport, which had not kept up with the rapidly growing airline industry. At this time Uncle Pete decided to remain at Albert Whitted and start his own flight program and maintenance service. He named it Florida Aviation Corporation, which expanded rapidly after World War II. Later on this will all come together if you will bear with me.

Uncle Pete had received his pilot training in the Illinois Air National Guard and as you have probably surmised, he was called back into active duty shortly after we entered World War II. He did not qualify to be a pilot because of deteriorated eyesight, but was made Chief of Maintenance in a B-25 Squadron stationed at Drew Field in Tampa, presently Tampa International Airport. His squadron was deployed to

New Guinea, where although not qualified, he flew numerous combat missions as copilot in B-25's. This was verified by many of his fellow squadron crew members that came down to St Pete after the war to work for him. While in New Guinea out fishing one day, his small boat capsized, injuring his right arm. He was sent to Letterman General Hospital in San Francisco to recover, which we will come back to later.

As I mentioned before, I was in my senior year of high school (York High) when America entered World War II, however, long before this, without any doubt or misgivings, determined that I wanted to be an Army Air Corps Pilot. Prior to our entering the war, I did considerable reading about the career of a military pilot and when each member of our senior English class had to give a talk on his or her chosen vocation, it was easy for me. I had read a pamphlet that explained if you went through military pilot training as a cadet, you would graduate a Second Lieutenant, receive a promotion every three years thereafter and retire after 20 years with a minimum rank of Full Colonel. Anyone could do it! You'll understand my point as you continue to read on, but it does seem that military recruiting promotional promises haven't changed much over the years.

I graduated in June of 1942 when I was 17 and immediately went down to Chicago to Join the Army Air Corps where I was nicely told to come back after I turned 18, which would be in December. I also needed to complete two years of college in order to become eligible to apply for entry into the pilot program. I guess I was very determined because after having been informed of a college program allowing for a two year deferment from the draft, I immediately applied. Acceptance into the program required the recommendation of the Dean of the school you intended to attend. I applied at Elmhurst College, in my home town. My interview with the Dean did not go at all well because of my high school grades. Maybe having already decided my future, my mind was in the sky rather than in my books. Nevertheless, I was accepted, but on probation. The first grading period went quite well, so I was allowed to remain in the program. About halfway through the second grading period I was told the two year college requirement was waived because so many aircrew members were being lost in combat. I was not the least bit discouraged because "nothing will happen to me,

I'm invulnerable," which is most young men's attitude at that age. Of course, after hearing about the change, I immediately made application. I was given a date to report for the written and physical exams which would give me time to finish the first semester of college. I am not proud of the grades I made after learning that college was no longer a requirement. I guess my mind had returned to the sky!

I had been told the minimum weight for acceptance into the Air Corps was 117 pounds, so the day I went down for the exams, I stopped to buy a bunch of bananas and drink a milk shake.

We were first given the written exam. There must have been about 100 applicants in the room and I believe the exam had about 100 questions, with a time limit. Unexpectedly, a few of the questions required identifying pictures of military airplanes. I did not know a Piper Cub from a B-17 so I missed all of those. When the time expired, we waited a short time to hear the results. That was a very anxious period for me as I had my heart set on being a pilot. It turned out to be just one of many anxious moments I faced throughout my flying career. Finally they started calling out names followed by, "Come back in thirty days," or report to an address, which we had previously been informed would be for a physical exam. I was fully prepared to come back in thirty days when my name was called. God answered my prayers and I reported to the address given.

This physical was a very comprehensive exam checking parts of my body I never heard of. Things went well until the blood pressure test. In those days the high side was considered important, with your age plus 100 being the norm. I recall the horrible disappointment I felt after being informed mine was above the limit. Apparently the technician giving the test recognized the dismay I must have shown and very assuredly told me this sometimes is caused by excitement or anxiety and suggested that I lay down for a period, try to relax and he would take it again. He was absolutely correct. Somehow I managed to clear my mind and actually fell asleep. When he awoke me, I breathed deep and slowly, during the test and passed well within limits. The final phase was an interview with a very senior officer. I think he was a Colonel. At that time I could not distinguish between a hotel doorman and a General. They both wore fancy uniforms. I was told to take my shoes off before entering his office so I figured he did not want his carpet soiled or maybe he had been stationed in Japan. Anyway, he asked me to be seated and then asked this question. "Where are the Aleutian Islands located?" War activity at the time seemed to be focused in the South Pacific, so of course, sounding very self assured, South Pacific was my answer. He looked me in the eye and very calmly said, "Off the coast of Alaska." I cannot recall the rest of the interview because I had already assumed I failed. The interview ended after he reviewed my physical exam results. He then said, "Everything is fine except you are under weight." You weigh 114 pounds and minimum weight is 117 pounds." This is one time in my life I gave the correct response. I remember very well saying, "Sir, I thought the army would do that for me." He said, "You are right," scratched out 114 and changed it to 117. I was dismissed and instructed to go home and wait for my orders. The testing took place in January, 1943 and after what seemed an eternity, I finally received my orders to report for active duty in April of that year.

CHAPTER TWO

I'M IN THE ARMY NOW

Now that we finally have me on active duty I will try to limit this to exciting, terrifying and gratifying experiences that occurred throughout my many years of flying intermixed with a few personal events or circumstances encountered along the way. I will break my activities down by the location in which I was stationed or working at the time. Because my memory must recall events that took place so very long ago, I may not relate them exactly in chronological order.

My first few assignments were quite uneventful. I went to Jefferson Barracks Missouri for basic training, learning how to march (drill,) do calisthenics and KP. (Kitchen police) KP was not as it sounded. We scrubbed pots and pans, moped the kitchen floor, or waited on tables. I did learn how one full time chef salted a huge kettle of soup. He leaned over the kettle while stirring and at the same time was sweating profusely. I will not go into detail where the dripping sweat was going, but I immediately realized how efficient and resourceful the Army was!

After completing basic I was sent to Carroll College in Waukesha Wisconsin. This was an intense three months of academics pertaining to subjects we would be concerned with while flying. This of course was mostly math and physics. I surprised myself how well I did when the books applied to my favorite subject, "flying."

We were bunked six to a room in the girls' dormitory. No, we did not share our rooms or even the dormitory with girls. In fact, to erase what your thinking from your mind, there were no girls anywhere on the campus! Waukesha was not far from Elmhurst, so one Sunday my Mom and Dad drove up for a visit. They found me walking alone along a rectangular course between several buildings with a gun on my shoulder. They immediately assumed I was doing guard duty when in fact, I was walking off a tour, "gig" (demerit) for some goof up I had been caught at. Each gig was punishable by completing a one hour "tour." They waited patiently while I completed my "tour" and I never spoiled their image of me. This was intended to be a five month course, however, because of continued excessive loses of combat air crews, the program was accelerated and completed in three months.

Next, I was sent to a classification center at Santa Ana California. Our group spent three hectic weeks taking every type of exam imaginable. This was to determine if we would be better qualified as a pilot, navigator, bombardier, gunner, or transferred to the army for immediate ground combat duty in the infantry. This alone, *motivated* me, to do my absolute best! The one questionnaire I mostly remember asked to give your crew position preference in numerical order from 1-4, pilot being # 1. I put pilot 1, pilot 2, pilot 3 and pilot 4. This either should have left no doubt as to my preference or eliminated me for impertinence. The day they posted our assignment was quite memorable. I expected to see "front line trenches," but to my amazement, after my name was, "pilot." I later determined those with the highest academic scores were made navigators so I really should not have worried about that! Up until this time we had been Aviation Students and now we were Aviation Cadets, in my mind, a very prestigious rank.

Now we were ready for pre-flight training on the other side of Santa Ana Air Base. Of course my thought was, "would we never start flying?" Pre-flight was all academics, drill and calisthenics. As at Carroll College the Aviation Cadet program had a demerit, "gig," system, which, after receiving a certain number of "gigs" you could expect automatic, "washout." (Elimination) We marched to the pre-flight side of the base and were dismissed in front of our assigned barracks. With arms full of baggage, I passed a very young Captain and did not drop my baggage to salute him. I then heard, "mister don't you salute officers in pre-flight?" "Follow me!" I was led to the orderly room and given a gig. I then walked out of the orderly room barracks, headed for my own barracks when I stepped on the grass while turning a corner. I again I heard, "Mister we don't walk on the grass in pre-flight!" I was led to the orderly room and received another gig. I believe the maximum gigs allowed were seven and in the first 15 minutes, I already had two. At that rate I did not think I had a chance of making it through the programmed six weeks, because there were so many "nit picking" items on the gig list. A couple of examples of the gig list included: A coin dropped on your cot must bounce, absolutely no non essential chatter during meals and eating with your left hand in your lap except when necessary to slice meat or spread something on bread. I carefully watched every move I made and thankfully received no more gigs in pre-flight.

After completing pre-flight, our class was assigned to Thunderbird Field, just outside of Phoenix, Arizona for primary flight training. (First phase of flight training) We lost a few of our class in classification and a couple more in pre-flight but now the possibility of being "washed out," after being informed of the high wash out rate in each of the three flight phases, made my future very uncertain.

The reality of becoming an Army Air Corps pilot and commissioned officer was possible, but definitely not certain at this point.

CHAPTER THREE

"OFF I GO, INTO THE WILD BLUE YONDER"

THUNDERBIRD FIELD, GLENDALE, ARIZONA

We were assigned five students to an instructor and I was very fortunate. My instructor was very experienced and flew the Stearman trainer like it was part of his body he was maneuvering. The Stearman was a bi-plane, open cockpit, with tandem seating. The student flew in the rear seat even when flying solo. It was a very maneuverable, forgiving plane in the air, but in a cross-wind, could be a little difficult when landing. It had a narrow landing gear and relatively small rudder. Because of this, I was having trouble with directional control on the ground during take off and landing. Thankfully my instructor had the patience and experience to help me overcome this. Recognizing my problem, he had me taxi to a remote side of the field and instructed me to maintain directional control while he controlled the throttle. He rapidly accelerated and decelerated while I was to keep the rudder pedals continuously moving but trying to go straight ahead. I suddenly got the hang of it and never again had a directional control problem. I used this same method later when I was an instructor. It always worked! After about ten hours of dual instruction I finally soloed on Dec. 24, 1943. This was a big day for me as we were told 12 hours of instruction was the maximum time allowed and I was getting close. Prior to soloing I would sit on the side of my cot at night imagining

I was landing, by easing back on my imaginary stick until I attained landing attitude and touching down. I do believe this helped. Today, I understand that imagining yourself through the steps of a complex task is very much part of modern training in learning any set of skills. Shortly after soloing, my instructor was made a check pilot, so our group was assigned a new instructor. He was very mild mannered and understanding. After soloing things went quite well until my first cross country flight

This turned out to be my first really frightening experience in flight. The procedure was to fly cross country with your instructor and then fly the same course solo. After completing the round trip the instructor got out and sent me on my way, solo. It was a right angle course heading straight West, to a check point, turn 90 degrees to the South and land at a designated field. We were to check in, take off and fly the same route home. Shortly before arriving at the landing strip, I noticed that I was running low on fuel. The fuel gauge was simply a tube mounted just in front of the cockpit below the upper wing. Knowing there was no fuel available at the auxiliary field, I determined that landing and taking off would use fuel I could not afford. I over-flew the field, however instead of flying the right angular route home; I opted to fly a heading that would take me directly to Thunderbird field. (Hopefully) The fuel level was indicating very low and I really thought I could not make it. We did not have radios in the Stearman so I was strictly on my own. I held my heading while looking for a suitable place to land. Also going through my mind, was the thought that no matter what happened, this would probably be my last flight. Was I told to refuel before taking off solo and did not hear it? I really did not know! Also, being very inexperienced at cross country and map reading, I thought maybe having already realized my situation when approaching the auxiliary field; I should have landed and let someone else worry about getting the plane back to Thunderbird. I was going to be "washed out" anyway! With the fuel gauge on empty, knowing I had passed the "point of no return," I continued to hold my course and prayed. I was mostly over desert when I suddenly saw signs of a populated area ahead. Lo and behold, straight ahead was Thunderbird Field. As I entered the traffic pattern for landing, I kept repeating to the engine, "please don't quit now! Please don't quit now!" I fully expected it to quit while taxiing to the parking ramp. I really wanted to stick around to see how much fuel it took but did not want to stir up a commotion. Nothing was ever mentioned as to why I did not land at the turn around point or why there was so little fuel remaining after landing. I certainly did not mention it anyone, not even to my instructor. Much later, I thought maybe it was the instructor's fault. He sent me on my way solo, without ever considering I would need more fuel. Any way it was a lesson well learned at an early stage of my career and never forgotten as a pilot and later as an instructor.

My second frightening experience in primary training was while attempting a landing. Our landing area was a rectangular grass field. We did not have a control tower giving landing instructions and there were no actual runways, so we landed in the direction indicated by the wind sock. At times this could be on a diagonal heading across the rectangular field. On the day I'm referring to, we were using a diagonal approach. There was another airplane already turning on the final approach, so I chose to land to his right. As I was descending, I realized I would be landing in a very small section on the corner of the field. I should have pulled up and gone around for another approach, but this would be admitting my bad judgment, so I continued the approach and landed. After touchdown I really did not think I could stop before hitting the field boundary fence or putting the plane on its nose using excessive braking. There was not enough landing field remaining to make a go-around and I was saying to myself "stupid, stupid, stupid," as I stopped just short of the fence. I thought afterward, going around really would have displayed good judgment in recognizing and correcting my error. I also carried this experience with me the rest of my flying career. Later on, admitting a mistake and making an immediate correction, was always emphasized to my students. Terror does have a way of making you remember things!

My final check ride was with my first instructor. I made the take off and performed several maneuvers at his direction and then he indicated he would take control. Of course I immediately thought I had already failed and he would take us home. Suddenly he started doing every acrobatic maneuver in the book with perfect precision. I was sure he was demonstrating how an aircraft "should" be flown. He then cut the throttle and started doing snap rolls in the direction of a deserted field. One to the right, one to the left, back and forth continuously descending until very low. Finally he leveled out directly over the spot he had selected for his simulated forced landing. He then indicated that I should fly us back to Thunderbird. Now I was really puzzled. I landed and taxied back to the ramp. We both got out without a word spoken and started walking back to operations. Finally he looked at me and said "congratulations, you're going to do fine." I quickly went from having a horrible inferior complex to a wonderful outlook as to my future as a cadet. I think he saw I really needed this comment. I know of only one other pilot that could match his acrobatic skill. This was Bugs Thompson, whom I will discuss later. Incidentally, I never tried that power off snap roll approach even at my peak.

LANCASTER FIELD, LANCASTER, CALIFORNIA.

After completing primary I was assigned to Lancaster for basic training. We flew the BT-13 which was about the same size as the Stearman, but was all metal, with flaps, a two speed prop, radio, wider landing gear and 450 horsepower engine. It was very stable, rugged and easier to land, but not as maneuverable as a Stearman. Also the landing gear being wider lessened the probability of a ground loop on landing. Did you ask, what's a ground loop? I'll try to explain. The tail wheel on most trainers is somewhat steerable by applying pressure to the rudder pedal in the direction you wish to turn. If you make too tight a turn the tail wheel will go into "full swivel," allowing the aircraft to pivot on one wheel in a very tight turn, usually, as a minimum, caused the wing tip to scrape the ground. If this happens, it is very embarrassing to the pilot, because it's an admission that he has lost control.

Our training area was the Mojave Desert which was surrounded by mountains, which made remaining within the boundaries pretty easy. I remember at the time being told I was the first in our class to solo, which was quite elating. Nothing exciting or scary happened in basic that I can recall, except I was having difficulty recovering from an intentional spin. I just vowed to myself I would never get into an accidental spin! In case you're wondering what a spin is, I will attempt to explain. Remember, it's been over fifty years since I was in my last spin! As best I recall, to enter an intentional spin, you fully retard the throttle, abruptly apply full rudder in the direction you wish to turn and at the same time briskly pull the stick to the full back position. That was easy, but now comes the recovery. Put in full opposite rudder until the wings are about to become parallel to the horizon then, "pop" the stick forward while simultaneously neutralizing the rudders. My problem was in not neutralizing the rudders. I was late in neutralizing the rudder and would start spinning in the opposite direction. (Very poor timing and coordination) I finally got the hang of it in advanced training. I don't even think spins are taught anymore because the maneuver is prohibited in most civilian trainers. This might be a good time to explain what a "snap" roll is. A snap roll is a spin performed horizontal to the horizon, as opposed to a spin which is performed perpendicular to the horizon. Again, back to my story. We completed another 65 hours and moved on to advanced training.

LUKE FIELD, PHOENIX, ARIZONA

Luke was near Phoenix so I was already familiar with the area. Now we were introduced to the North American T-6. It was quite sophisticated compared to the BT-13. It had a 650 horse power engine, retractable landing gear and hydraulic system to operate the landing gear and flaps. I remember I had to position a lever, to actuate the hydraulic system, prior operating the flaps or landing gear. In addition to improving my piloting skill, I do remember a couple of incidents that occurred while in advanced.

Our class, 44-F was told, although we were training for single engine, because of unpredicted bomber losses in combat, we were very likely to end up as copilots in heavy bombers. (B-17 or B-24)We were given an option of volunteering for night fighters and eventually flying the P-61 (Black Widow). It was twin engine, but at least I would remain in the fighter program. Later on I'll explain why I believe it got that name. I was assigned to one of the two designated night fighter squadrons and although we remained at Luke, our training program was quite different than the standard advanced course. We received additional instrument training, night flying time and also had gunnery training just prior to graduation, *if* we got that far. I would like to emphasize at this time that I never once heard an aviation cadet say "when" I graduate. By the same token you never heard a cadet say, "If" I graduate. Everyone remained very silent on that subject!

My first incident in advanced that I recall was during a night cross country flight. I looked up after studying my navigation chart and saw a red light that appeared to be at my same altitude and coming directly at me. At that time aircraft lighting consisted of a red light and green light, one on each wing tip. Without hesitation, I immediately did a split S which is to roll into an inverted position, pull the nose down by applying back pressure on the stick until the nose comes back up to the horizon and finally leveling off in the opposite direction after losing considerable altitude. It was a maneuver used by fighter pilots during combat. After completing the split S I made a 180 degree turn to resume course and observed the red light was still there in front of me but now little higher. I had forgotten that mountain peaks were identified with red lights! Two lessons were learned here, since I had not considered the loss of altitude this maneuver would require and had reacted on impulse. I could have easily done myself in. I learned to meticulously look the situation over and then make a deliberate decision as to the best action to take.

My second incident was very embarrassing and also taught me a long lasting lesson. I had taken off from Luke one night to complete a black out (no lights) landing requirement at an auxiliary field. Upon approaching the field, I attempted radio contact to receive landing instructions. My radio appeared dead and considering we were not using lights, radio contact was essential. I headed back to Luke using the "radio out" landing procedures we had been taught. Upon pulling up to the parking ramp the crew chief was waiting for me. He quickly was up on the wing, reached for the headset cord which was dangling on my left side, connected it and my radio was working! He never said a word, but his look indicated his thoughts. Is this guy going to be a combat pilot? I later realized that I had been transmitting, but not receiving. Everyone on the ground was aware of my problem well before I landed. Lesson learned, what is the first thing to check when suddenly your radio is not receiving?

On a routine daylight cross country flight in clear weather, over mountainous terrain near Flagstaff Arizona, I suddenly started losing altitude. I applied power until I had full power, but still kept sinking. I finally realized I had entered a downdraft. This was one phenomenon not covered in our weather course. I always liked to fly as low as possible, but this was one time I had a strong desire to have been higher. I knew I was going straight into a mountain side at full throttle. Finally, after I had given up all hope, the T-6 finally stopped descending. I now knew how unpredictable and deceiving weather could be.

The last two weeks in advanced was spent at Gilabend, Arizona taking gunnery training. This consisted of air to air and air to ground strafing. Practicing air to air we shot at sleeves being towed by another T-6 with a very "brave" pilot. Five cadets were assigned to an instructor. Ours' insisted on flying a very tight formation. We took off in formation and remained in formation, except during actual passes at targets during which time we flew in close trail. While in formation the instructor always flew lead, continuously saying, "number so and so, close it up." If you were number six, you felt you were on the end of a whip especially in turbulent air. The entire gunnery course was a real challenge. To goof up now, this close to graduation would have been very disheartening to say the least. I did have one close call. During an air to air mission I experienced something that we had been warned about which was, "Target fixation!" While trying to get as many bullets as possible in the target sleeve, it was suddenly right in front of me. I abruptly banked to the left and dove knowing my right wing would strike the sleeve. Again, someone up there was protecting me, as I somehow cleared it. Our bullets were color coded, so practice missions were always scored. Needless to say, I did quite well that day, either because I was in so close or someone up there was looking out for me, or both! The ground target phase was what I liked best. We could legally descend as low as we dared which was where I liked to fly.

Finally we headed back to Luke to await graduation and purchase our officer uniforms. I don't know about other cadets, but I held out until my final landing as cadet before I spent one cent on a uniform. This reminds me to explain that officers must purchase and pay for their own uniforms except for clothing such as flight suits and combat fatigues. I've spoken to a lot of people that never knew this.

CHAPTER FOUR
PILOT, OFFICER, GENTLEMAN

June 27, 1944 was an extremely momentous day for me. By direction of the President of the United States and act of Congress at the ripe old age of 19 1/2 I became a commissioned officer and a pilot in the Army Air Corps. What I did not realize at the time, this was to open the way for most of my productive life. It was customary for new second lieutenants to give a dollar to the first enlisted person to salute you. I immediately headed for the nurses area and received a salute from a very pretty nurse. She was grateful for the dollar but that was as far as it went!

After receiving orders to report to Mather Field, Sacramento, California, our night fighter class received a short leave. I went home to Elmhurst by train, to show off my bars and wings. To my disappointment it seemed no one in Elmhurst knew the difference between a Private and a General. My bars and wings did not seem to impress anyone except my Dad. He was very proud after having been an Army Private in WW 1.

I thought it would be nice if I visited the parents of good High School friends, all of whom were in the service and overseas. On my first visit I was greeted with, "My Arthur has been at sea for six months. I know how you officers have it!" I had been an officer for a week and did not have any idea how officers had it. That was my one and last visit to a parent. I did shortly re-learn that I could talk while eating with both elbows on the table. I also learned that I could walk without being in step and in formation. I certainly had a lot of new advantages! My pay was now $150.00 per month with an additional $75.00 flight pay. Later this was called hazard duty pay because it looked like air crew members were given special treatment. The foot soldiers in trenches overseas did not receive this benefit.

MATHER FIELD, SACRAMENTO, CALIFORNIA

I received multi-engine training in the B-25 Mitchell. I felt very fortunate because the B-25 was a great airplane and I believe it was the most stable plane I ever flew. After checking out, most of our flights were at night, however, several noteworthy incidents come to mind.

One day I was scheduled to practice instrument flying. A hood was placed in front of the pilot's windshield (mine) and the copilot was the observer. There was a lot of air traffic in the area so the copilot really had to keep his eyes open. After practicing some air maneuvers I made a simulated radio range let down and low approach to Mather. A few other aircraft were doing the same thing. After completing the approach I signaled the copilot to take the controls while I removed the hood. When he did not respond, I looked at him to see why. He was sound asleep! I had no idea how long he had been sleeping or how many aircraft we may have caused some anxious moments. I was furious but never mentioned this to any one. I did make sure I never flew with him again.

A good friend of mine, John Keig, had a frightening experience one night. He was returning to Mather when his left engine caught fire. He completed the normal emergency procedures without success and the fire started increasing in intensity, threatening structural damage to the engine nacelle and left wing. John instructed his copilot to bail out and he would follow right behind him. The escape hatch was a few feet behind and below the pilot's station. The copilot proceeded to open the hatch and eased himself out. John stood on the ledge above the open hatch and dove for the opening. He over shot, striking his forehead on the sharp metal bordering the far side of the hatch. He did not remember leaving the plane or opening his chute. His first recollection was floating toward the ground. After landing safely, somehow, he and the copilot found each other on a hilltop overlooking a small town. John had a large gash on his forehead but was able to gather up his parachute and head for the town. A short time later they were picked up, John's gash was treated and all ended well. When asked why he salvaged his chute, considering the condition he was in, John replied, "I did not want to be charged for it." Of course the lesson learned was; consider the possible consequences and alternatives before you "dive!"

Another frightening experience happened, but this time it was to me. I was returning to Mather not paying much attention to where we were while listening to some music on the radio compass, which is meant to be used as a homing device, intended to be a navigation aid. It had frequency bands capable of being tuned to standard radio stations and radio ranges. It was an excellent homing device, with usable range depending on the altitude of the aircraft. As usual I was flying at an altitude as low as permissible and fortunately it was a bright moonlight night. Not realizing I had drifted quite a bit off course, I suddenly saw the side of a mountain very close, directly in front of me. While making a sharp left bank I just knew we would not clear it. Again, someone was watching over me!

My Mother prayed on her knees for my safety every night before bed and I can't help but think this was a contributing factor toward my many recoveries from such situations. She did this throughout my entire flying career. (Thank Goodness)

While at Sacramento, my parents informed me that uncle Pete was at Letterman hospital in San Francisco, recuperating from his boating accident. He was to be discharged from the service after recovering. A short time later I received a note from Uncle Pete asking me to visit him at my earliest opportunity. I invited Craig to join me to spend a weekend in San Francisco, so shortly thereafter, on a Sunday afternoon, I made the visit. Uncle Pete was in bed but suggested we take a walk. After getting dressed he took a cane off the wall, which puzzled me so I asked, "why the cane when the injury was to your arm?" He had been in the National Guard for twenty years and was still a captain. If he carried a cane, he did not have to salute all the high ranking officers roaming the grounds who were much younger and inexperienced. This was definitely an ego thing but perfectly logical to me. His purpose in having me visit was to convince me that civilian aviation was really going to "take off" with a plane in every back yard after the war. He wanted me to get discharged as soon as possible to join him in St. Petersburg, Florida and he was very persuasive. Craig thought I was very fortunate in having such an opportunity. Little did he know! (I will explain that later).

We decided to go to the top of the Mark Hopkins Hotel before going back to the base. It was a restaurant and cocktail lounge, known as a San Francisco landmark, a "must," for any visitor. In the elevator going up we saw large signs posted. "If you are not 21 you are not allowed in the top of the Mark" We were 19, but 2nd Lt's in the Army Air Corps, so naturally the signs did not apply to us. There was also a Sergeant in the elevator. Everyone wore a uniform at all times during the war so our rank was easily recognized. Upon stepping out of the elevator we were approached by an employee who asked to see our ID. Then he firmly said, "Sergeant, come on in, you two, back in the elevator" This was a lesson in "humility" I've carried with me all through life.

Our class was the last class to take B-25 transition at Mather. After we completed the course, all the B-25"s were ferried to Douglas Air Base, Douglas Arizona. This was our next base assignment so some of us were able to fly down as copilot. My pilot made me responsible for navigation. After landing, he commented on what a fine job I did. I mention this as I intend to mention my navigation problems later.

DOUGLAS AIR BASE, DOUGLAS, ARIZONA

At Douglas we were placed in a pilot pool awaiting assignment. I believe the base was primarily used to train navigators. The instructor pilots assigned to Douglas frequently took B-25's on weekend cross countries. We could go along, riding as passengers, in the rear of the plane. On one weekend a couple of the guys in our group of friends decided to take one of these flights. I do not remember their destination, but clearly remember what happened during take off, when heading back to Douglas. For some reason the copilot attempted to raise the landing gear before the plane was off the ground. Both props struck the concrete runway, the gear collapsed and the plane skidded on its belly to a stop. The friction caught the fuselage on fire, which immediately grew very intense when the fuel tanks ruptured. The persons in normal crew positions up front were able to escape by releasing the canopy over the pilots' heads. My friends in the rear were unable to get out because the escape hatch was on the floor, held closed by the concrete runway. Rescuers could not penetrate the skin of the fuselage in the short time the trapped persons had to survive. Witnesses could hear them screaming for help, which is the part of this accident I most remember. When word of this got back to us at Douglas, there was a long silent period. We had been with those pilots all through pilot training and it was quite a shock realizing that any of us could have been passengers in that B-25.

After a short time at Douglas, we received our orders for the next training phase. Quite unexpectedly we were told the night fighter program had an overage of pilots at this time, so some of us would be ordered to another program. I thought, "Here I go, to become a B-17 or even worse, a B-24 copilot." Then we were told half the class would go into photo reconnaissance and fly a modified version of the P-38. It would be equipped with cameras instead of guns. If selected, this would be a very exciting turn of events. I had seen the P-38 in action, dog fighting with navy aircraft over Luke Field. Also, just before graduation at Luke, Major Bong, the P-38 fighter pilot holding the overall record for enemy kills in combat, gave us a motivation talk. Not that we needed it! He was on temporary duty in the states touring fighter bases. His departure was quite impressive. Immediately after raising the gear, he "feathered" one engine (cut the engine and turn the prop blades streamlined with the air flow to cut drag) and did slow rolls while climbing out on one engine. I immediately developed an inferior complex realizing I could never do that! I did have mixed emotions about dividing our group up because I had become especially close friends with four other pilots. To be separated now would not be easy. I will name these friends at this time because their names will come up throughout the rest of this story. They were Craig T. Anneberg, from Long View, Washington (who is still a great friend,) Bob Dagget, from Eugene Oregon, John Keig, from a suburb of Chicago and Lloyd Fish, from Phoenix Arizona.

We were told the selections would be made by taking an alphabetical roster and picking every other name. To our amazement, all five of us were sent to photo recon training at Will Rogers Field, near Oklahoma City, Oklahoma.

WILL ROGERS FIELD, OKLAHOMA CITY, OKLAHOMA

Our stay at Will Rogers was quite brief. Half the class was sent to Coffeyville, Kansas for training. I have no idea how they determined who would go, but most improbably, all five of us went to Coffeyville.

COFFEYVILLE AIR FIELD, COFFEYVILLE, KANSAS

Before starting training in the modified P-38 we had to complete an instrument course using BT-13's, the trainer we flew in basic training at Lancaster California. Strangely enough, Craig and I were assigned the same instructor. His name was 1st. Lt. R.B. Rothey, who I remember well, because he really put our careers in jeopardy. After flying with each of us once, he would meet us at the aircraft, tell one of us to take his place as observer in the front seat and after landing, put his name in the form one, (flight log) making it appear that he was on the flight. We completed the entire course this way. Well, someone finally reported this to his Squadron Commander and Lt. Rothey was put up for court martial with Craig and I as witnesses. At first we were considered accomplices, but thankfully this was dropped. We were briefed to only say "Lt. Rothey was our superior officer and instructor, so we had no choice but to follow his orders." At his court Martial, it came up that he was also accused of taking a B-25 to Kansas City, loading it with cases of whiskey and selling the whiskey for a big profit in Coffeyville. Kansas was a dry state at that time so it brought a premium price. It was also disclosed that he had been at a port of debarkation several times en route to combat duty overseas, but each time was too ill to travel and his assignment was cancelled. This guy was some officer, a great example for us 2nd Lts. Craig and I got off unscathed, but Lt Rothey received one year at hard labor and a dishonorable discharge. I later heard that he was hired by an airline because they were desperate for pilots due to rapid expansion.

A B-25 was scheduled to go to Kansas City for some reason, so I asked to ride along just to observe. There were a couple of us going and I was put in the nose gunner's position. It was enclosed in glass panels allowing excellent visibility. As luck would have it, the pilot appointed me as navigator. The regular crew positions received comfortable heating, however in my crew position I became so cold, I fell asleep.

After a while I was awakened by the pilot saying, "navigator, what's our position?" "Right on course' I replied, not having the vaguest idea where we were. Things did not look right to him so he orientated himself using radio equipment. A short time after arriving back at Coffeyville, I was called into the commander's office. He read me a report from the B-25 pilot stating how poor my navigation ability was. Perfect navigation was essential in photo recon so as a result I was scheduled for a check ride in a B-25. This time I rode in the copilot's seat and as the pilot wandered all over the country side, I continuously told him our position. He seemed like an understanding guy, so I decided to explain to him what happened to require this ride. His evaluation of me was very good and I was completely absolved of my problem. I must admit, I again had some very anxious thoughts.

Check out in the P-38 consisted of a few hours of ground school learning the aircraft systems and a short piggy back flight while an instructor demonstrated flight procedures. I remember being hunched up in a very small space behind the pilot's seat. My Instructor was a tall broad shouldered man so I could not see a thing he was doing. After my "demonstration" flight I was cleared for solo. My first solo flight in the P-38 cost me ten dollars and a lot of embarrassment. All went well until I attempted to land. I overshot the runway and had to go around. While on the final approach the plane did not descend at the rate I expected and on my second approach I realized the problem. The flap lever had two positions. "Dive brakes"- to accelerate a descent and "full flaps," which were used for every landing. Dive brakes were intended to improve maneuverability during combat. I had merely pulled the flap lever straight back which gave me dive brakes, just a partial flap position. Full flaps required pushing the flap lever forward, then full back. I landed after the second approach and was immediately called into the commander's office. He took ten dollars from me, saying this was customary for having to go around. I kept quiet about the lever goof up because you can't be absent minded when flying high performance aircraft. I preferred he just consider me a lousy pilot.

My second incident in P-38's was my first near mid-air collision. I was on a photo training mission at 35,000 feet concentrating on positioning myself directly over an assigned simulated target, when I looked up and saw another P-38 directly in front and heading straight for me. We both turned at the last second barely avoiding a collision. I'm sure we were the only two aircraft at that altitude within hundreds of miles. Very few military aircraft and no civilian aircraft had that altitude capability at that time, so this was completely unexpected. Again, was it luck, a guardian angel or my Mother's prayers?

I did something else that I kept to myself. I think I almost blew up an engine. On a training mission in the local area, practicing different maneuvers, I decided to feather an engine, wondering how well the plane performed on one engine. The procedure was to completely retard the throttle and then either push or pull the feather button. (Don't remember which} It was red, on the instrument panel easily recognized and reached. I retarded the throttle and then inadvertently actuated the button for the <u>opposite</u> engine. I heard "pow, pow, pow" and suddenly realized what I had done. In preparing for the decreased airspeed with one engine shut down, I had applied extra power to what was to have been the "good" engine, which was now feathered, adding tremendous stress on the engine. Luckily I was able to get things back to normal before any "obvious" damage was done, or at least that I was aware of. Once again I was being protected. I began to think-how many chances do I get? I know I will never win the lottery because I have used up all my luck!

A few of us at were scheduled to make a night flight. To be safe we were assigned specific boundaries to remain within and altitudes to maintain. I was cruising in my assigned area and altitude when the control tower instructed me to give a short count. This meant counting from 1 to 5 and back to one. I was asked to do this several times, but not given a reason or further instructions. After landing, I was called into the commander's office. (Again) He asked how the town of Coffeyville looked from "there." Thinking he meant from my assigned area and altitude. I replied "great." He then accused me of buzzing the town at a very low altitude. It happened that one of our P-38s had actually buzzed the town going back and forth, over the town. The control tower had a direction finder capable of detecting the exact direction a radio signal was coming from. That was the reason for the short count and my position when giving the count, was directly in line with the town and the tower. When I realized what had happened, I adamantly insisted it was not me and tried to explain why it appeared to be me. I was dismissed, but informed this was not over. I was totally distraught; convinced this was the end for me. I thought of Lt. R.B. Rothey. Strangely enough, nothing more was ever said to me about the incident, but I was kept dangling for a long time. I later found out who it was but did not snitch. His wife lived in town and he wanted to show off.

Another very unpleasant thing happened to me on a routine training flight. While at 35,000 feet, with several hours to go before landing, I urgently had to urinate and attempted to use the pilot's relief tube, which all fighter aircraft were equipped with. It was positioned just below the pilot's seat, a funnel connected to a hose that drained out of the bottom of the fuselage. Urine sprayed over whatever land surface you happened to be flying. This was later modified so the urine went into a container and emptied by the crew chief after landing. I mention this so you don't take shelter every time a military aircraft flies overhead. Anyway, I completed urinating and, whoops! Urine suddenly backed up spraying all over the cockpit. I had navigation charts spread around along with other gear so had a real mess. I was wearing an oxygen mask, helmet and goggles so at least my face was spared. The cockpit heat was on, so you can imagine my plight for the rest of the mission. (Odor) After landing I informed the crew chief of my problem and left clean up to him.

After completing photo recon training, we were ready for overseas duty. We thought! Very unexpectedly, part of the class was selected to go to Chanute Field, near Champlain, Illinois, to attend weather school. This was an awful disappointment. We were informed that selection was based on our class standing in the photo recon course. Unfortunately Craig and I were very competitive so finished at the top of the list. Again, unbelievable, all five of us were selected.

CHANUTE FIELD, CHAMPAGNE, ILLINOIS

I really disliked weather school. We attended class eight hours a day and flew in the back of a B-17 about once every two weeks. It was equipped with all the apparatus needed to obtain information that a weather station would use making forecasts. We took the first exam after about three weeks and a classmate named Bill Hubbard turned in a blank paper. He was removed from the program and we were told that he was sent back to Will Rogers Field and shipped over seas to join a Photo Recon Squadron. Of course, that gave me a great idea. When given our next exam, I also turned in a blank paper. I was called into the Commander's office and was very emphatically and firmly informed I would receive a zero grade, that we were graded on a sliding scale and if I did not bring my grades up to a passing level, I would be held over to attend the next scheduled class.

Now, like it or not, I really had to buckle down and I did.

In order to receive flight pay we had to fly four hours a month. Base Operations had BT-13's and T-6's, which we could fly all we wanted depending on aircraft availability. Very often the five of us and a new friend that had been with us a long time, John Barry, headed straight for the flight line after a dull day in the classroom. This was great flying! No instructor looking over our shoulder and no limit to what we did in flight provided we broke no regulations. Most time was spent flying very tight formation, dog fighting and playing follow the leader. Once, while flying lead, in follow the leader, I attempted a vertical slow roll. The BT-13 was not the plane in which to attempt this. Too much drag for the power. About half way through the roll, it stalled out and I completely lost control. The plane was falling through the sky on its back. I had absolutely no response from the stick or rudder. Finally, after what seemed like an eternity, the weight of the engine pulled the nose through and I came tearing over the ground at 400 feet. I was at 4,000 feet when starting the maneuver. We normally did not fly that high but again I lucked out. The guys behind me saw the futility of the maneuver and did not attempt it. Of course, I won the follow the leader contest that day.

One Saturday Craig and I decided to take a look at my home town, Elmhurst, Illinois. It was about 100 miles from Chanute. I lead the way and after arriving over town, took us down to 500 feet over York Street, the main street in town. It was about noon and looked very busy. We flew up and down York Street doing snap and slow rolls. We were in BT-13's which, in flat pitch for acrobatics, were extremely noisy. We hadn't thought about this. After several passes while inverted during a slow roll, which requires a lot of side pressure on the stick, I was sure I heard and felt the stick crack. I could just see myself trying to recover with just a stub to hold. I completed the roll and motioned to Craig to head for home and I judiciously flew back and landed at Chanute Field. I reported what happened to the crew chief, but never heard more about it. That night I received a call from my Dad. It happened he just got off the train coming home from work and was walking down York Street when we arrived.

He said we had all traffic stopped and people were coming out of the stores to see our show. Unfortunately he assumed it was me and made sure all his friends heard about it. Now I knew I was in deep trouble! This type of flying was strictly prohibited, a court martial offense. Craig and I really sweat it out for several weeks, but apparently we were never reported.

After completing weather school we were ordered back to Will Rogers Field. We were now called "photographic weather reconnaissance pilots," having an additional rating of, "qualified weather forecaster."

WILL ROGERS FIELD, OKLAHOMA CITY, OKLAHOMA

We were placed in a pilot pool waiting for orders to our next assignment, which was an air base in Rapid City, South Dakota.

While having nothing to do, I heard my old friend, Jim Cronin, from Elmhurst, had returned home after having been in a German prison camp for two years. I felt I just had to see him. I was doing nothing but checking the bulletin board each morning, so convinced myself, it would be OK to leave the base for a couple of days. I rode the train to Elmhurst which took a whole day and was able to see a lot of Jim. After being gone for three days, I started getting very nervous. I was actually AWOL, (absent without leave) another court martial offense. The fourth day, the return train trip which again took all day, was the longest day of my life. That evening I finally arrived back at Will Rogers Field and immediately looked for Craig. He was still there, "thank goodness," having received no orders. I vowed to myself, never again, would I put myself in that sort of situation.

Finally we were told that Rapid City was not yet ready for us and were given a short leave. Craig, John and I decided we would not try to go home, but would visit a resort lake in Missouri. We also decided we needed a car to get there so took a bus to some small town in Missouri and immediately went to a used car lot. During the war used cars were at a premium and very scarce. The salesman showed us a 1931 Pontiac Chief, which was within our price range and it appeared to be in excellent condition. We bargained a little and finally agreed to pay $225.00 cash plus two cartons of cigarettes and a bottle of Canadian Club Whiskey. Craig and John donated the cigarettes and I had a bottle of Canadian Club given to me by an old Elmhurst neighbor, Kelly Poole. He was the most knowledgeable person I knew concerning the war He had maps of the participating countries in his basement, keeping track of combat areas with marked pegs. Both times I went home he gave me two bottles which were almost impossible to buy. The "chief," as we named it, was a great car and gave us a lot of faithful use.

At last we received our orders. Craig, John and I received them at the same time, so headed out in the Chief, which got us to Rapid City without a problem. Bob Dagget, Lloyd Fish and John Barry received their orders a few days later and pulled into Rapid City in a 1929 chevy. It also was a "going machine."

For some reason we decided to combine our ownerships of both cars between the six of us. Gasoline was rationed and we had used up our ration cards on the trip to Rapid City. We were told that when a car changed ownership a new ration book was issued. We always had plenty of gas by changing ownership when we ran out of ration stamps.

The P-61 "black widow" fighters we were to use in our mission had not yet been delivered. They were being modified with weather observing equipment, cameras and additional fuel tanks. We had a couple of unmodified planes which were used to check us out. The base also had a couple of B-25's which we could fly to maintain our proficiency.

Craig and I heard about an annual celebration called "The Days of 76" in Deadwood, South Dakota. It was a very notorious town back in the old West and the tradition had been carried on throughout the years. The streets in town maintained the old western appearance. The 2004 TV series "Deadwood" was based on stories that originated in this famous old Western town. It was a four day event with residents from hundreds of miles coming to town. We decided to each check out a B-25, meet over Deadwood and provide a little entertainment. As it turned out, I never did find Deadwood, but Craig found it and shook things up a little. Someone reported him to the Base Commander and he was in hot water for a while. For some reason, nothing came of it, but I was grateful for my poor navigation ability this time.

I was finally scheduled to check out in the P-61, "Black Widow." This consisted of a ride in the Observers seat behind the pilot. Again I learned nothing, but I had paid attention in ground school this time so it probably did not matter. Immediately after the checkout flight I made my first solo flight. It handled just like a B-25 except for two things. While using cruise power settings, both engines overheated and I had to reduce power to remain within temperature limits, secondly, rounding out for landing required a lot of back pressure on the control column even after applying an unusual amount of back trim. I cannot imagine why it was called a P-61. "P," meaning "pursuit," like the P-38. What a difference! The P-61 flew more like a B-17 than a fighter. That was my only flight in a P-61, as the war ended shortly after that. The Japanese probably heard I was coming over in a P-61, so surrendered!

We had been told our mission was to go alone over a designated enemy target, take photos and then radio weather conditions back to headquarters. Targets had to be identified by visual contact before radar became available so they would use that information to determine whether or not to launch the bombers. Considering being over enemy territory in a lumbering P-61, was difficult to imagine. With luck, we might have completed one half of a mission.(if you get what I mean) I think this would have been a very important mission but in my opinion, considering the plane selected for the job, the Government spent a lot of time and money training me for a heck of an impossible mission. The "black widow" was an appropriate name. I'm sure it made a lot of "widows!"

All of us were called into a meeting hall and told, as our names were read off, to state our intentions concerning getting discharged or remaining on active duty for an indefinite period. We had what was considered a "critical job" rating because of the weather course and many of us were offered a regular commission. This meant we could make the Army Air Corps our career. We would be transferred to a base in South Florida and fly weather reconnaissance missions all over the world. This was very tempting, but Uncle Pete was pressuring me and I elected to get out.

All six owners of our car pool chose to get out. John Keig wanted the Pontiac chief to use while going to Northwestern University. No one wanted the Chevy so it was decided the last one to leave would attempt to sell it, which happened to be me. I had my orders and had not yet found a buyer. On my last day I was talking to a bartender in town and when I explained my problem. He said he needed a car for getting to and from work and would give me $100.00 if it would get him home, which was on a hill one mile from work. I said, "Let's go!" The old Chevy did a great job and he purchased the car. I sent an equal share to each of the owners.

I rode a train home and stayed eighteen days before heading for Florida to make my fortune. Before leaving, I purchased a 1938 Desoto. It ran perfect, except on the first day of my trip, I ran out of oil before I needed gas. I purchased six cans and kept my eye on the oil pressure gauge during the rest of the trip. I'll explain later why using a lot of oil was not a problem after I arrived in St. Petersburg.

CHAPTER FIVE

GETTING STARTED ON MY FIRST "MILLION DOLLARS"

ALBERT WHITTED AIRPORT, ST. PETERSBURG, FL

I arrived at Albert Whitted about three o'clock, on a weekday afternoon, in October, 1945. This I can remember, because Uncle Pete was talking to a friend when I presented myself. He introduced me and then told me to take the friend home to Sarasota, Florida. (I guess I was already working for him.) Pete pointed to a PT-19 parked on the ramp and said, "Use that." I had two problems. I had never seen a PT-19 before and had no idea where Sarasota was. Pete saw no problems. The PT-19 was just another airplane and the friend would give me directions to the airport in Sarasota. The PT-19, like the Stearman, had tandem open cockpits, so the friend gave directions by pointing since it was too noisy to talk We landed on a sod field next to Ringling Brothers winter headquarters. I dropped him off and hoped I could find my way back to Whitted. I had no chart and was not at all familiar with the area. I was too busy trying to get acquainted with the airplane during take-off and departing Whitted, to pay attention to the surrounding area. I did find Albert Whitted directly next to Tampa Bay, between the Bay and the city of St. Petersburg. Even I could not miss it! I mention this flight because I quickly learned this was a typical example of how Uncle Pete operated. I never knew what to expect from him, but if I was to become a "millionaire," I really didn't care. Considering this and being almost 21 years old, I felt I could drop the "Uncle" about this time.

Pete operated a flight school (it would now be called fixed base operation) and leased two large hangers with a very well equipped shop in one of them. He stored privately owned planes, as well as his own planes and did extensive airframe repairs, overhauls and inspections. At that time aircraft required 25 hour inspections, which were mostly oil changes and 100 hour inspections which were very thorough. I remember, during inspections, all the panels were removed to inspect cables, electrical and hydraulic lines. Not having ever performed a 100 hour inspection, my job sometimes was limited to removing and replacing the panels. The actual inspections were very thorough and had to be signed off by a qualified A & E mechanic. I do remember that A stood for aircraft and E stood for engine. This rating required very extensive training.

Most pilots are completely dependent on the expertise of mechanics performing routine maintenance and scheduled inspections on their aircraft. I have gone into detail concerning qualified mechanics because the general public does not realize and is uninformed about the responsibilities placed on that aspect of aviation. After an accident, the first thing checked by the FAA is the aircraft's flight and inspection logs. They must be accurate and up to date. Throughout my career in aviation I always tried to express my gratitude to persons responsible for providing me with a very airworthy plane to operate. I must mention that the used drained oil was poured into a 55 gallon drum left setting in the hanger, so now you understand why oil consumption in my 1938 Desoto was no problem.

Pete's business was called Florida Aviation Corp. The company was well known throughout Florida and pilots from all over the state flew in for repairs, inspections or parts and sometimes to drink beer with Pete. He seemed to be known everywhere we went, but was also known to be quite eccentric. I was proud to be introduced as his nephew.

The flight school had Cubs, Aeroncas, a Stearman and Cub Cruiser. The cruiser could seat two persons in the rear seat which had a stick and rudder pedals which was unusual for a sight seeing plane. It was fun telling passengers, "take the controls." Normally within a few minutes they would have the knack of straight and level flight. After landing

I would hear them tell friends how they "flew" the airplane and there was "nothing to it." Little did they know! The cost of a 15 minute flight, which normally consisted of proceeding directly the Gulf Beaches, briefly parallel the beach and return to Albert Whitted was $1.50 per person. Because I let them fly the plane, I frequently received a tip which I really appreciated because I had no income.

The U.S. Coast Guard had a small detachment on the South side of the field. Young enlisted men frequently would ask for a ride in the Stearman to experience some acrobatics. After making sure they were securely strapped in with a parachute snugly attached, I performed a standard flight routine. This consisted of climbing to about 1,500 feet, then after positioning myself just east of the St Petersburg Municipal Pier did a slow roll, a snap rolland a loop followed by a one turn spin recovering at a position to enter the Whitted traffic pattern. The flight took about 10 to 15 minutes and we charged $5.00. I looked forward to those flights and usually received a small tip.

I was living in a small one bedroom apartment with Pete and he paid for our meals and rent. The tips were my beer money and I kept gas in the car by lending it to Pete's friends.

Fortunately I had a commercial pilot's license which allowed me to fly for hire. While on active duty at Chanute our class had been ushered into a room and to our surprise, we were given commercial licenses with single and multi engine ratings. No exams were administered! At that time I really did not realize the significance of having this and how difficult and expensive it was for civilian pilots to obtain pilot ratings.

Ernie Baker was the chief pilot and he immediately began preparing me for my instructors rating. Until I received that rating, I "hopped" passengers and was "chief hanger boy." That meant I serviced and parked the planes in the hanger, at the beginning, during and at the end of each day. I also learned how to "prop" a plane. Light aircraft did not have starters so the prop had to be manually pulled through compression to start the engine. As the engine started sputtering and coughing, you thought, "I did that!"

My first charter was to take a passenger to Fort Meyers in an Aeronca Champion. It had a 65 horsepower engine, with tandem seating and primarily used as a trainer. Ernie introduced me to the passenger and his wife who was there to see him off. She looked at me and said, "He's too young to be flying passengers." Again I was put in my place! Ernie gave her no alternative, assured her I was qualified and she finally, reluctantly, consented. She said goodbye to her husband like she would never again see him, or else they were newly weds facing their first separation. It was a very emotional good- bye.

My next experience was after I was asked to test fly a BT-13 that had been modified in Pete's shop to have it conform to FAA standards (Federal Aviation Authority) for licensing. The owner had heard of my previous experience in the BT-13. It had a fuel tank in each wing and for take off; the selector was put in position to draw fuel from a tank that had some sort of standpipe to provide an added safety feature. I cannot remember which tank it was now, but I went through the before take-off check list making sure everything was positioned properly. I took off to the East, which after clearing the runway; put you directly over Tampa Bay. As I climbed through about 100 feet, the engine quit. Fortunately, the Army Air Corps had trained me well in emergency procedures, which called for immediately switching fuel tanks. It started coughing and sputtering and I recovered just a few feet above Tampa Bay, able to complete the test flight. Now you are wondering what I did wrong. Any pilot will tell you, while silently chastising me, always, without exception, remove the caps from the fuel tanks and visually check or dipstick each tank during the pre-flight inspection. I had not done this! Another lesson painfully re-learned!

On a Sunday morning in January of 1946, (this I can never forget,) Pete said he had five passengers wishing to go for a sightseeing flight over the Gulf Beaches. I reminded him we did not have an airplane capable of carrying more than two passengers. I was then informed a friend of his had flown a UC-78 (Twin engine five place Cessna) into the Albert Whitted the night before. He had recently purchased it surplus from the Army Air Corps and had it licensed and reconditioned for carrying passengers. Again I reminded Pete that I had never ridden in a UC-78, much less flown one. Well, he reminded me that it was just another airplane and I did have a multi-engine rating. I did know a pilot that had recently flown a UC- 78, so was able to get some information about power settings, airspeeds and fuel tank sequence; because this is critical information no matter what airplane you fly.

By this time Jim Cronin had arrived in St. Pete, was also working for Pete and he asked to ride along. If you will remember, Jim was my idol and mentor as a young boy and now we were working together. Jim was still recovering after having spent two years in a German prison of war camp. I was very excited when I was told he was coming down to Florida.

We were informed that our passengers were the Great Grandson and family of Teddy Roosevelt and instructed to give them the VIP treatment. Boy did I ever do that up right! Take off went smooth and I gave them a very nice smooth flight over the Gulf Beaches. I returned to Albert Whitted and entered the traffic pattern to land to the East on the East/West runway, which is no longer there. I positioned the landing gear switch to the "down" position and then back to neutral. This was the procedure used in another plane I had flown with a switch to activate the landing gear. Everything looked fine as I came over the fence to begin my flare. I did notice Pete alongside the runway waving his arms and thought he was waving the Roosevelt's a welcome back. I was holding the Cessna off in landing attitude when I felt a terrible vibration. As I appeared to be settling closer to the runway than expected, I realized the vibration was the props digging into the concrete runway so knew the landing gear was not extended. We slid a short distance and stopped at an angle to the runway. Until I looked at the landing gear switch, I thought the gear had collapsed. The switch was in the "up" position. I really did not want to get out of the airplane and face Pete. Kermit's wife just looked at me in disgust. They thought I had forgotten to put the gear down. Pete had seen the gear come down and then back up while I was on the downwind leg. He knew exactly what I had done. I quickly learned the switch was to remain in the down position. Also I later found out that while the gear was in the fully extended position, it could be seen from the cockpit by looking over the leading edge of the wing. The District Manager for the FAA, Ames Ulrich, was over from Tampa early the next morning to investigate the accident. I'm sure because he was a friend of Pete's, all he said to me was, "you were an Army Air Corps pilot I've been told." From this remark I knew what he thought of military pilots. Ames, of course, was an old time civilian pilot and had no idea how intensive our training program had been and I did not provide a very good example with this disgusting landing.

Pete decided to purchase a couple of surplus Cessna's to either use for multi-engine training or re- sell. The Army Air Corps had stored them on a closed air base in Cuero, Texas. By this time several more of his Air Corps pals had arrived in St. Pete to make their fortune working for him. He had two of them drive Alfie Frieberger and me out to Cuero in order to select two that were flyable and bring them back to St. Pete.

We had dozens to choose from but most had very spongy fabric and engines that would not turn over. Finally we selected two, did a thorough pre-flight, agreed Alfie would take off first and we would take turns leading. I watched him take-off and as the landing gear came up; his plane started settling toward the ground. He dropped out of sight behind some trees and of course I thought he crashed. What seemed like an eternity, he reappeared, slowly climbing out. I then apprehensively took off not knowing what caused Alfie's very erratic performance after becoming airborne. I found out later that just as he broke ground, he heard a loud bang from his left side and at the same time his seat slid fully back. He could just barely reach the control column but not the rudder pedals for leverage, so was not able to apply back pressure to raise the nose. At the last second he unbuckled his seat belt, somehow eased forward in the seat and regained control of the plane. The loud noise was when a large section of fabric on his upper left wing had torn loose leaving a big gap. He lost some lift from the wing, causing the plane to feel left wing heavy. Shortly after departing Cuero we had encountered a heavy rain storm that stayed with us until were abeam New Orleans. Alfie was getting very left wing heavy with accumulated rain, so he signaled me to land there. At this time I was unaware of his problem, but followed him in. After taxiing to the parking area I looked at his wing and saw the accumulation of water and section of missing fabric. I was amazed that he was able to maintain control.

Considering what happened on take-off and then the left wing problem, I wondered how many pilots could have handled the emergency as professionally as Alfie did. We had the wing patched and again headed for St. Pete. After landing at Whitted, Alfie turned off the runway and headed straight for the parking ramp, not using the paved taxiways. The bottom of his fuselage struck an object, tore the fabric and broke a couple of wooden ribs. Alfie tried to explain his precarious take-off and left wing problem to Pete, not exploiting his obvious skill in saving the airplane, but all Pete could see was the damaged fuselage. He really showed his anger.

Alfie later became quite a celebrity. He was called back to active duty at the time of the "Berlin airlift" in 1948. This was a very difficult mission and important enough to have a movie made called "The Big Lift" Alfie was given the part of copilot on the crew selected to demonstrate the activities of a typical airlift crew during a routine mission.

The movie starred Montgomery Clift, a very renowned actor and several other well known actors. Alfie had a very large speaking part and it seemed strange to see him on the screen, as we had paled around a lot before his recall. He seemed very natural on the screen and I fully expected him to make acting his career after leaving the Air Corps

A young pilot named Johnny Greene had a Stearman that he parked next to Pete's ramp area. He did not work, so spent full time tinkering with his plane. Johnny and I practiced for our instructor's rating together. He was an excellent pilot and frequently he would take me up in his Stearman. He and I would take turns doing acrobatics. Several times he motioned to me to take the controls, while he got out of the front cockpit (without a chute) and crawled all over the airplane.

One time I noticed he was making full stop landings; landing toward the North on the North/South runway. He would stop short and then disappear behind a hanger while taxiing back for another take-off. There was quite a delay while behind the hanger, so I walked out to where I could see what he was doing. He was out of the airplane smoothing the loose gravel between the concrete runway and seawall. Actually he was seeing how close he could put the Stearman tail wheel to the seawall. In those days we made "three point" landings meaning both main wheels and tail wheel touching down simultaneously. A slight miscalculation would put him and his Stearman in Tampa Bay!

Several times I saw Johnny sitting on the upper wing of his plane holding a rope tied to posts extending out from each side the engine cowling. One day he asked me to sit in the cockpit while he propped the engine to get it started. After the engine started, he crawled to his position on the upper wing, took hold of the ropes he had attached to steel posts mounted on each side of the engine cowling and motioned me to rev up the engine. He seemed to be enjoying it and we did this several more times during the following week for his strange, unusual "enjoyment." He asked me to take-off with him on the wing, but I flatly refused knowing the pilot flying the plane is responsible for activities during flight.

This was absolutely forbidden without prior FAA approval, which we would never get. One evening, after everyone on the airport had gone home, Johnny asked me to taxi around the airport with him on the wing. I saw nothing wrong with that, as everyone seemed to be gone, so I consented. First thing I knew, we were in take-off position on the active runway which headed North/West. The flight path after take-off on this runway went directly over downtown St. Pete. Johnny motioned me to rev up the engine, which I did. He then urged me to release the brakes which I did. (The expression, "the devil made me do it," was not popular then, so I had no excuse.) First thing I knew we were accelerating down the runway. Johnny was sitting upright on the wing causing so much drag I could not get airborne. By the time I realized this, it was too late to abort and I was certain we would go right into the airport boundary fence. Johnny being the pilot he was, sensed the predicament and leaned back, streamlining his body and we leapt into the air barely clearing the fence. With all that drag, I was hardly able to climb and felt like I was flying on an egg shell about to crack. We staggered over downtown St Pete and just then, Johnny sat up. The Stearman started to shutter and thankfully, Johnny recognized this and just as I thought we were going "in," he again leaned back; I judiciously nursed the plane around the traffic pattern and somehow safely landed. When I taxied back to the ramp, there must have been over one hundred people waiting for us. I was too anxious to get out of there to hear what they were saying but I did hear later that we scared the daylights out of many people. The next morning, Ames Ulrich, the regional FAA inspector whom I've already met, was waiting for Johnny and me. He directed us into the airport manager's office, Cliff Pyatt and really gave us a going over. His final words were to the airport manager and I remember exactly what he said. "If you ever see these two walking toward the same airplane, call me and neither of them will ever pilot an airplane again." I feel sure we got off this easy because of his being an old friend of Pete's. Pete never said a word about this and I'm sure it brought back a lot of his "crazy Pete" memories.

One evening Pete informed me I was to fly a "friend" of his, the president of St. Pete Junior College, to Miami the next morning. I was to use the Cub Cruiser which carried sufficient fuel to make the flight without making a fuel stop. We took off very early because he was to make a luncheon speech. We should have made it in plenty of time, but I did not anticipate an exceptionally strong headwind. Cars were passing us by on the highway below us. With still a long distance remaining, we were running low on fuel, necessitating landing as soon as possible. The chart indicated an airstrip at Belle Glade, on the South tip of Lake Okeechobee. The field was deserted, however, there were a few aircraft scattered about. I did see a Stearman, probably used for crop dusting, with the fuel gauge indicating about half full. I found an empty 5 gallon fuel can nearby, so opened the fuel petcock on the Stearman and "borrowed" five gallons. I poured this into the Cruiser fuel tank and we were on our way. The college president did not say a word, but he was looking at his watch. We arrived at the Miami airport about one thirty and he immediately left for his luncheon. A short time later he returned, fuming mad. The luncheon had apparently ended early, without a "guest speaker." I felt I had done my best, even "stealing" fuel, so did not feel guilty, but just sorry for him. Pete had told me the president was an aviation enthusiast, so with the cruiser having a stick and rudder pedals in the rear seat, I let him fly all the way home. This, I could tell, pleased him, so by the time I talked him through a landing, he was quite congenial. I never heard any more about it.

I had been taking an instrument course with United Flying Services, which was also located on Albert Whitted. The instructor, whose last name was Lindsey, took three students at a time in a UC-78. (twin engine Cessna.) We would each practice for an hour and spend the other two hours in the back seat. It had recently been licensed by the FAA and the interior was nicely lined with very pretty upholstery material. We always flew about two thousand feet, where the air can be quite turbulent especially during summer. One morning, after I had consumed a few beers the night before, I started getting airsick. Having no burp bag, I decided to open the cabin door, so I would not throw up on the nice upholstery. As soon as the door opened, the suction pulled most of the lining off the sides and ceiling. Mr. Lindsey, rightfully so, was quite angry and let me know this, but I feel sure, because he was a friend of Pete's, allowed me to complete the course. He usually came to work smelling of booze and was chewing gum, so he should have understood my predicament.

On the day I was to take my instrument flight exam, who should show up as my check pilot, but Ames Ulrich. I really considered canceling out, but Pete would never understand. He had been pushing me to get the rating. Just like during practice, we were only allowed to use needle/ball and airspeed. We also had an altimeter, rate of climb indicator and magnetic compass. As I explained earlier, ask any old pilot and he'll verify, this is not a very accommodating instrument panel. I was required to perform a few maneuvers, such as steep turns and a radio range let down. All turns had to be timed adjusting for lag and lead, when turning to North and South headings. I managed to perform the check to Ames satisfaction, so he passed me. Later, I began to think he actually liked me, because he made a point of telling Pete I was a good instrument pilot. Maybe I also reminded him of his younger flying days! In June, 1946, I took my flight instructor check with one of Ame's assistants and he also passed me which pleased Pete because now I could actually earn my keep.

CHAPTER SIX

BIRTH OF TAMPA INTERNATIONAL AIRPORT

At this time the Army Air Corps was pulling out of Drew field in Tampa and the entire field with all its facilities was to be turned over to the city of Tampa. Pete had been doing some wheeling and dealing with the Mayor of Tampa and he also became good friends with the Air Corps officers responsible for preparing Drew for closing.

DREW FIELD, (TAMPA INTERNATIONAL AIRPORT) TAMPA, FLORIDA

Shortly after obtaining my instructor's rating, Pete informed me that Florida Aviation was about to open a flying school on Tampa International and I would be "manager and chief pilot." He had rented a building on the East end of a large ramp adjacent to what was known as "the big black hanger." He had also rented the black hanger, which had a large shop on the South side, with a loft above it. The building on the East end of the ramp would be our flight operations center and the loft in the black hanger our ground school class room. With each aeronautical rating, a certain number of hours had to be spent in ground school, followed by a written and flight exam administered by the FAA, or a designated representative, so we had the facilities to become operational.

My first responsibility was to obtain whatever FAA licenses were necessary to prepare students for pilot ratings of private, commercial, multi-engine, instrument and flight instructor. I was to have the school operating as soon as possible, but Pete did not tell me how to go about this. I was also to hire a ground school instructor and flight instructors as needed. Because I already knew the Regional FAA Inspector, Ames Ulrich, I decided his office was a good place to start. I had flown over to Tampa International and checked the facilities we were to use there and then drove over to the FAA office in Tampa to make application for the flight school ratings. I was not surprised to find that the people working in the FAA office already knew Pete's intentions, so they were ready for me. I really cannot remember all the details, but I'm sure because of Pete, they made it easy for me. Also, at this time, I believe there were only two other flight schools in Tampa and they were on Peter O Knight Airport on the other side of Tampa. Everyone, including the FAA, was anxious for us to start operating off recently acquired Tampa International Airport.

At this time I was living with my Mom and Dad in St. Petersburg. They had moved down in the spring of 1946 along with my two sisters, Betty and Joanie and my aunt Claire, Pete's twin sister with her two children. My other uncle, Ted, was already running the shop on the Albert Whitted. Pete had lured the whole Hubert family to join him in Florida! We were all to become "millionaires," under Pete's leadership.

While living with my Folks, I commuted by plane to Tampa each day from Albert Whitted Airport. Whitted did not have a tower, nor did Tampa International and radar did not exist, so I would never get above about ten feet while flying over Tampa Bay. Occasionally I would see a really large fish and I remember pulling up to clear Gandy bridge. Interstate 275 had not yet been constructed.

Before long we had the required licenses and ratings so we were in business. Pete had provided me with several Aeroncas and cubs, a Stearman and Cessna UC78 for multi-engine and instrument training. He had fully equipped the shop and hired a few mechanics. We were the only facility of any kind on the entire Tampa International Airport. You can imagine the depth of nostalgia I sense whenever I see the airport as it is today. Word of our operation got around Tampa very quickly and I had no problem hiring flight instructors. I lucked out in finding a ground school instructor. His name was Lueman Stevens, (Steve) and he was also a flight instructor. He was extremely well qualified at both. The students admired and respected him.

Our student enrollment grew very rapidly because of the GI bill. I personally processed all the applications and turned them in to the regional V.A center. It was in the hotel on St. Pete Beach now called the Don CeSar Beach Resort. During the war it was used as a rest and recuperation center for returning veterans. I went there every Wednesday afternoon and after completing business would have a couple of beers at one of the open beer bars on the beach. There was not much else on that part of the beaches at that time. I also gave all the multi-engine and instrument instruction.

The shop was taking transient aircraft in for inspections, repairs or modifications and if required, I would make the test flights after planes completed repairs. In so doing, I had the opportunity to fly just about every make and type of light planes in operation. I also flew charter flights in the Cessna which sometimes was very interesting. I should also mention that about the time we opened shop, Pete got married. He had rented the former Base Commander's home, which was on Tampa International and he invited Jim Cronin and me to live with them. I really don't think we had a choice. Anyway, it was very convenient and cheap. We paid no rent.

I had a couple of interesting things happen in attempting to make some test flights. While doing a slow roll in a BT-13, I suddenly felt a severe vibration. In checking the cockpit, I saw that a large section on the left side of the fuselage was gone. I still had good control so went into a steep left bank hoping to see the panel floating down. Sure enough, it was going side to side gently descending over an open field. I watched it land, marked the spot in my mind and quickly returned to Tampa International. Without saying anything to anyone, I got in my car and drove to the exact location. There the panel was, without a scratch or dent! I tied as much of it as possible in the trunk, put a rag on the end and headed back. Without hesitation, I took a screw driver out of my tool box, put the panel in place on the fuselage, tightened the zeus screws holding the panel in place and returned to flight operations. I told no one for two reasons. On a test flight, knowing the panels had been removed during maintenance, I should have checked them during preflight. Also the mechanic responsible for Okaying the plane for flight would have been severely chastised by Pete. I had seen Pete chew people out before. He really had a knack for it. However, at the end of the day, he would return to the shop and invite as many as could go, to the Little Beaver for beers. It was about the only bar on Dale Mabre and just a short distance from the field. Jim and I ate and drank beer there just about every night after servicing the planes and putting them back in the hanger.

My other experience was also in a BT-13 that had also been in the shop for maintenance. In attempting to taxi, when I pushed the left rudder pedal, the plane turned right. The tail wheel, being steerable, was controlled by the same cable system as the rudder, so it also was rigged in reverse which would have made steering on the ground difficult but possible. As stupid as it seems now, I was really tempted to attempt to take off. Both the rudder and tail wheel were essential for directional control during take off and landing, so this was a real challenge to my coordination and presence of mind. Thank Lord, I did not try it! I'm the first to admit, I never really was that good! This incident was also kept from Pete.

I found instrument instructing very boring. I had a hard time staying awake. When the student would start his simulated instrument orientation, let down and approach, I would always file an "instrument flight plan." This would give us priority over all aircraft flying VFR, (visual flight rules) in the local area, so the tower would give traffic advisories concerning our position to other aircraft. Our destination was Tampa International and the south leg of the radio range, which was part of the simulated instrument approach, went directly over MacDill Air Base at their traffic pattern altitude. This was a very busy military field with mostly B-29 training taking place. The B-29 was the largest plane in operation at the time, so I became alert and enjoyed watching this "monster" leave the traffic pattern so we could come through, usually, in a BT-13 or later on in a Bonanza.

I had a "reserve assignment" in one of the B-29 squadrons and when the pilots found out it was me disrupting their training, they acted angry, but actually got a kick out of knowing I was the pilot. I was still only a 2nd Lt. and not qualified in the B-29 and yet, I had priority.

During my second year of instructing instruments, I received a message to report to the FAA regional office. Of course now, I thought what had I, or one of the students or instructors done? The assistant inspector that had given me my instructor's check flight was waiting for me. I thought, this is a relief; thank goodness it's not Ames Ulrich! He asked to see my pilot's license and then looked up, showing disappointment and said, "Are you really only 22 years old?" I felt apologetic so answered "I'm sorry," still not knowing why. He then explained he wanted to make me an instrument flight examiner, but the minimum age for this rating was 24. It would have been a very prestigious rating. I believe I would have been the only instructor in Tampa to have this privilege. It would have been helpful to have this rating since I had been taking my students to the St. Pete Clearwater Airport to receive their instrument check flight from a very experienced pilot named, Vic Carmichael. You will hear more of Vic later. Incidentally, all of my students passed on their first attempt.

I also had some other interesting charter flights while working for Pete. There was a lady (I use the term loosely) living in Thomasville, Georgia, that chartered the twin engine Cessna a number of times. Her husband had died leaving her with some oil wells in Louisiana and she was 29, which I considered quite old. I would fly to Thomasville, pick her and sometimes her good looking niece up, take them to their destination, wait for them at her expense and then return to Thomasville. The Cessna did not have air conditioning so the cabin stayed very warm. She always boarded with a thermos of martinis, I assume to give her courage to fly with me! As soon as the cabin door closed, she and her niece, if along, would disrobe down to bra and panties. Of course I never objected, but it was quite a distraction. (Pleasant) They did not want to soil their dresses. Sometimes, while in a public place, after a few martinis, she would get vulgar. This happened in Havana, Cuba. (Back when we could travel there at random) We were in a very plush restaurant, when she stood up and started cussing out the waiter. I wanted to crawl under the table. Luckily, we were quickly ushered to the door before the police were called.

She really did scare me onetime. The back seat of the Cessna had a sort of armrest on each side. Actually, it was just an opening in the interior lining, with a piece of wood as the armrest, with only fabric between the cabin and outside. I smelled smoke and looked back intending to have her put out her cigarette. What I saw was an ashtray on the armrest and she, without looking, was fumbling with her lit cigarette over the ashtray, scattering hot ashes everywhere except in the ashtray.. Fabric skin on an aircraft is heavily covered with dope, which is extremely flammable. I had read that an aircraft covered in fabric, that caught on fire took 18 seconds to become just a frame. Not very airworthy! My last charter with her was to Baton Rouge Louisiana. She was going back there to live and I actually felt relieved.

Don Hartung, one of our instructors about my age, wanted to ride along. He was building up multi-engine time in order to get a multi-engine rating. We had an unexpected head wind and were running low on fuel (again) which I had not anticipated. I located an airfield on my chart close to our route, so decided to land and refuel. As we approached, I could see the field was very short for a Cessna to land and had trees in the approach flight path which meant I could not "drag" it in as you do in attempting a short field landing. Don turned the controls over to me, I think, for two reasons. He did not want to take the blame if we hit the far end fence and of course he wasn't experienced in landing the Cessna. I cleared the tree tops by inches, cut the power, applied the brakes right after touchdown and stopped a few yards short of the fence, after some very doubtful moments. I hoped that taught Don a good lesson! I really had not planned the flight very well. Incidentally, Don entered the aviation cadet program in 1948 and retired after 35 years as a Brigadier General. His brother Paul, one of Don's students, entered the cadet program shortly after Don and retired at the same rank. I'm sure Don benefited from my poor judgment in attempting that landing.

We had a policy in which we gave what was called a "dollar ride" to any potential student. The instructors did not get paid for this flight and I was on salary, so if available, I would give the ride. The purpose of course, was to motivate the person into wanting to enter the flight program. Actually, there was no charge for the ride. I always tried to reassure them that learning to fly was not as difficult or complicated as they may have expected.

One day a nicely dressed young man indicated a desire to sign up, but was reluctant, because he did not feel it was safe. I assured him his "dollar ride" would satisfy that problem. I put him in the front seat of an Aeronca Champion and taxied out to wait for my green light from the control tower for clearance to take the active runway. We would be taking off to the West, following a National Airlines DC-4. (4 prop driven engines.} When the DC-4 was well down the runway, I received a green light from the control tower and proceeded to take off knowing I would be far enough behind the DC-4, to avoid it's prop wash. I was wrong and so was the man in the tower. After attaining about fifty feet of altitude, the prop wash hit us. We were tossed into a near vertical bank to the left, with the nose dangerously high. I applied full power, full forward and right pressure on the stick along with full right rudder, all without a response. We were sides-slipping at that angle, in a very rapid descent when finally, at the last second, the plane responded to my corrections and we resumed a normal climb. Without exaggeration, the left wing was just inches from the runway as I regained control. In talking to the tower operator later, I was told he thought a crash was inevitable and had already pushed the emergency alarm button. He also was surprised that I hit the prop wash, which should have been well cleared of the runway at the time I hit it. Back to the potential student! As I climbed to altitude he frantically pointed back to the field, indicating that he wanted us to land immediately. After landing, without a word, he hastily got out of the plane, went directly to his car and drove away. Needless to say, that was his first and last flight. Another lesson learned and from that time on, I gave plenty of spacing prior to taking off behind another plane.

One Sunday morning, Pete asked me to start up the Cessna and taxi it to line up with the nearby taxi-way. He was with his good friend, Charlie Banks, from his National Airlines days, who was now head of maintenance for National. Occasionally, he would come up from Miami and he and Pete would have a fling. I could tell they had both been drinking and to the best of my knowledge, Pete had never flown the Cessna. In fact, I'm not sure Pete had ever flown as pilot in a multi-engine plane before and I know he had not flown as pilot for a long time. Of course his physical, which must be renewed every two years, had expired long ago, because Pete didn't have time to bother with such petty things. Pete was insistent and it was "his airplane," so I followed his orders. I lined up on the taxiway got out, but left the engines running, because I wasn't sure Pete remembered the starting procedure. They climbed on board while we all watched and without hesitation, or stopping, he taxied to the take-off position and immediately took off.

I noticed the landing gear never came up as he climbed straight out to about 1000 feet, made a left 90 degree turn, followed by another left 90 degree turn, which put him on the downwind leg, with the landing gear still down. At that time I had to rush into operations, as the phone was ringing. It was the control tower, asking in a very angry tone of voice, who was piloting the Cessna. He had taken off without clearance and this was a serious violation! When I responded "Pete," he said. "No kidding!" As if, this is what's expected of Pete. Anyway, Pete turned base, then final and made a very nice landing. He taxied back to where they took over and gave the plane to me to park. I had two questions for him, never mentioning the tower call. Why didn't he raise the landing gear and what was the purpose of the brief flight? His response was that he was afraid he would forget to lower the gear and he and Charlie had a bet. Charlie had bet Pete that he could not get the Cessna in the air and successfully land it. I think the bet was for a beer!

After returning from a charter in the Cessna one day, a mechanic was waiting for me as I parked. He was there to claim his flashlight which had an extended flexible neck for looking into hard to get at places. He searched the interior and then started on the outside. He found it in the left wheel well and started nonchalantly walking away. I stopped him to emphasize the serious damage it could have caused to the landing gear supports during retraction or extension. I easily could have had the gear collapse on landing, jam, or damage structure so as to render the gear inoperable. To me, this was a very serious, careless, mistake but for a change, this time I was not at fault! Again I did not mention this to Pete.

Another time, two things happened which were because of my neglectfulness. Late one night, while returning alone in the Cessna from a charter to Miami, I lost all electrical power. I did not have a flashlight, which is required during night flights, so I was really handicapped not being able to read the instrument panel. That was mistake number one. Upon reaching Tampa, I could not contact the control tower, nor could they see me. I had to "hand crank" the landing gear down and would have no flaps for landing, which wasn't a big deal. I would just come in a little faster, but had plenty of runway. After a long period of cranking, I had to assume the gear was down, as there was no way to visually check it. It was too dark to see it over the leading edge of the wing. With no landing lights, it reminded me of my blackout landing while at Luke. At least I would know what to expect. There was no moon and all I had were the soft blue lights on each side of the runway. Making sure there was no other traffic, I entered the traffic pattern and landed. It went better than I expected and I was glad when I was safely down. I went into our flight operations and called the tower in case they saw me taxiing in. My phone call was the first time they were aware I was even in the area. I hate to admit it, but the only time I filed a flight plan in those days was when I had to fly on instruments, only because it was an absolute requirement. Not filing a flight plan was my second mistake. Had I been forced "down" somewhere, no one would have known where, when why, or even if I had taken off.

I frequently had to take passengers to Crystal River, Florida. There was an airstrip just south of the city along U. S. 19 which I assume was also a pasture because of cows grazing on it There was just one short grass strip running North/South, suitable for landing. Quite often I would have to "buzz" cows, to chase them off the strip and then swing around very quickly to land before they returned. It was a fun maneuver and only once did I have to do it a second time.

Pete decided he wanted to compete for an FAA license to start an interstate commuter airline. Somehow he had obtained what was called a "docket number," which allowed him to compete for the commuter permit. One of the prerequisites was to prove he could maintain a scheduled route for three months. The airline obtaining the permit would be carrying mail, which would automatically generate a steady income. My job was to fly the scheduled route in the Cessna three times a day at the same times each day. The selected route was from Tampa International, to Albert Whitted to Sarasota Airport and return by way of the same route. Scheduled airlines did not service Whitted or Sarasota. Pete had a step made for easy boarding of the Cessna for the women and elderly. At Tampa International, I parked in front of the terminal building with the step in place for about 30 minutes before each scheduled flight. The ticket agents for Eastern and National, the only airlines operating out of Tampa, had been briefed on our operation and Pete and the station managers for both airlines were drinking buddies, so both airlines were very cooperative. At take off time I put the steps on board, flew to the next scheduled destination, parked where I thought any passengers might be, waited 30 minutes, threw the step on board and followed this routine at every stop. I was ticket agent, ground crew and pilot. After three months, without missing a flight, Pete was informed the contract was awarded to a cab company in Orlando. They were using a Beech D-18, which was much more suitable for the service. I think I carried two passengers during the entire operation. In order to help subsidize the operation, I sometimes took a multi-engine student along and charged for dual instruction. Actually it was excellent experience for the student who probably had aspirations of becoming an airline pilot. I taught him all phases of an efficient one man airline operation.

One time I had a charter to take a passenger to Orlando and used a Cub PA-11. As usual, I had a headwind, therefore was flying as low as possible because the wind gets stronger as you go higher. I suddenly received a tap on the shoulder from the passenger. He pointed down, which made me think he was airsick and wanted to land. I started looking for a suitable field and he tapped my shoulder again. This time he yelled "cigarette!" Now he had my full attention! He pointed to the base of the control stick in the rear seat where there should have been a covering over the hole in the floorboard at the base of the stick, but the covering was gone. Now I realized what happened. His lit cigarette fell through the hole unto the fabric which covered the bottom of the fuselage. It was very hot that day so I was flying with the cabin window open which is why I did not know he was smoking and I absolutely would have forbidden. Again, I thought of it taking only eighteen seconds before I would be attempting to keep an engine and airframe airborne. If we were to catch on fire, I felt sure this would happen before I could manage a landing and I did not see a suitable field anyway. After many tense moments I finally decided we were safe. From then on, I would very positively emphasize, "no smoking," to my passengers. I don't know who learned the greater lesson, the passenger or me. I think I did because he didn't know about the eighteen seconds.

Another time, Pete asked me to take him and an airline Captain from somewhere in South America to Atlanta, Georgia in the Cessna to conduct some business. As we approached the Atlanta area, we encountered a huge thunderstorm which appeared to be directly over the airport. I did not have sufficient fuel to orbit while waiting for the storm to pass over, so opted to land at a small landing strip nearby. The storm had already passed over the clay strip so I should have realized it would be slick. The runway ran North/South and had a string of high tension lines crossing the approach to the South end. The wind sock indicated a light wind from the West so I chose to land to the South in order to drag it in for a short field landing. I touched down close to the strip boundary at the North end, but when I applied the brakes, the wheels locked and we skidded, like on ice. The South end of the runway was coming up fast and I considered going around until I saw the high tension wires which I did not think I could clear. We had slowed down considerably, but when it appeared inevitable that we would slide into the barbed wire boundary fence, I attempted a "ground loop" to the right. This would pivot the plane on the right landing gear, hopefully causing no damage. I applied full right rudder and full power on the left engine, turned almost 180 degrees while sliding sideways to the left. We were almost stopped when the left wheel dropped in a shallow dip, which put too much side stress on the gear strut collapsing it. The left engine nacelle and prop dug into the clay causing severe damage. We got out and Pete looked sick. By this time the wind sock now indicated a slight wind from the North which made him question my judgment in landing to the South. (Downwind) Worse than that, in my haste to attempt the ground loop, I neglected to unlock the tail wheel allowing it to freely swivel 180 degrees which is why the plane skidded sideways instead of pivoting on the right wheel. I could really sense his disgust! We had the plane towed into the hanger and took a bus to Atlanta. After they finished their business we took a bus back to Tampa. I cannot describe how horrible and embarrassed I felt. It definitely rates number "2" in my long list of embarrassing "plight" incidents!

I had been giving my "little" sister, Joanie, flying lessons for several months in the Aeronca champion and determined she was ready to solo just prior to her sixteenth birthday. Sixteen was the minimum age to solo, so it seemed like a good idea to let her solo on her birthday, which happened to fall on a Sunday. Without Joanie knowing, I arranged to have my Mom, Dad and Sister Betty watch the event while hiding behind a hanger. My Mom really showed her displeasure about Joanie flying, but reluctantly agreed to join us for the occasion.

The procedure for soloing a student was for the instructor, while shooting a couple of landings with the student, to intentionally jerk the controls just before touch down, causing the plane to touch down in an unusual attitude forcing the student to recover from a "bad" landing. If this went well, the student was ready to solo. Joanie did well, so I got out of the Aeronca and sent her on her way. For a successful first solo, the student had to make three full stop landings with the instructor briefing the student after each landing. Joanie made two perfect landings, but on her third approach, she struck a bird with her right wing strut, not very far from the windshield. This scared the daylights out of me, but Joanie retained her cool and landed with the bird still attached to the strut. I shudder to think of the consequences if it had gone through the windshield.

My Mom, Dad and Betty came out of hiding and we all congratulated Joanie. After Joanie left, my Mom let me know in know in no uncertain words, how much she was opposed to Joanie flying. This got me to thinking about my being fully responsible should Joanie have an accident, so proceeded very cautiously with her training. As required, she completed three solo flights and started working toward her private pilot's license. I never told anyone, but for some reason I began having misgivings about her progress and could not determine if that was the case, or maybe I was being too critical because of my Mother's attitude and she was my "little" sister. It seemed to me her control of the plane was more mechanical than by "feel" and perhaps she was not gaining the "self confidence" normally observed as a student pilot built up flying hours.

One day after she had about twenty hours, the only plane available to fly was the old Cub Cruiser. It handled just like the Aeronca, but I shot a couple of landings with her before turning her loose to go solo. At her scheduled landing time, I watched her approach. She was landing to the East on the East/West runway. There was a boundary fence in front of the runway and Joanie mis-calculated her approach, descended below the top of the fence and pulled up at the last second, just barely clearing it, before plopping down on the extreme end of the runway. She should have recognized that her approach would bring her in too low, long before the abrupt pull up. Also, she did not apply power when she pulled up, which should have been automatic, considering her experience!

This convinced me that I would no longer encourage Joanie to fly and strangely enough, she never again asked to be scheduled. Later on, I would brag about her soloing on her sixteenth birthday and never let on that I was very relieved when it was over. My Mom certainly was too! As far as I know, Joanie never piloted an airplane again even though her future husband owned a flight school on the Albert Whitted Airport and held an instructor's rating.

CHAPTER SEVEN
EASY COME, EASY GO

In late fall, 1947 Pete informed me he had sold the flight school. He assured me the buyers would allow me to remain as manager and chief pilot. There went my "million" dollars! The buyers were Pat Johnson and Ray Bustler. Pat would be the promoter (not at Pete's level,) and Ray would be a silent partner. They were both great guys to work for. Although Pat was in charge of the school, he was around very little. He was always out promoting. He did not change a single procedure as far as the operation of the school went. He hired his sister in-law to be office secretary which eased my work load. I still made the weekly trips to the VA but she processed all the paper work. I was to remain at the same salary, but as an incentive, would receive one percent of the gross income. I agreed not to start collecting it, until they became better acquainted with the operation. I never should have agreed to that, because it was never mentioned again. The office secretary was to keep track of the account.

Just before the change of ownership, Jim Cronin left for Elmhurst to be with his ailing Mother. He was an only child and felt it was his obligation. That was another reason I was glad to see Pat's secretary take over the paper work. I really missed Jim for many obvious reasons.

The Beach Bonanza had just become operational, so Pat was awarded the distinction of becoming one of the few Florida dealers. It was a beautiful five place airplane, far ahead of it's time. He immediately purchased one to use in the school and also as a demonstrator. It was very economical to operate, so I used it for instrument instruction and charter.

Pat had a large sign made up indicating charter prices. We put a desk along with the sign in the terminal building and either Steve or I would be there at three o'clock every afternoon seeking passengers. Eastern and National were still the only airlines operating out of Tampa at that time and that was by far their busiest hour. I had become good friends with most of Eastern and National's ticket agents, so they would make announcements introducing our charter service during Steve's and my absence. A couple of the agents were students in our school.

The Beach factory equipped a Bonanza with additional fuel tanks and initiated a sensational sales program.

Bill Odem, a prominent Beach salesman, flew a Bonanza non stop from Hawaii to New York, setting a distance record for single engine aircraft. Bill then toured the country in his modified Bonanza, visiting Beach dealers. Pat made arrangements to join up with him over St. Pete with two escorting Bonanzas, circle St. Pete and Tampa and land at Tampa International. Hillsboro County Aviation Authority planned a dinner dance in his honor for that evening. Pat flew our company Bonanza, borrowed a Bonanza for me and we met Bill at a scheduled time over downtown St. Pete.

This was my first opportunity to fly formation since leaving the Army Air Corps and I tucked in very close to impress Bill Odem. Pat did not have formation flying experience, so hung back a little. After circling Tampa, Bill called Tampa tower requesting a straight in approach, landing to the west. As we approached the runway, I started dropping back for the landing, but Bill motioned me to keep in close. We landed in a very tight formation. After parking on the ramp, we introduced each other. Bill's comment to me was, "you must have been a military pilot." I considered this a nice compliment and one I sorely needed coming from an aviation celebrity as I recalled Ames Ulrich's derogatory comment after my "wheels up" landing.

Pat and I attended the dinner dance and the next morning saw Bill off. The next I heard of him sometime later, he had entered a race, flying a P-51, did half snap roll while rounding a pylon and dove straight into the ground. He was only 29 years old and I thought, "What a waste." It was determined that he had no previous experience in high performance aircraft, which the P-51 certainly was and should never have attempted entering that extremely dangerous race. Another example of "know your limitations."

I'll give you an example of how things have changed concerning airline passenger concern and comfort. I was returning from Daytona Beach one afternoon after picking up two passengers intending to catch an airline out of Tampa International when I encountered a huge thunderstorm between Lakeland and Tampa International. It was so extensive that I could not attempt going around it and get my passengers to Tampa on time for their departing flight. I decided to land at Lakeland and wait the storm out. I was very good friends with all the traffic controllers in Tampa tower, so before landing, I radioed the tower, to inform them, I had two Eastern passengers with me and I was about to land at Lakeland to wait out the storm which, they could no doubt see toward the East of the field. I requested they contact the Eastern pilot and ask him to delay his take-off until I arrived with the passengers. The tower quickly radioed back acknowledging that the pilot agreed to wait. My passengers were surprised and pleased which they demonstrated after landing at Tampa, by giving me a sizeable tip. Just try to ask an airline captain to do that now days!

The Bonanza was great for generating tips. The control wheel could be released and swung over in front of the person sitting in the copilot's seat. To the surprise of my passengers I almost always did this while flying in smooth air, preferably over the Gulf of Mexico. I would place the wheel in front of the person and say, "you've got it," while holding my hands above my head. Invariable I heard, "I can't fly" and then I would ask, "Do you drive a car?" When they responded, "yes" I would demonstrate how to keep the nose on the horizon, wings level and steer the plane like a car. You can't imagine how thrilled they were to realize they were actually flying the airplane.

Pat introduced me to C. M. Washburn, owner of Honeymoon Island. It was just West of Dunedin, Florida and only accessible by boat or plane. The landing strip was seven or eight hundred feet long, running parallel to the beach. It really was a beautiful place. He had about a half dozen thatch covered huts for sleeping and a large community building with a fully equipped kitchen. He was promoting the Island to be used as a getaway for business executives in large Northern cities. We were to ferry passengers from Tampa International to Honeymoon Island and pick them up when ready to return to Tampa. It was a great idea, but was never really successful.

One incident comes to mind. I was to pick up passengers one evening to carry back to Tampa in order to catch an airline returning them home. There were no lights on the landing strip and I arrived just before dark but it was totally dark by the time they ready to leave. There were four adults, one child and lots of luggage. The Bonanza was licensed to carry five persons, had a very limited amount of luggage space and I was aware that I was quite a bit over the maximum weight limit. I placed one person in the copilot's seat and the rest in back along with the luggage. There wasn't near enough room in the luggage compartment, so part it and the child were on the lap of the rear seat passengers. What little wind there was came directly out the South, so I had to taxi in soft sand to the extreme North end for take-off. In attempting to turn around into the wind, two male passengers had to get out, one on each wing and align me with the runway. I was very slow to accelerate in the soft s and and with all that weight, finally broke ground at the very south end of the runway. It was pitch black out over the Gulf, so I immediately had to go on instruments. That would not have been bad, but the Bonanza was extremely tail heavy so it took a lot of forward pressure on the control column to hold the nose down. I had put in full forward trim and still had to hold forward pressure on control column to maintain level flight. It was very scary and a most unusual feeling. As I made my approach to Tampa International, instead of putting in back trim and easing back on the control column, I slightly eased off on my forward pressure in order to maintain the proper airspeed rate of descent and landing attitude. It was the strangest landing I ever attempted. I kept easing off pressure until finally the main gear touched down while I still had full forward trim in. Taking into account weight distribution had never before been a consideration for me. From that time on it most certainly was!

C.M. always wore a very well pressed pin stripped suit, well starched white shirt and expensive looking tie. He had distinguishing looking gray hair, was tall and carried himself very erect. He was a very impressive looking person. For financial reasons, he was looking for a buyer for Honey Moon Island. He had been a very successful stock broker in New

York, had many upper class friends and was trying desperately to sell the Island to one of them.

He frequently chartered the Bonanza and I flew him to New York several times. He always introduced me to his friends as "his pilot" and always suggested that he and I together with friends go out to dinner. I never saw him offer to pay the check which was embarrassing to me having them pay for my dinner. That was always the only decent meal I would get on the entire trip. For breakfast we would go to a deli bar and drink some concoction of mixed vegetable juice. It was horrible!

We stayed at the Lemmington Hotel in Manhattan, but picked up his mail at the Waldorf Astoria. He continuously operated in a manner intended to impress people.

One time we stopped in Raleigh on the way home. He supposedly was to meet Arthur Godfrey, the most popular radio talk show host in the country at that time. We had to remain over night because his good friend, Arthur was delayed. The next day C.M. was told that Arthur could not make the meeting, so immediately got ready to return to Tampa. When we attempted to check out of the hotel C.M. had absolutely no money and credit cards were very rare or unheard of as far as I knew, except for purchasing fuel. Guess who paid the hotel bill? But I must say, I did get reimbursed by a friend of C.M.'s, after we returned to Honeymoon Island. When I heard that C.M. died before he sold the Island, I felt bad, especially when I heard how much it was sold for. I honestly believe that C. M. died from stress as a result his unrelenting efforts in attempting to sell the Island. Today it is a very well known public park.

Pat purchased about 20 Culver's directly from the Culver manufacturer. The plant was closing down for lack of business. After flying a Culver for the first time, it was easy to understand why the planes were not selling. It had a very poor lift ratio, carried two persons seated side by side and was highly underpowered. Pat purchased them for very little money, so we used them in the flying school, mostly with students taking the commercial course. One of the requirements for getting a private license was to make an extended cross country flight of at least one hundred miles, land and then return to the point of take-off. Depending on a student's progress we sometimes used the Culver for the cross-country. I might add, we always made students file flight plans for that flight. I guess you would call that, "do as I say, not what I do."

I had not been back to Elmhurst for a long time and we had a student in the commercial course named Jim Dunn, from a suburb of Chicago. Therefore we planned a flight cross country flight to Chicago's Midway Airport in a Culver. The flight up was uneventful except when we had to climb to clear some mountains. We started climbing exceptionally far back, knowing the poor climb performance of the Culver but when we reached the mountain, we had to circle for a time to attain an altitude that would clear the top which was only about 4000 feet. I never before made that much of a miss-calculation. I mention this to illustrate the exceptionally poor performance of the Culver which I was soon to dramatically experience. I dropped Jim off at Midway airport in Chicago and proceeded to Elmhurst Airport. It seemed strange landing on the airport so instrumental in starting my aviation career.

When I departed Elmhurst airport, I distinctly remember the take-off. I took off to the West and used every bit of the grass runway available. It seemed the Culver used the full runway on every take-off no matter what the length. I picked up Jim at Midway as planned, again using most of the runway when taking off. Midway is buried in the middle of a very densely populated, congested, section of Chicago. We climbed out very slowly, finally reaching 500 feet, at the base of an overcast, which was prevalent all the way to Louisville. My point is, we were quite low over a very congested area, for an exceptionally long period. You will understand my concern as you read on. I planned to refuel at Louisville, but if the weather conditions did not improve, would remain there until they did improve after considering our limited visibility in light rain, 500 foot ceiling and rugged terrain in our flight path. The weather forecaster at Louisville assured me that thirty miles South of Louisville, the weather would quickly improve and remain excellent the rest of the way to Florida. I took his word for it and we took off.

Just as he forecast, after thirty miles the rain stopped and the overcast started quickly breaking up. I told Jim to climb because we were both uncomfortable at 500 feet. As he advanced the power, the engine sputtered twice and stopped. I changed fuel tanks, but did not get another sputter out of it. Jim gave me control of the Culver and I immediately made a ninety degree turn to the left, (East) turning into the wind. The Culver had a glide ratio about the same as a B-29 which was not very much mostly as a result of the inverted gull wing design. From 500 feet I had very little time to select a suitable landing surface. Rolling hilly forests were all I could see when I spotted a small corn field directly ahead. Beyond it was a very short cleared area. I knew I could make the corn field, but the clearing was doubtful. I reasoned the corn stalks would provide a cushion, hopefully allowing a safe landing. If I was lucky I might even make the clearing? I left the gear retracted, which was the normal procedure in a "dead stick landing." This extended my glide just enough to clear the far corn field boundary fence, but what I had not seen was the deep ditch just beyond the fence where the cleared field started. I extended the glide as long as possible and cleared the ditch by a few feet, sliding to a stop a couple of yards short of the East boundary fence. I had not noticed, but there was a farm house a short distance south of the clearing. The farmer was watching our landing and was at our plane as we were getting out. He was very congenial, offering to call for a flat bed truck to haul us and the plane to a nearby landing strip. In very short order, there must have been twenty people observing the Culver. The only obvious damage was to the prop and air scoop beneath the engine. Most of the damage was to the plywood fuselage which we landed and slid on, which could not be seen until the truck arrived and everyone present helped lift and load the Culver onto the flat bed. Luckily, the Culver had a very short wing span, because the truck driver took us down the main street of Campbellsville, Kentucky. I think everyone in town was watching us maneuver through town.

We finally arrived at a small grass airstrip with several Luscombs parked in front of a building adjacent to a shop. The man that greeted us was the airport manager, flight instructor and shop mechanic. He mentioned he saw us fly past the airstrip, heard the engine quit and suggested that we should have made our emergency landing on the strip. He had never flown a Culver, so was unaware of its flight characteristics. I'm sure we could never have made more than our one turn and landed safely.

He was very hospitable, inviting us to stay at his home until we were picked up. I called Pat Johnson explaining our predicament and was told he would pick us up in the Cessna the next day, Sunday.

After an early breakfast Sunday morning we were invited to accompany him to the airport. Being Sunday, he had a very busy student flight instruction schedule. When we arrived at the airport, he was right because there were five students waiting for him. I had informed him that I had an instructor's rating, so he politely asked me to take a couple of them up for flight instruction. He briefed me on their progress to date and there I was, flying over unfamiliar terrain, with a student I just met and in an airplane I had never flown before. The flight instruction went very well and I actually enjoyed it.

That afternoon Pat arrived in the Cessna, looked over the damaged Culver, arranged for its repair and we headed for Tampa with Pat piloting. About half way back we encountered bad weather, so Pat had me take control in order to file an instrument flight plan. The rest of the flight was uneventful, but this was another experience I would never forget.

Pat was talked into buying a Stearman, outfitted to tow banners. He also bought all the banner letters and had me get checked out on the pick up, in flight and drop procedures. My checkout consisted of one demonstration flight which included all three procedures, with the salesman leaving immediately after we completed the flight. I quickly realized why he did not hang around, because he sold Pat something he just wanted to get rid of. There was a small empty shack next to our flight operations which we used to store the letters. I strung a rope back and forth along the inside walls 0f the shack and hung the letters in alphabetical order. There were three or four of each letter, so I could make up more than one banner at a time.

We needed approval from the FAA to conduct the operation and demonstrate the number of letters we were capable of towing. Pat had me make up a banner with forty letters and invited Ames Ulrich to watch the demonstration. I made the pick up, circled the field once, dropped the banner and landed. I did not want to stay up long enough for Ames to recognize our problem which was that every time I towed a banner I would lose several letters from it's tail end, but I will get back to our remedies for this later.

Pat was a good banner salesman, so with everything else I was doing; I really put in a full day. I'll try to explain. The entire operation was completely my responsibility with no assistance provided. I took the letters out of the shack, laid them out on the ramp in the proper order, fastened them to the tow rope then rolled up the banner along with the lead rope and put the package in my car trunk. After coordinating with the tower as to where on the airport I could lay the banner out for pick up, I drove out to the pick up position and unrolled the banner. I then attached the 150 foot lead rope to a rope tied between two six foot vertical poles standing about 10 feet apart. The lead rope followed by the letters were laid out starting from between the vertical poles in the direction of my line of flight

The Stearman was equipped with a bar hanging beneath the fuselage with a small hook at the end. The position of the hook was controlled by the pilot and the banner was picked up or released by positioning the hook. After take-off, the bar which was attached to the fuselage was lowered, but because of the wind pressure did not drop below the landing gear level. The pickup speed was 90 mph. and the approach was made with the gear lower than the height of the horizontal rope strung between the vertical posts. The pick up was made by passing between the vertical posts and abruptly pulling the nose up into a steep climb. The abrupt maneuver swung the bar out so the hook would be lower than the wheels and attach to the horizontal rope. The pickup was so exciting, the tower operators frequently asked me to make the pickup directly in front of the tower which was also in front of the terminal building. This would also put on a thrilling show for passengers in the terminal.

The drop was made by approaching low to the side of the active runway and then position the hook to release the banner over the designated drop area. After the release, I would land, park the Stearman, get in my car, drive out to the banner, rolled it up, put it in the trunk and drive back to the ramp. I then unrolled it, unhooked it and sorted the letters to hang up alphabetically in the shed. I mentioned losing letters which happened on almost every flight. The banner whipped so badly that it shook the plane. This was even after flying as slow as possible without stalling. Pat tried many ways to stabilize the banner, but the most extreme, was when we attached a very heavy lead weight on the tail of the banner. On the first flight with the lead weight I lost it. One minute it was there and then it was gone. I had no idea where I lost it and since I was always over congested areas, was very lucky it did not kill someone or go through someone's roof.

One time on Gasparilla day I was circling the float parade at about 800 feet I became so engrossed in the floats, I let my airspeed drop a little. Before I could make a correction, the Stearman stalled and did a half turn spin before I was able to recover. This put me at about five hundred feet, much too low according to FAA regulations. This must have looked very strange from the ground and I must have been heard and seen, because I applied full throttle during the recovery. Strangely enough, I never heard a word about it.

I finally had lost so many letters I was not able to put a banner together. About the same time I ran out of letters, Pat was told the letters were made of the wrong material. They should have been made from a very porous, light weight material land our letters were made out of heavy canvas. I could not understand why we were certified to carry them. Actually I don't think Ames Ulrich knew any more about banners than we did. Also that is why the guy that sold Pat the "business" left in such a hurry. I was very pleased when we closed the banner business down.

I might mention that shortly after we went into the banner towing business one of the instructors wanted to give it a try. He had watched my performance several times, so knew the procedure. On his first and only flight he did not abruptly pull up, so the bar never swung out to attach to the horizontal rope, but he did catch the horizontal rope with the landing gear. He did not know he was towing the banner with his landing gear until attempting to release it. After several attempts to make the release he landed, dragging the banner on the ground until coming to a stop. Just about the entire banner was ripped up, (I should have thanked him for that). Pat firmly informed me that I was the only one allowed to tow banners after that happened. There went the only help with the program I ever had.

One of the owners of the Flight Service, Ray Bustler, had a daughter in high school. She was in the drama class and Ray had at least one thousand leaflets printed, advertising a school play. I was asked to take his daughter up in a cub so she could drop the leaflets over the high school campus. At about five hundred feet, enough upwind from the campus to allow for drift, I told her to make her drop. The instant she let go, the leaflets started spreading out. We watched for a short time and it was very obvious that leaflets were going to widely scatter and saturate a large part of Tampa so I got out of the area as quickly as possible. The next day she informed me that as far as she knew, none of the leaflets landed on the campus. I expected to receive a severe reprimand and sizeable fine for littering, but never heard a word about it. I should hold the record for being the area's worst litter bug!

I mentioned "Bugs" Thompson earlier. Don Hartung introduced me to Bugs and we immediately became good friends. I never knew him during pilot training, but we graduated from Luke in the same pilot class, 44F. He now was an instructor at Peter O'Knight airport in Tampa. Shortly after I met Bugs, Don and I went to an air show at Peter O'Knight Airport where Bugs was to perform acrobatics in a T-6. It was a very windy day for an air show, so most of the performances were cancelled. A forty mph cross wind did not stop Bugs. He put on the most professional and daring performance I have ever seen. The T-6 did not have the advantage of the engine continuing to operate while inverted, like modern stunt planes, so it required a lot of forward pressure on the control stick to hold the nose up while inverted. As Bugs broke ground on take-off, he "crabbed" into the wind to compensate for the severe cross wind. Then, as the gear retracted, to everybody's amazement, he did a snap roll while still crabbing into the wind and his wing tip barely missing the ground. On his recovery, he was still in a crab, further demonstrating his skillful control of the T-6. This is an abrupt, precision maneuver and being performed in a T-6 so shortly after take-off would be unbelievable unless you have actually witnessed it. Bugs climbed to about 500 feet and continued his performance. Again he amazed the audience, demonstrating every acrobatic maneuver heard of, while keeping his entire performance in perfect view, directly in line with the active runway, never neglecting to compensate for the crosswind. I understood why after graduation from Luke, he remained at Luke as an instructor.

Now for another unbelievable story about Bugs. This is true because later on my copilot, Monroe Hatch, saw the exact same story in some men's magazine. I had related it to Monroe earlier and I think he doubted its authenticity. Bugs and a student had been drinking before a scheduled instruction flight. No one could understand why, but they concocted a plan to rob a bank in Naples, Florida. After taking off in a cub from Peter O'Knight Airport, they flew to some airfield enroute, left their cub and stole a another light plane. Next they landed at Naples, hitched a ride into town and entered a bank, waving guns. I understand they shot a few rounds into the air, when leaving the bank with $18,000.00. Still waving their guns in the street they commandeered a car, instructing the woman driver to take them to the airport. They took off in the same stolen plane and then landed on a golf course to bury the money under a tree. Being basically honest, they returned the "borrowed" airplane to its home field, got in their original cub and returned to Peter O Knight. All went well until the student, still drinking that night, was stopped for a traffic violation. Again, no one knows why, but he blabbed the entire escapade to the police. Bugs was immediately arrested and sentenced to eighteen years in prison. Strangely, the jail term amounted to 1 year for each $1000.00 of stolen money. To end this story, Bugs was released from jail after ten years and went back to his instructor's job.

Sadly enough, not very long after his release from prison, while giving a student multi-engine training at night; he crashed just after take-off, killing both he and the student. I was never able to learn the cause, but I cannot believe Bugs could lose control especially after watching his T-6 performance. I could not help but think, what a wasted life for such a great pilot and person, discounting his stupid bank episode.

Back at the flight school, now called Florida Aviation College, Pat somehow made an agreement with the Dean of Tampa College to give flight training to College students, as a credited course. On the day the students were to select courses for the next term, I set up a table and attempted to solicit students. We enrolled a few each term and this gave the school, ("college)," a certain amount of prestige. Of course now I was a college teacher!

Florida Aviation Corporation was still very active in the aviation business on Tampa International. My Dad was finance officer, so commuted every day from St. Pete. My sister, Betty was a secretary, so most of the Hubert family was still involved in Aviation. Pete, his wife

Ruth and I were the only pilots, but I think people thought all Huberts were pilots. My Dad liked to have people think that!

One day, Mr Shallenberg, the airport manager at Peter O'Knight Airport, flew into Tampa International in a rented Ercoupe to conduct some business with Pete. The Ercoupe carried two passengers, had side by side seating and had one unique feature. The control wheel steered the nose wheel while on the ground, just like a car. It was also supposed to be spin proof, which I found to be true the one time I flew one on a test flight. When Mr. Shallenberg was ready to depart, he needed his engine propped. My Dad happened to be walking by, so he was asked to sit in the plane at the controls, while Mr. Shallenberg propped it. Most light airplanes did not have starters in those days. He had set the throttle in start position (almost idle,) but apparently did not set the brakes. The FAA required someone in the cockpit and wheels chalked while starting. Mr. Shallenberg pulled the prop through compression and the engine started. My Dad had apparently pushed the throttle in with his knee while climbing into the cockpit, so the ercoupe jumped the chalks and started accelerating across the ramp and continued on across the airport. Having driven a car, my Dad, not knowing any different, managed to keep it going strait, but as the plane accelerated to near take-off speed, he grew panicky. What would he do if it became airborne? Without hesitation he jumped out of the side window and slid over the wing. This occurred at the intersection of two runways, so he landed on concrete. Without a pilot, the Ercoupe quickly went into a turn which tightened up and ended up doing a cartwheel, wing tip to wing tip. By the time it stopped it looked like a ball of metal! The persons in the tower, witnessing the entire incident, pushed the crash button as they saw the plane about to lift off the ground and the pilot jump out so help arrived at the scene very quickly. I had just arrived back from downtown Tampa and by the time I arrived at the accident scene, an ambulance had taken my Dad away. When I first arrived, I had no idea who was piloting the plane and my first exclamation after listening to a brief description of what happened, was "who was that damn fool?" I knew no one could live through that! Then someone said "Bill, it was your Dad!" I said, "Oh my God, is he still alive?" As it turned out, he was severely scraped from the concrete, but had no broken bones or other injuries.

My Dad had a great sense of humor and after recovering he claimed to hold the distinction of being the first pilot to bail out of an airplane without a parachute. Poor Mr. Shallanberg lost his job and was in trouble with the FAA for using an unauthorized person in the cockpit while starting the engine. I felt very bad, because my Dad was too proud to say he was not a pilot. Being a Hubert and listening to him talk, one would certainly think he was.

Florida Aviation College was expanding. Pat rented a building on the North side of Tampa International in order to open up a black flight school and put me in charge. We hired a black flight instructor and black ground school instructor. Several of our least desirable planes were put on the ramp in front of the building and we immediately started enrolling students. All went well until I received a phone call from one of the students. I can remember the conversation quite well. It went, "suh, I had a forced landing." I asked; "Are you OK?" His response was "yes suh, but the lady got hurt." My next words were not asking the extent of her injuries, "but, in a very angry, demanding voice, "were you carrying a passenger? You know, a student pilot is not allowed to carry passengers?" His reply was, "Oh, no suh, the lady in the house." He then explained that he overshot the field he had selected to make his forced landing, rolled into a farmer's back yard and his right wing knocked over their "outhouse!" I then asked the extent of her injury and he said, "She does not seem too badly hurt and the other lady wasn't hurt at all." I'll let the reader's imagination take over from here.

Somehow, the black instructor and ground school instructor arranged to ferry a Lockheed Lodestar to Belize, a large city in Central America. The Lodestar is a twin engine airplane very stable and I would compare it to B-25 in size. It was being used by some airlines to carry passengers or freight.

Belize is on a heading of about 200 degrees from Tampa. The Lodestar had a radio compass to use as a navigation aid and apparently neither of them knew how to use it. They had been told it would "home in" on any frequency that it was tuned into, with no mention of its limited range. Before take off, a station in Belize was tuned in. After take-off, the directional indicator was pointing west, (270degrees) so they turned to that heading and held it until they approached the coast of Texas. Just then the fuel tanks went dry and somehow, they managed to land, with the landing gear down, in a large open field, causing no damage to the Lodestar. I guess someone then explained the limitations of the radio compass and they finally arrived safely in Belize. It was difficult for me understand how an experienced flight instructor and ground school instructor, who taught navigation, could make this mistake. and every pilot knows the first thing you do after tuning in a station, is to identify that station.

More about navigation. I was on a charter, I believe to either Raleigh or Ashville North Carolina in the Bonanza, flying low because of an overcast and limited visibility, when I came to a fork in the road I was following. One of the roads would lead me directly into my destination, but stupidly, I took the road to the right and first thing I knew, I was over a small lake surrounded by mountains. I'm quite sure it was Lake Lure. The visibility grew worse as I was circling, looking for a pass in the mountains. In every direction I pointed the nose; a mountain side would suddenly appear. I knew my destination was to the West of the lake, but I was trapped between the mountains. Finally, in desperation, I contacted Raleigh radio, meekly explained my situation and requested an instrument flight clearance to permit me to climb in an orbit over the lake to a safe altitude and proceed to where I was going. Climbing in the orbit was scary, because I was on instruments in the clouds and not knowing the wind direction, I expected to drift into a mountain side. When I finally broke out of the clouds, I saw the sky was perfectly clear west of the mountains, in the direction I should have taken. Had I not made that stupid mistake at the fork in the road, I would have avoided the terrible predicament I put the passengers and myself in. I think the passengers were so terrified that neither of them said a word.

After landing at Raleigh Durham Airport, I went into the weather station to check the weather for my return trip. As I entered the room unseen, I over heard a couple of persons discussing "that stupid Bonanza pilot that was lost over Lake Lure." While getting a weather briefing, I never disclosed that I was the "stupid pilot." My only explanation was, "I was lured into Lake Lure," which allowed me to forgive myself.

About eight o'clock one night I received a call from a man who desperately needed to get to Atlanta by Midnight. There were no airlines going to Atlanta until the next morning so someone recommended he call me. I met him in the terminal building and told him we could take off after I checked the weather. The weather station was on the 2nd floor of the terminal building and I knew most of the men working there and trusted their forecasts. I was told to expect a line of severe thunderstorms that stretched from Jacksonville to the West coast (of Florida) directly in my flight path. I would encounter it just South of Cross City. The design of the Bonanza V tail was not conducive to withstanding turbulence and had a tendency to "wander," in turbulent weather making it difficult to maintain a steady heading. There had been a number of Bonanza accidents contributed to the instability of the V tail. I explained the weather problem to the passenger, not mentioning the V tail problem, but he would not listen and insisted that we take off, insisting that it was imperative for him to be in Atlanta before midnight. I reluctantly agreed to give it a try, but made him understand the chances were slim and he would be charged for whatever time we were in the air.

The flight was very smooth until we approached Cross City. It really looked "wicked" up ahead so I contacted Cross City Radio and they verified what I had been told by the weather forecaster. The squall line had just passed over Cross City and it was now clear there, but extremely active a short distance to the South, directly in my flight path. It was not a very wide squall line and I thought I might find an opening in it. I followed the leading edge almost to Jacksonville, without finding a way through and then reversed following the line to the Gulf coast. Sometimes, due to the land/water temperature contrast, storms dissipated over the Gulf, so I followed the squall line as far West, out over the Gulf, as I thought feasible. I did not like the idea of flying over water in a single engine plane at night, especially without any life preserver equipment. I flew back to Cross City and was informed the weather conditions had not changed. I had spent so much time attempting to circumnavigate the storm that I just had enough fuel remaining to return to Tampa. This was decision making time. All this time the passenger was nudging my back, insisting we "must" get through to Atlanta.

Before heading back to Tampa, I thought I would prove my point, so I flew directly into the storm, but immediately started a shallow left turn. The rain was beating down on the Bonanza cabin, making a tremendous noise and the sky stayed lit with constant menacing looking lightning. The passenger was then poking my back pointing back toward Tampa. The turbulence was bouncing us all over and what he did not realize, I was probably just as scared as he was. At that time, the Bonanza had a partial instrument panel and the turn and bank indicator was bouncing back and forth like a windshield wiper making it very difficult to determine my bank angle. Even though I was in a hurry to get out of the storm, it was imperative that I maintain a shallow bank and reduce my airspeed to lessen the structural stress. We finally completed the 180 degree turn, left the squall line behind us and headed back to Tampa. After landing, the passenger profusely thanked me, paid the fare and gave me a ten dollar tip. We both learned a lesson and I'm sure that about the time our nose hit the storm, he decided getting to Atlanta by midnight, was not really that important.

Joey Chitwood, owner of the famous Joey Chitwood Auto Daredevil Show, spent a lot of time in our operations building when he was not traveling all over the country with his show. Pat sold him a Culver and we were checking him out in it. He was a very adept student. To my dismay, Joey and Pat came up with a publicity gimmick to advertise Joey's road shows. They removed the front seat from a Cub trainer and mounted a loud speaker system in its place. The system consisted of a gasoline driven generator, which powered an amplifier, record player, microphone and loud speaker. I did the test flying of the "contraption." I'll try to describe why I used that term. First, the noise from the aircraft engine combined with the generator noise was almost overbearing. The two engines were not "synchronized" which any multi-engine pilot will tell you is annoying and the propellers are continuously adjusted to avoid this. Next, the heat from the generator blasting up in my face forced me to frequently stick my head out of the open side window. Third and most important; the generator exhaust pipe got extremely hot and it was just inches from the heavily doped cabin fabric. Joey and Pat thought that problem was remedied by wrapping the pipe in asbestos, but it did not resolve the danger of sparks shooting out of the end of the pipe inside 0f the cockpit. Because of the intense heat and carbon monoxide being exhausted into the cockpit, I had to keep the window open, causing a lot of wind circulation. This aggravated the spark problem and I kept thinking about the "eighteen seconds" before becoming an airframe and engine. They kept assuring me there was no problem with the system, but neither one of them offered to fly the

Cub! Speakers were mounted beneath the support struts between the wing and fuselage and I had the option of playing a record, or using the microphone. I was to go from town to town in advance of a scheduled performance and advertise the coming of Joey's auto show. I certainly was not looking forward to participating in this crazy scheme.

About this time I started thinking of one of the jobs I had been offered prior to becoming involved in Joey's fiasco. I began thinking maybe I should have accepted the opportunity because it sounded quite promising A young pilot I had put through our instrument training program had family very much involved with Northwest Airlines. He had written, offering me a pilot's job. I declined the offer because I did not want to live in Minnesota and I had never heard of pilot's being able to commute like they do now. I was also offered a job as an aircraft traffic controller on Miami International Airport which I also declined because I did not want to leave the St. Petersburg area.

CHAPTER EIGHT

New "horizons," (non-scheduled airline pilot)

Shortly before I was to depart on my advertising tour with Joey Chitwood, the instrument check pilot, Vic Carmichael, began operating a non-scheduled freight airline out of St. Pete-Clearwater Airport. He had hired Henry Gonzales, a pilot friend of mine and asked Henry to see if I was interested in being his copilot in a DC-3. It was the first airplane most scheduled airlines used at that time having been designed and first flown back in the 1930's. I can best describe it's dependability by mentioning that some of them are still being used for a variety of flight operations. The military version was called a C-47 and was widely used during World War II. Thousands of them were manufactured by Douglas. Henry had already made a few trips so knew a lot about the operation. I mentioned that I had never been in a DC-3 and Henry assured me that was no problem; he would instruct me of my duties on our first flight which was to be the next day.

Steve was ready to take over my responsibilities in the flight school except for multi-engine and instrument instruction. At that time I did not have any students in either phase and I really was getting tired of instructing.

The name of the airline was Aravias Sud Americanas and being a new operation, it looked like a good opportunity. I certainly did not want to tour with Joey Chitwood and this was a gracious way out.

Henry informed me that the only uniform required was a short sleeve white shirt. I would just need one, because we were scheduled to fly to Carmen, Mexico, pick up a load of shrimp and return to St. Pete-Clearwater Airport. Sounded quite intriguing, but in realty, continue reading and you be the judge!

We took off early the next morning for Carmen and Henry showed me how to raise the landing gear and operate the cowl flaps which completed my copilot training. We had an uneventful flight, mostly over water and homed in on the radio beacon as we neared Carmen.

This is when I was first informed of an additional, unusual, duty. The radio compass was used for our homing capability and it operated on DC power. The instrument inverter which changed AC power to DC was inoperable, so Vic had generously provided us with a 12 volt DC battery. The same battery used in most cars. Maybe it was from his car! The battery was stored in the forward part of the passenger cabin, so my job on Henry's signal, was to connect cables to the battery terminals, while Henry operated the radio compass and determined a heading to steer. I was advised not to connect the cables for too long, because we could not get the battery recharged until getting back to Tampa and we would need it for navigation position fixes if the weather was bad. Actually, it was the only navigation aid we had because we were over open water during most of each flight.

When we arrived at Carmen I was surprised to find a very nice, lengthy, asphalt runway. What Henry had not told me, was that we had to refuel from 55 gallon drums which we carried down with us. We did not have a pump, so got the fuel flowing by sucking the end of the transfer hose and immediately putting it in the fuel tank to gravity feed. We had a barrel for each wing tank and two hoses, so we could refuel both tanks simultaneously. After getting the transfer started, we left for town and checked into our hotel, the only one in town.

The next evening we went down to the shrimp docks. Now Henry put on his "second" hat. As the shrimp boats came in, he bargained with the representatives of shrimp dealers waiting at the dock to transport a load of shrimp to an American market which had just been purchased from a shrimp boat Captain. Henry was raised in Spain, so was very fluent in Spanish which made him easily capable of bargaining with the "shrimpers." I quickly found out that shrimp were delivered to the most lucrative market place, which could be anywhere in the States. Henry did not seem surprised that our first load went to Miami. He consummated a deal and we departed that night.

About half way to Miami, both engines suddenly quit! Henry casually retarded both throttles, advanced the mixture controls and both engines re- started. When we were again underway, I asked Henry what caused the engines to quit. His reply was, "I don't know. This happened on my last flight," like, what's the big deal? Of course I was thinking what would happen if this occurred just after take-off, or on landing approach. Also, we had absolutely no water survival gear on board and as I mentioned previously, almost the entire flight was over water. I know Henry must have thought the same things, but appeared very nonchalant about it.

Before I learned my third job I should explain. The shrimp were packed in gunny sacks which had been loaded with about an equal amount of ice. The gunny sacks were placed in the forward end of the passenger cabin, however during flight, the ice melted, with the water accumulating in the rear of the cabin. My job was to run a hose from the huge puddle of shrimp juice and siphon it out through the cabin door. Of course I had to manually push the door open and cling to the door frame, to keep from getting sucked out. It then occurred to me that we did not have parachutes and I had recently read that an Eastern steward had been sucked out of a DC-3 door, while trying to secure it during flight! This certainly did not add to my appreciation for the job!

We landed in Miami, rested up and departed for Carmen the next morning. This time we waited three days before arranging for another load. A storm had passed through the shrimping area, which churned up the water causing very poor shrimping conditions. In addition to that, another airline using C-46's began operating out of Carmen, so we had serious competition. C-46's, like C-47's were also widely used during World War 11 but I do not recall the civilian designation of it. After the war they were purchased from the military as surplus equipment. It was capable of carrying a heavier pay load of shrimp than the DC-3 for about the same price. The C-46 crew got the first load after the storm and then it would be our turn.

Living in the hotel in Carmen was not very inviting. We dared not eat the food or drink the water, so we ate bananas or hard boiled eggs and drank beer or soft drinks. One other thing I should mention. Our room had one bed and one hammock. Guess who slept in the hammock? Hammocks may be OK for a nap in the back yard on a nice summer day, but as a bed, it was miserable. I got very little sleep and had a permanent "back ache." By now, my one white shirt was looking pretty raunchy, so I did try to rinse it out. We did not have an iron and it was pure cotton, so always looked like I slept in it.

Our next load was taken to Brownsville, Texas. After arriving in Brownsville that evening, we had a great steak dinner and went to a movie. I still remember it was a great movie named Red River, with John Wayne and Montgomery Cliff. About half way through, I noticed people sitting near us were moving to seats in other sections of the theater. Then I thought of my shoes. The heels and soles were crepe, very absorbent and I had been wading in shrimp juice before each landing. I guess I was used to the odor, but if you have ever smelled dried rotted shrimp, you will understand. While in Brownsville I purchased another shirt and pair of shoes out of necessity!

We made a couple more trips, always to Brownsville, before a "Blue Northern" came thru and churned up the water for days. This time it was three weeks before we arranged for another load. That was really a long three weeks in that hammock!

One day we decided to drink some lemonade, using bottled water we had brought back from Brownsville. We stupidly put ice from the hotel in the lemonade and guess what happened? You are right; Henry and I had a severe case of dysentery! We forgot the ice was made from their local water. Never again! We finally started getting shrimp loads again, but always to Brownsville where the market was best. I was really getting tired of Carmen and the DC-3 had not been looked at by a mechanic in the more than the two months we were gone.

Finally, after a trip to Brownsville, Henry received a telegram from Vic requesting we take a load back to St. Petersburg/Clearwater Airport as soon as possible because some the control cables needed replacing. The metal skin on the emphanage (tail end of the plane) was badly corroded and when I personally examined it, I felt like I could easily put my finger through the metal surface. I already knew shrimp juice was very corrosive so this did not come as a complete surprise. We had flown through some very rough weather at times, putting a lot of stress on the plane, which was kind of a frightening thought. I suggested to Henry that we forget the next load and head right back to St. Petersburg. We both knew the plane was way overdue for an inspection. Henry was a great company man! He decided to return to Carmen and attempt to get a load to carry back to St. Pete. I informed Henry that I was going to wire Vic, requesting he send a replacement copilot to Brownsville immediately. Vic quickly wired back that a copilot was on his way, so I boarded a bus and headed for home.

I had not received any pay since starting and Henry charged all our expenses to the Company, so at $250.00 per month, I had over $600.00 coming. It took about two months of pleading before I finally received the back pay and I wondered if all non-scheduled airlines ran that type of operation. Even if they do, what would a copilot earn today?

I went back to Pete's home to live and now I did not have a job. Pat let me again take over instrument and multi-engine instruction and I started flying charter flights again in the Bonanza. Instead of a salary, I was paid at the same rate as the other instructors. During the time I was manager and chief pilot, my salary was $60.00 per week and the other instructors always made close to $100.00 per week. After resuming my multi-engine and instrument instructing, I was making far more money than when I "ran" the school!

Glen Durst, a mechanic and commercial pilot, was hired by a company that raised and sold tropical fish. He was modifying a Lockheed Lodestar to transport tropical fish from Tampa to cities up North. His shop was on Tampa International and we became good friends. Occasionally, when I wasn't busy, I would help him with his modification. He was mounting shelves on each side of the cabin holding a total of 100 containers, each capable of carrying 100 tropical fish. Glen had installed a pump with hoses to provide air into each individual container which was a very unique arrangement. Glen did not have an instrument rating, so asked if I would be his copilot when delivering fish to dealers up North and I was to receive $25.00 per trip. The round trip would take twenty four hours, so I could schedule my instruction flights accordingly.

Glen completed the modification, which checked out very well and we made our first flight. A crew from the fish farm loaded the fish and we prepared for a midnight take-off. All went well, so after our first flight we alternated routes each week, naming them East Route and West Route. Flying the East route we landed at Lumberton for fuel, (because it was cheap) and then unloaded containers of tropical fish at Washington, Baltimore, Philadelphia, Newark, Hartford, Boston, Syracuse and Pittsburgh. In route back home we again landed at Lumberton to refuel, arriving back at Tampa International around midnight having no rest stops. Glen always called ahead giving the dealers our estimated time of arrival to their city. With the dealers help, we unloaded his fish order and put the empty containers from our previous flight in the cargo compartment. After twenty four hours of either flying, or unloading & loading, we were pretty well pooped out. The West route went to Dayton, Cleveland, Detroit, Milwaukee, Chicago, Indianapolis, Louisville and Nashville and did not stop at Lumberton for fuel.

We frequently encountered some very severe weather. If we flew through a front or squall line going up, we could count on meeting it again on the way home. I remember one time; it got so rough, we both held the steering column. Another night, flying well clear of a thunderstorm, a bolt of lightning struck directly in front of us. That shook us both up! We always plowed on despite what the weather was like up ahead. I might add that we always filed an instrument flight plan. I was getting smarter!

One night, coming back from the West route, Tampa International had a very low ceiling and limited visibility. We had taken on just enough fuel at our last stop to get back to Tampa because we did not stop at Lumberton. I requested an instrument approach from Tampa Approach Control and they replied that the ceiling and visibility were below our minimums and we should proceed to an alternate field. I informed them of our fuel situation, but they would not clear us to attempt an approach. We were advised the nearest suitable field with weather above minimums was Daytona Beach. We calculated this was beyond our available fuel range, but had no choice but to head there. Of course, we did not have parachutes; we were flying on instruments, on a very black night and extremely tired after continuously being on the go for twenty four hours. Can you imagine a worse scenario? Our tanks indicated empty long before we arrived at Daytona, so we sat there waiting for both engines to quit. Finally, we could see the runway lights at Daytona Airport but could also see a fog bank just east of the Airport that looked like it was rolling in. We really needed that to add to our desperation and suspense. Glen made a straight in approach from the West to land on the East West runway. At this point, we did not care what the wind direction was; we just wanted to get on the ground! That was the longest approach, other than at Thunderbird Field in primary, I ever sat through. Thunderbird was during daylight, in a much lighter plane and plenty of vacant land to set down on. That wasn't much of a comparison, except, here I would probable get killed, whereas at Thunderbird, I would have washed out of cadets, which at the time would have seemed worse than death. Well, we landed safely and spent the night in Daytona. The next morning Glen put a dip stick in each tank and could barely see a trace of fuel. I think we were operating on fuel "vapor" when we landed.

One morning I intended to sleep late because I had been out drinking beer the night before. Suddenly I felt someone shaking me and it was Joey Chitwood. He had to get to Brownsville Texas that day to make arrangements for a scheduled show. The weather report indicated bad weather en route, so he wanted me to fly with him in his Culver. I felt lousy, but he was very persistent and assured me that I could return in a couple days. Actually the only thing I had scheduled was the Lodestar trip and that was uncertain because of engine problems. I reluctantly agreed to go with Joey after he offered me fifty dollars and expenses. He flew the airplane and I was to assist him navigating if necessary. I tried not to show it, but I felt very nauseated all the way to Tallahassee, our first fuel stop. The minute we pulled up to the parking ramp, I ran to the men's room in the terminal building. After throwing up, I felt a little better, but very sleepy. After refueling, Joey took off and the weather looked pretty good up ahead, so a short time after he reached cruise altitude, I dozed off. I slept quite a while, because when Joey awoke me, we were again running low on fuel. Joey made a comment like; he really didn't need me after all. I don't think he liked me going to sleep on "his time." Of course, I did not know he had been flying over a cloud layer for some time and had absolutely no idea where we were. That did not seem to matter to him, because he had "me" along. Our only navigation aid was a low frequency band radio capable of picking up radio range signals. We had been airborne long enough to be somewhere near New

Orleans so I tuned in New Orleans radio range and did a radio range orientation procedure. Joey had no idea what I was doing, but was surprised when suddenly the New Orleans Airport appeared in front of us. He then finally admitted he was glad I came along.

We arrived in Brownsville late that afternoon and checked into a hotel room which Joey and I shared. Most of his drivers and crew were already in Brownsville so we met them for dinner in the hotel dinning room that night. The next morning Joey and I went to a local used car dealer. He needed three old used cars for the show's "dive bomber" act. I had no idea what that consisted of and Joey simply told the owner that he needed three old cars for his show and he could pick them up immediately after the end of the show. In return the dealer would receive two free tickets to the show and could sit in the center of the oval track with the drivers and crew. The dealer gladly accepted the offer and Joey had his drivers pick the cars up.

It had been raining for the past day so the dirt track was very wet, with large ruts caused by previous traffic. Joey had asked me to hang around a few days in case there was bad weather between Brownsville and his next show location, so he put me to work driving one of his stunt cars around and around the track to flatten it down as much as possible. I did this for the rest of the day.

Joey's show cars were well identified with the name of his show printed in large letters on all sides. When he sent me on an errand in one of his cars people thought I was one of his drivers and I did nothing to have them think otherwise.

Joey had a big turnout for the show and he placed the used car dealer next to me in the center of the oval track. I was told to help the crew set up ramps and other props and that was ok with me, because now I could tell people I was in the show.

The last act in the show was the dive bomber feat. Two cars were lined up side by side, with a ramp placed a short distance in front of them. Then a car (the third used car from the lot,) sped up the ramp and dove straight into the windshields of the two other used cars. The used car dealer was flabbergasted! He started yelling at me, when thankfully, Joey walked up. Before the dealer could say a word, Joey casually said; "You can pick up your cars now." All three cars were totaled. When the dealer started yelling at Joey, all Joey said as he walked away was, "we made a deal." It was easy to tell that Joey did this in every city his show performed. The next day we checked the weather and it looked good, so Joey gave me bus fare back to Tampa and the $50.00 and that ended my relationship with Joey.

Glen Durst had two Cubs a man in Havana had purchased for resale and he already had buyers waiting in Cuba. This was before travel restrictions to Cuba were in force. He asked if I would fly one of them down with him. I gladly accepted and we headed for our first refueling stop at Everglade City after which we then proceeded directly to Key West. We had absolutely no radio or water survival equipment, but could see land off to our left most of the way down, so didn't think much about it. In Key West we were to get clearance from the Cuban army and intended to depart for Havana early the next morning. That night, I think Glen and I had a beer in every bar in Key West and there were a lot of them. The next morning neither of us could get out of bed we were so hung over. We spent the entire day recuperating and finally departed for Havana the next morning.

There is a saying, "over water, out of sight of land, planes with a single engine go into automatic rough." I found that to be true because when I lost sight of land my engine seemed to be running rough. I put the carburetor anti-icing on and started looking for ships I could glide to. I spotted quite a few of them, which was reassuring. After about an hour and a half, we landed in Havana. The buyer was waiting for us and it was obvious he was plenty mad. He had been waiting at the airport the entire previous day, attempting to soothe his buyers. Glen tried unconvincingly, to explain that our delay was caused by the Cuban army because they would not give us a clearance. We got paid and departed as soon as possible.

After arriving back in Tampa I borrowed Ray Bustler's Bonanza and flew to Miami. Ray had demolished his Culver in attempting to top a thunderstorm over the Everglades. He stalled out, dove into the storm, lost control and spiraled into the ground. Miraculously, he survived the crash, made it to the only highway crossing the everglades and was picked up by a doctor and his nurse. His only injury was to his left foot. He was fitted with a brace and immediately purchased a Bonanza. He asked that I give him a few hours of instrument instruction, to prepare him for the next time he encountered a storm. I gave him some lessons but emphasized that the best way to survive a thunderstorm was to positively avoid it. In return for the instruction and words of wisdom, he allowed me the use of the Bonanza.

In Miami, I applied for a pilot's position with Eastern Airlines. My qualifications were excellent, but the application indicated five feet eight as minimum height and I was almost five seven. Wearing the right shoes, I might qualify, so I entered my height as five feet eight. If necessary I would explain that I thought they meant with shoes on. After all, I would have shoes on when I walked up the isle to the pilot's compartment. I'm sure the minimum height was to "impress" the passengers.

In June of 1950, the United States entered the Korean conflict. It was a "conflict" because Congress never declared it a "war." At this time I held an "M Day" (mobilization) assignment at Macdill and was assigned to a B-29 bomb squadron. It was inevitable that I would be called back to active duty to join the bomb squadron, because the purpose of the M Day assignment was to augment the active duty units. Being recalled did not bother me because I had not heard from Eastern and I certainly would welcome a change. If you will remember, I was not anxious to leave the military in the first place. My only problem was, I did not want to go into the very "unpopular" Strategic Air Command, (SAC) and fly bombers.

I was explaining this to a friend; Bill Spranza and he made a suggestion. Bill worked at Warner Robbins Air Base, in Macon Georgia and commuted to his home in Tampa each weekend. He explained that he had a very good friend, a Lt. Col. that was responsible for all recalls in the 14th Air Force. The Air Force was now a separate branch of the service and Macdill was a part of the 14th Air Force. Bill suggested I fly him to Warner Robbins the following Monday and he would introduce me to the Lt. Col. who may have a different assignment for me. I again borrowed Ray Bustler's Bonanza and we departed for Macon early Monday morning. To be honest, considering I already had a critical assignment, I did not have much hope for anything to materialize from this. Being a Reserve Officer, I was permitted to land at Warner Robbins and we immediately went to the Col's office. Bill introduced me and it was evident that they were good friends. I explained my predicament and that I really would like a single or twin engine assignment. At that time he had only one assignment to fill which was a single engine unit in Waco, Texas. Waco was an advanced flying school in the Training Command, so I would undoubtedly be an instructor in T-6's. He was expecting additional assignments, but did not know when they would come in so I could accept either the Waco assignment, or wait for something else. I knew I would receive my orders to join the Bomb Squadron at Macdill at anytime, so I gladly accepted Waco. I really did not know how he would get me out of my "M Day" assignment, because SAC had a very high priority for personnel in the Air Force. I began to doubt my being released and actually did not expect to hear anything from the Lt Col., but to my amazement in just three or four days I received orders releasing me from my M Day assignment and new orders assigning me to Waco, Texas.

CHAPTER NINE
HAPPY TO BE BACK IN THE AIR FORCE

I had traded my Desoto for a 1948 Chevrolet convertible to impress Barbara, my girl friend at that time. It was beautiful when I purchased it, but the maroon paint quickly faded in the hot Florida sun and the convertible top also rapidly deteriorated. It did not look too good, but the engine ran well and I arrived in Waco sometime in August, 1950, two months after the U. S. entered the Korean conflict.

I reported in and was assigned to a T-6 instructor's squadron. I was immediately checked out in the T-6 but would not be assigned students until I became acquainted with the training program. There were about twenty of us that had been recalled and assigned to Waco, but I was the only one with recent flying experience, so I was told my training would be accelerated.

One day I was called in for an interview with the Base Personnel Officer and was asked what I had been doing during my break in service. That's when I really messed up by proudly telling him I managed a civilian flight service, had an instructor's rating and had flown many models of light airplanes. His eyes lit up as he informed me I would immediately be assigned to the Air Force Liaison School located on the Base, behind the officers club. I had never really noticed the landing strip since arriving on base.

Shortly after arriving at Waco, My Folks forwarded a letter to me from Eastern Airlines asking if I was prepared to start copilot training. I wrote a nice letter back to Eastern explaining that I had to decline at this time, however, may be available in about a year. Recalled pilots had a one year commitment before requesting release.

I reported to the Commanding Officer of the Liaison School, a Major who expressed how glad he was to have me in his squadron and I quickly found out the reason.

Without wasting any time, I was given a forty five minute ride in an Aeronca with an instructor, in what the Air Force called an L-16 and on the next day I was assigned five students. These Aeroncas were modified having an 85 horsepower engine as opposed to the 65 horsepower engine in the Aeronca Champions I had been flying. Other than that, here I was back to instructing in a light plane which I so much wanted to get away from.

The five students were Army Officers, some of the first to join the Air Arm of the Army after the Air Force separated from the Army in either 1947 or 1948. Apparently, the Army did not want to totally give up to what was once called the Army Air Corps.

None of my five students had ever flown an airplane before, so I had my work cut out for me. The Air Force would not be as tolerant as we were in the civilian school, because as you may have already surmised, we needed the money to continue operating. I was now training Army Officers to eventually fly liaison missions in Korea so they had to be pretty good if expected to survive this extremely vulnerable combat assignment. Incidentally, I was still a second Lt. and I'm sure, setting a record for time in grade as a Second Lt. During my interview with the Commanding Officer of the liaison school, he noticed my time in grade, but made me understand, he would have to observe my performance before I could be promoted. This took until the following January, 1951, with then almost seven years in grade. You may remember this is not what I was led to believe when doing my research in high school!

My five students did very well, so nothing interesting happened for the first five months. For my next class, I was assigned three officers from the Italian Army. They spoke a little English, but having them understand me over the noise of the engine was a challenge. We had no interphones back then. They had a lot of pressure on them, as they were to go back to Italy and organize the Air Arm of the Italian Army.

One of my students, Capt. Stradiotto, was to head the Air Arm so he was especially aware of his responsibilities and the prestige the position would provide. He was extremely emotional, so I had to be very careful not to have him think I was yelling at him when I was merely trying to overcome the engine noise. Several times he let go of the control stick, reached in his back pocket for a handkerchief and started wiping his tears. I would then have to attempt to cheer him up and reassure him he was doing OK, when actually, he was not. I had to work exceptionally hard with him while being very tactful, so he would not go home in disgrace. He had a difficult time maintaining directional control on take off and landing, which brought back memories of my control problem in primary flight training. I used the same technique that my primary instructor used with me and he improved somewhat. It was easy to identify him as the pilot of a plane taking off because the tail of the plane swayed back and forth, but somehow, thank goodness, he always maintained control. After each dual flight, I critiqued students immediately after landing while still on the flight line while standing by the airplane and the flight was still fresh in their mind. Twice, while being critiqued, Capt. Stradiotto took out his handkerchief, leaned face down against the fuselage and cried. I had to be so very careful about what I said and how I said it. I always felt that a big Part of an instructor's job was to instill confidence in his student, without making him feel to cocky. Capt. Stradiotto needed confidence, but he would never feel cocky. One day early in the course, I could smell liquor on his breath when he arrived at the flight line after lunch. Students that went to ground school in the morning flew in the afternoon. This procedure was alternated every other week. I asked if he had been drinking. His reply was "just one liter" of wine while he indicated with his fingers, that it was a very small amount. I think he did it to build up his courage, but I am sure it never happened again!

All three students made it through the course and went on to the next phase at a different flight facility. One other instructor, Bob Eldred, also had three Italian students, but one of them did not make it. Believe me that Italian student received a lot of sympathy from his fellow Officers but I later heard he was made the chief of maintenance in the Italian Air Arm which I was happy to hear.

It was customary after the engine was started to have one of the students remove the chocks from in front of the wheels just before taxiing out for take-off. I always strongly emphasized to hold the wing strut with one hand while bending down to remove the chocks. The chock removal procedure put the student's head close to the spinning prop, so by holding the strut, it should not be possible to be struck by the prop. About a month after the Italians left, I was informed that Capt. Savanni, one of my students, was struck in the head by a spinning prop while removing chocks and died immediately. I felt terrible about this and wondered if I had not put enough emphasis on my procedure of holding the strut. In my mind, I was also blaming his present instructor, because apparently, he did not insist on, or did not use the procedure I taught and diligently used.

Our flight school was given a T-34 Mentor and T-35, right off the assembly line, to evaluate their performance. Our evaluation would help determine which plane would be most suitable to use as a primary trainer for the Air Force. The T-34 was made by Beech and was very similar to the Bonanza, except it had a conventional (vertical) rudder and was a two seat tandem style. It was known that I had a lot of Beechcraft Bonanza time, so I was assigned the job of checking the other instructors out. The T-35, (I cannot recall the manufacturer,) had side by side seating and a tail wheel. I also did those checkouts; I guess because of my wide variety of light airplane time. My mind was made up immediately as to which plane would make the best trainer. The T-34 was by far my preference because of its excellent flight characteristics, maneuverability and forgiveness. Forgiveness, meaning that when the pilot goofed up, the airplane, because of its inherent desire to stabilize itself, enabled the pilot to recover. One thing that seems to make a huge difference today was that the T-35 had a tail wheel and the T-34 had a nose wheel. Aircraft with a tail wheel made three point landings, touching down on the main gear and tail wheel simultaneously. This required attaining "landing attitude" just prior to touch-down which is a precision maneuver. Aircraft with a nose wheel have more leeway in attaining landing attitude prior to touch down. Touch-down must be made on the main landing gear with the nose gear being eased down as airspeed decreases during the landing roll. That fact had absolutely no bearing on selecting my preference, but I certainly imagine it would by pilots today. I have been told how tricky "tail draggers" are. The clay runway we used at Waco was very short and the T-35 had a tendency to float prior to touch down, therefore each approach had to be carefully planned. Whereas, the T-34 had far better landing characteristics.

One day I had been up solo for some reason in the T-35 and when I attempted to flare just before landing could not ease the control stick back to establish a three point landing attitude. I floated halfway down the runway and had to make a go-around by establishing a climb attitude strictly with trim tabs and adjusting the power accordingly. I was very cautious because I thought I might lose complete control at any time not having immediately identified the cause. Fortunately, I looked down at the floor and noticed, wedged between the floor and a counter weight at the base of the control stick, was a ball of twine. Some mechanic had left it on the floor and it made its way to that hazardous position. I am relating this incident just to demonstrate how an unexpected and unforeseen event could accentuate weaknesses already built into the aircraft, thus resulting in a potentially fatal accident.

After about a year at Waco, our flight school was moved to an abandoned military base in San Marcos, Texas. The Liaison school was expanding rapidly, with new potential instructors arriving daily. A new squadron was established solely to train new instructors. I forgot to mention that after being at Waco for about four months, I had been promoted to First Lt. and made assistant Flight Commander.

When a Flight Instructor Training Squadron was formed to train incoming instructors my good friend, Captain Bert Brown, was put in charge. I was made Flight Commander, therefore did not have regular students assigned. I gave progress spot checks and the final flight check. Some of the new instructors had not flown for five or six years and it seemed that most of their flying time had been in B-17's or the like (heavy aircraft). It was difficult to get them to approach for landing at less than 100 miles per hour instead of sixty. No matter what, this was an improvement over having five new students assigned every five months.

I was invited to become a helicopter instructor, in a new squadron formed at San Marcos, but emphatically declined the offer.

Base Operations had several pilots assigned for administration flights, so I made it a point to become acquainted and hounded them until I was checked out in the one B-25 available. I guess I was the only liaison instructor interested or persistent, because I was the only L-16 instructor they checked out. My check pilot was Sam Castleberry, who will come back into my story later. I was mostly called to fly the B-25 on weekends, which is understandable, but I enjoyed the change and opportunity to become current in twin engine because I hoped to some day start doing something different. San Marcos did not have the capability to refuel the B-25, so before landing we went to Austin, Texas and filled up on fuel. Things weren't too bad now, but I still wanted to go to Korea.

Bert Brown, Andy Anderson and I, were sent to Waco to put on an air show Armed Forces Day. Imagine attempting to put on an interesting air show in an L-16? It was not stressed to withstand acrobatics or any negative pressure, like inverted flight. We pondered over the possibilities as to what might be interesting to the spectators and I came up with this idea. Take off in formation, climb to about 1000 feet and while in a V formation, in view of the grandstand, go into a two turn spin. Bert was to fly lead and on his signal Andy and I would simultaneously break into a spin in opposite directions. A few seconds later, Bert would enter his spin. We would be spinning very close to each other, which I hoped would excite the audience. (It did me!) After recovering from the spin at about 500 feet, we would enter the traffic pattern in close trail. Depending on the landing direction either Andy or I would be number three and intentionally too close behind number two for a safe landing. At about 150 feet, the announcer would excitedly yell over the P.A. system, "number three, you're too close, pull up and go around!" Number three would perform a loop, which then provided adequate spacing for landing. Most people understand what is meant by "go around," so a loop that close to the ground was definitely not what the audience expected. Andy and I practiced performing loops making sure that 150 feet altitude was adequate to complete the loop.

Two maneuvers we taught were obstacle clearance take off and short field landings over a barrier. The take off required climbing at a steep angle just above stall speed until an obstacle was cleared. In making a barrier landing, the approach was made at minimum speed in a slight sideslip to make the approach angle steeper. After barely clearing the barrier, wings were leveled, power cut and the plane would plunk down on the runway stopping in a very short distance. Since it was my idea to demonstrate these two maneuvers, Bert and Andy decided I would perform them at the air show. I was hoping Andy would perform the low altitude loop!

We flew three Aeroncas to Waco the day before the show and that night we realized we did not have a barrier for my landing. I mentioned the wing of an Aeronca was about the height of our practice barriers, so that problem was resolved.

When it was our turn to perform, the spins and loop went very well. Andy did the loop to my relief! He admitted he cheated and started it at about 200 feet and I think I would have done the same. Now it was my turn. We put the barrier (Aeronca) in place and I took off and I really goofed up! Attempting to show off, I climbed too steep and fully stalled at about 150 feet. I immediately lowered the nose while trying to keep the wings level and not go into a spin. We taught this maneuver, called a rudder control exercise, but this was neither the time nor place for it. If my barrier landing demonstration went like my take off, I was going to wipe out two planes instead of only my own. The barrier landing did go well, but I really did not want to get out after parking. How could I face the audience, much less Bert and Andy after my lousy take off demonstration? To my surprise, they thought my climb out was quite spectacular and intentional. I had climbed at an angle that would allow me to clear the imaginary obstacle and once cleared, lost a little altitude allowing me to accelerate to a normal climb speed. Who was I to convince two very experienced instructors they were wrong. I only hoped they didn't go back and teach students short field take offs using that method!

I had been at San Marcos about a year when I was assigned "Officer of the Day." I believe this was November of 1951. This duty was rotated among all officers, so we seldom were scheduled for it. Officer of the Day is actually misnamed. The duty was performed after normal working hours, filling in for the Base Commander while he was "off" duty. He monitored all incoming phone calls and messages and if thought important enough, relayed the information to the applicable person.

On this Particular night, the Base received a message, which had been directed to all bases in the Training Command, requesting former B-25 and B-26 pilots to volunteer for duty in Korea. I answered the request immediately, without going through the normal chain of Command. Two days later I was called into the Deputy Commander for Operations Office and informed he had received orders transferring me, providing the Commander of the Liaison School approved. The following day all instructor pilots were called to an emergency meeting in the base theater. Using very strong language, the Base Commander stressed how critical our jobs were and there would be no transfers approved. I knew I was the only pilot that saw the request, so I was responsible for this meeting.

We were dismissed and as I was walking through the theater lobby, the Deputy Commander came up beside me and put his arm around my shoulder. I was wondering how severe my punishment would be for not going through the chain of Command and of course my transfer would be denied. To my astonishment, the Deputy Commander said, "Bill, your transfer has been approved" and he wished me the best of luck.

My then former girl friend, Barbara, had come to San Marcos in June to get married. I had traded my Chevrolet convertible and purchased a new 1951 Chevrolet so Barbara would be left with a good set of "wheels."

My orders allowed me a short leave and then to report to Camp Stoneman, in San Francisco. We drove, with all our possessions, which consisted only of clothes, to St. Petersburg and stayed with my Mom and Dad. After a few days, I caught a flight to San Francisco and Barbara remained with my Mom and Dad. Tours in Korea were one year, so we planned accordingly.

CHAPTER TEN

FOR ME, COMBAT WAS NOT MEANT TO BE!

I checked into Camp Stoneman in December, 1951 and was told my assignment orders had not yet been received, but to check the bulletin board twice a day. Every day I expected to see my name, but was disappointed day after day and then week after week. I began to think I had been forgotten, but was assured by personnel this had not happened.

Other pilots had reported in after me and transferred out a short time later, mostly assigned as T-6 spotter pilots. They were to fly over battle areas and direct our ground troops to enemy positions. It was a very hazardous mission known to have heavy combat losses. I felt sure that would be my assignment because I had a lot of recent T-6 time and I heard of no one going to B-26's. Finally after more than a month, I was assigned to the Philippines as a photo reconnaissance pilot. I had no idea as to what type aircraft was used, but assumed I would be taking photos over Korea, while operating out of the Philippines. My assignment was a result of having attended photo recon training during World War 11.

I shipped out in an old troop carrier ship, the USS Ainsworth, shared a stateroom with six other officers and spent twenty one days at sea. One of my roommates was Frank Borman, later to be an astronaut. He was grounded shortly after graduating from West Point and flight school, because of a punctured ear drum and by the time we arrived in the Philippines Frank and I had become very good friends. He was destined for a ground job but desperately wanted to get back on flying status.

On the day we finally arrived at Clark Air Force Base it was about noon, so before reporting in, we went to the Officers Club for lunch. After lunch Frank and I separated, intending to report into our individual assignments.

As I left the Club, I heard someone from behind me call out my name. It was a Lt. Col. Hendman. I do not recall where I knew him from, but he was as surprised to see me as I was to see him. When he asked where I was assigned, I explained I had just arrived and was on my way to report to some Photo Recon Squadron. He said it was a lousy assignment, flying long missions in B-17's, photo mapping the Philippines. The crews were on temporary duty (TDY) most of the time, stationed in small towns all throughout the Islands. He asked if I would like to be assigned to Base Operations. One of the pilots was leaving in a couple of months and I could take his position. In the meantime, he could put me in the Base Photo Lab, as the officer in charge was in the process of leaving. This sounded great to me, even though I knew nothing about a photo lab, or what my job would be in Base Operations. I soon discovered that Lt. Col. Hendman was Deputy Commander for Operations assigned to the Thirteenth Air Force, which had Headquarters at Clark. He definitely had the authority to change my assignment, even though the Recon Squadron had a high priority for attaining personnel. I realized I had been at the exact right place at exactly the right time!

The Base Photo Lab had a Master Sergeant, Sgt. Kilmer, assigned, who had been a glider pilot during World War 11. He still held his Second Lt. rank in the reserves and I immediately determined that he was perfectly capable of running the lab and definitely did not need me. I made it clear that I would not interfere with his routine. In turn he taught me how to use the photo equipment, develop and enlarge pictures and order supplies. This was in case anyone asked me what my job was and I could make it sound like I knew the business and was earning my pay.

Col. Patenude, my Group Commander, saw I wasn't busy enough, because I kept flaunting Sergeant Kilmer's capabilities and stupidly made it known that he did not need me. Actually I would have liked to see him get recalled as a Second Lt.

I feel sure that as a result of my praise of Sgt. Kilmer, Col. Patenude assigned me the additional duty of Base Small Arms Range Officer. The firing range was off base, which required that I drive through a small village of Negritos to get there. They were very small people and the women did not wear anything over their breasts. Very distracting! The Sergeant running the firing range was also very efficient and responsible. I was relieved, because I never liked being around firearms. Anyway, this position and the photo lab were temporary, because I would soon be assigned to Base Operations.

However, when I finally was transferred to Base Operations Col. Patenaude informed me that I could do my job in operations and keep the photo lab and firing range as additional duties. Before me, these were a single assignment for each officer in charge, but I dared not complain, because then I would be admitting I was not capable of handling the combined responsibilities. Also I knew that neither of these positions required supervision, but it provided me with a reason to act over worked, but like a dedicated officer, never complain.

As it turned out, my job in Base Ops was more than full time. Clark field had over 150 "behind the line" pilots and I had to make sure each pilot flew four hours each month to maintain flight proficiency. Each pilot also received ten hours of instrument training each year, followed by a flight check. In addition, the Base Operations Officer or I had to check out each new pilot in either the T-6, or C-45 (twin engine Beech.)

I also had to provide crews for every administrative flight out of Clark. All this required a lot of record keeping, so I did have a Philippine civilian to maintain flight records and record each pilot's monthly and annual flight activities on a large blackboard next to my desk. Toward the end of each month Col. Donahue, the Base Commander, checked the board to personally make sure that all requirements were completed. My big problem was getting these behind the line pilots to fly. In the Officer's club during happy hour everyone acted eager to "get in the air," but with a few exceptions most pilots had to be scheduled several times before they actually completed their monthly requirements. While spending a lot of time on the phone attempting to work up a flight schedule, I frequently heard, "my boss won't let me off work." I checked with most of their bosses and was continuously told they instructed all assigned pilots to take off work anytime they were scheduled to fly and encouraged them to maintain their flying proficiency. I quickly discovered that many pilots maintained their flight status strictly for the extra pay!

The Base Flight Operations job required that he be an instructor, qualified to check out pilots in all types of aircraft assigned to Base Operations. I had immediately become an instructor in the T-6, C-45 and C-47, so was getting plenty of flying time. Also each day at nine o'clock in the morning and four o'clock in the afternoon, I had to send a C-45 to Manila in order for base personnel to conduct business. Manila was 65 miles South of Clark, so it took a little over half an hour to get there taking about an hour and a half for the round trip, including time on the ground. Very frequently I could not get a crew, so took the flight myself.

Once a month around payday, while in Manila, we picked up a couple of canvas sacks filled with pesos. (Philippine currency.) Two pesos equaled one American dollar. On those trips we always carried an armed guard which I was grateful for, but not for the obvious reason. I could not dispel the thought of, while flying over a small village, emptying a sack of pesos. Most of those people were destitute so you can imagine what the outcome of this thought would be. Guess I would have been a court-martialed, national hero!

Fortunately, after a couple of months, Frank Kelly, was assigned to Base Operations as instrument training instructor and we quickly became very good friends. I could always depend on Frank to help me and he immediately relieved me of a large amount of my workload. I was finally able to enjoy my job.

I cannot recall how long we had been at Clark when Frank Borman finally passed his physical exam and was qualified to be back on flying status. I was required to give him several flights in a T-6 to determine if he was capable of flying again. Of course, this was a formality, because he immediately demonstrated he was exceptionally well qualified. After checking out, he was assigned to a fighter squadron, flying F-80's, the first single engine jet in service. Frank was concerned that he was behind his contemporaries in flight time and experience, so volunteered to fly with me anytime he was off duty and I needed a copilot. We were able to fly a lot together.

After Frank and I were at Clark about six months, we were assigned base quarters, (homes) and our wives came over. Sue Borman and my wife came over on the same boat, so they were already friends before they arrived. I've always been proud of the time I spent with Frank and I knew at the time, that he had a great career ahead of him and I was right. He was the first astronaut to leave the earth's orbit, circumnavigate the moon and return to earth making a splashdown landing in the ocean. After leaving the Air Force as a full Colonel, Frank joined Eastern Airlines, which had been headed by Eddie Rickenbacher, a famous Army Air Corps pilot and Frank eventually became President and CEO of Eastern Airlines.

The Commanding General of the Thirteenth Air Force, a Lt. General, had a C-47 and B-17 assigned as his personal airplanes. I learned a good lesson from him. He was a gruff old guy that did not waste words.

Each year every pilot was scheduled to get link trainer time. When the General's turn came, I sent him a pre-printed form indicating the date and time he was scheduled. I might explain the link trainer had a cockpit designed like that in an airplane and was used to provide instrument practice time. The pilot was on instruments from take-off until landing. Anyway, when the General received his schedule, he must have borrowed his secretary's lipstick, because when I received the form back, in large red letters, he had printed, "leave this to the junior airmen and never send me this again!" and I didn't!

Fortunately, soon after that he was replaced by Lt. General Sessems, an exact opposite personality. General Sessem's Aide, Frank Bowen, was the only pilot allowed to fly his B-17. and Frank Kelly and I were the only pilots allowed to fly his C-47. When a VIP arrived on base and needed air transportation, either Frank or I would take the flight. The C-47 had four plush seats mounted in the front of the cabin and the B-17 was pretty plush throughout. Also whenever an interesting flight was scheduled, I would put myself on as instructor.

One time a C-54 cargo plane had engine failure when landing at Hong Kong. I was told to find a crew capable of delivering an engine to Hong Kong in the one other C-47 we had. A Lt. Col in charge of maintenance at Clark wanted to take the flight as pilot so he could supervise unloading the engine, because it was a tight fit through the cabin door. He had flown the C-47, but was not current at that time so I convinced myself I had no choice but to go along as instructor. We had a very thorough weather briefing and were told the weather at Hong Kong was marginal and at times below minimums, but by our time of arrival it should start breaking up. Never having landed at Hong Kong I was apprehensive about taking off from Clark after receiving the uncertain weather forecast, but decided to make my decision at the point of no return. To go beyond that point, we would not have sufficient fuel to return to Clark. Except for Hong Kong, the entire China coast was "Red China," and if we landed in Red China, the plane would be confiscated and no telling what our fate would be.

We took off early in the morning and encountered instrument flying conditions about two hours after take-off. I was continuously checking the Hong Kong weather and was told it was holding at minimums, or slightly below. There was a British aircraft about thirty minutes ahead of us also headed for Hong Kong and I could hear his anxious transmissions. He also had planned a point of no return and was rapidly approaching it. Finally I heard him inform air traffic control that he was turning back. British pilots had a reputation for being excellent instrument pilots, because of England's normal bad weather conditions, so when he turned back; I was convinced there was no hope for us. We were rapidly approaching our point of no return, so it was decision making time. I made one final check of the Hong Kong weather condition and it sounded encouraging. The present weather was slightly above minimums and expected to slowly improve, but there was no guarantee of this! Anyway, I decided to proceed on, knowing what the consequences were if I was wrong. Further weather checks had the ceiling and visibility marginal or slightly improving. Believe me, I was very uneasy the remainder of the flight.

Finally, after arriving over Hong Kong, the weather was slightly above our minimums, so we proceeded to make an instrument approach. As I recall, the approach procedure called for flying over the station and after turning to an Easterly direction, start descending and then make a procedure turn, (turn forty five degrees left and then one hundred eighty degrees right) to intercept the inbound heading to the station. We were informed by approach control that after completing the procedure turn at the prescribed altitude, some small white islands should be seen out of the left cockpit window. Just as I spotted the islands, the left engine started misfiring. This was a terrible time to lose an engine! I pushed the mixture control full forward and retarded the throttle. The engine started idling smoothly, so I slowly advanced the throttle as it continued to run smoothly. Of course I expected it to act up again at any second. We had the field in sight off our right side and turned to line up with the runway and it was then that I saw the mountains practically surrounding the airport. I realized I could never make a "go-around" on one engine at our weight but the engine was kind to me and continued to run smoothly. After parking on the ramp, I could not duplicate the sputtering problem, but I was apprehensive when we took off two days later. The flight back to Clark was uneventful and after landing I reported the problem to the crew chief, but he was never able to determine the cause of our problem.

I frequently had to fly VIP's to Bagio, a rest and recuperation center buried in the mountains about one hundred miles North of Clark Field. I would either take a C-45, which had passenger seats, or the General's C-47. Bagio had a very short, narrow, landing strip which I believe was about five thousand feet above sea level. Landing was not too difficult, but the take off could be exciting. It seemed the wind was normally out of the West, so immediately after take off; pilots had to make a slight turn to the left while flying through a narrow mountain passage and accelerating to climb speed. A few clouds in the area would add to the anxiety. Frank Kelly and I were the only pilots allowed to land at Bagio other than Frank, the General's Aide. I assume, being only a First Lt., I was expendable. Philippine Airlines had stopped going into Bagio sometime earlier when a C-47 crashed while landing but for some strange reason I always looked forward to flying in out of that airport.

One night I had to take General Sessems to Manila in order to attend a banquet. I let him out in front of the Philippine Air Force Operations building and taxied to the parking ramp. I had to be careful because the ramp in front of operations was under repair. It had a large gap with the bottom about twelve to fifteen inches lower than the ramp with a sharp, abrupt edge. The General gave us a time he would return to operations, so we went to a nearby restaurant. I cannot recall who my copilot was, but the crew chief that normally flew with the General did not accompany us on this flight. The substitute crew chief knew that the General always received first class service, so before the General's time to return for the flight home, he attempted to taxi the plane to a position directly in front operations. Upon our return from the restaurant, to our surprise, the C-47 was already in front of the building, but to our dismay, the tail wheel was bottomed in the gap, butted against the sheer edge of the ramp. While making a one hundred eighty degree turn so the General would not have to walk around the plane to enter the cabin, the crew chief miscalculated his turn radius and put the tail wheel in the gap. I realized that applying power by revving up the engines would not work, because the thrust required would have put the plane on its nose. As we were pondering over the problem, General Sessems returned. He probably assumed I was responsible, but graciously did not ask for details. There were a few Philippine officers standing around offering their help so the General calmly asked if they had a jack and in about two minutes he had a jack. He removed his white mess dress blouse (formal uniform) and began to place the jack under the fuselage as close to the tail wheel as possible. I immediately asked if I could do that and he said "I have it," as he started jacking up the tail. When the bottom of the wheel reached the height of the ramp he stopped and instructed me to start the engines and ease the plane forward on his signal. I was told later, he asked everyone standing around to hold the leading edge of the tail wing up to prevent the wheel from dropping back into the gap as the plane pulled forward off the jack. His plan worked perfectly and the entire procedure took about twenty minutes. He thanked everyone for their help and we headed back to Clark. I never heard another word about the incident and I thought when I become a three star General, I want to handle problems the same way!

On the last day of each month I had to send the C-47 to Formosa with the payroll for contingency forces stationed there. It was about a five hour flight with a stop at Hanoi and then proceed on to spend the night in Taipei. I frequently made the flight while giving instrument checks to behind the line pilots. Col. Hendman and I had become good friends and played golf together almost every Sunday, so one Sunday I mentioned he was due for his annual instrument check and suggested he and I take the next Formosa flight. I explained that I could give him his check which he thought was a good idea, so I scheduled the flight. After departing Clark, all went well until we attempted to take off from Hanoi. While we were on the ground a ground fog moved in which required him to make an instrument take- off. Immediately after becoming airborne, the artificial horizon slowly began indicating we were in a bank. I checked the needle in the turn and bank indicator and it indicated level flight. Lt. Col. Hendman had started following the artificial horizon which actually did put us in a bank. I told him to ignore the artificial horizon and refer to the turn and bank indicator but he continued to follow the artificial horizon, so I said, "I've got it" and took control. The artificial horizon continued to roll doing a full circle which, had we followed it, would have put us on our back half way through the roll! We shortly broke out of the ground fog and I had Lt. Col. Hendman cage the instrument. This locked it in a horizontal position rendering it unusable. I wanted to make sure it was not referred to again. After a few minutes I uncaged it, made a couple of small turns and it seemed to operate normal.

This was very important because the weather at Taipei was a little above minimums, with an overcast and poor visibility. The instrument let down required that you track outbound going between two mountain ranges, make a procedure turn and then track inbound to the station. The distance between the two ranges did not allow much leeway while tracking. Lt.Col.Hendman could not see the mountains, but "I" certainly knew they were there. While proceeding outbound he had a little crosswind, so started drifting off track. I asked him to make the proper correction using the radio compass and he seemed completely confused. I made the correction for him and then gave him back control. All this time I was watching the needle very closely because of the artificial horizon malfunction after taking off from Hanoi. He again drifted off course and obviously had not flown precision instruments in a long time because of his desk job. I then continued the let down giving him back control when we had the field in sight. After landing I discretely let him know he needed practice making instrument approaches.

The next morning we took off in poor weather conditions and he had the same tracking problems. We were on an instrument flight plan and if I remember correctly, we were told to level off at 7,000 feet. A little later while still in the clouds, we heard a strange noise. I looked out the side window and saw another C-47 at our exact same altitude passing just off our left wing. Lt.Col.Hendman calmly said, "Boy, that was close," and I called the ground control center to report the near miss. I was informed they had no other reported traffic at our altitude or anywhere close to our position. This was long before radar, so they could not observe airborne traffic. Even though the visibility was very limited, we both kept our eyes open because it was obvious that Chinese pilots did not always file an instrument flight plan while flying in instrument conditions. I might mention here, that the two things I feared most in flying were mid-air collision and fire.

The rest of the flight went well, however, after landing, I informed Col.Hendman he "failed" his instrument check. Failing a check flight put a stigma in a pilot's permanent records and for the Deputy Commander of the Thirteenth Air Force, who was ultimately responsible for all flight activities, to fail a check ride when he should be setting an example, was unheard of. I realized in his position, he had little time to maintain proficiency, but I felt there should be no double standards. I told no one of the check ride except my immediate boss, the Base Operations Officer, who reviewed all flight check results. Of course Col Hendman was our boss and when I informed the Operations Officer why he failed, he looked at me in amazement and said, "Do you realize who Lt. Col. Hendman is?" I said, "Certainly I know, he got me this job, I play golf with him almost every Sunday and we knew each other before coming to Clark." He said, "Can't you do something about that write-up?" I started feeling extreme compassion for Lt. Col. Hendman, so I changed the evaluation to "incomplete" and immediately called him. He thanked me and agreed to go up a couple of nights after work to practice instruments and complete his check. We continued playing golf together and I really believe he appreciated both my integrity and ability to cope diplomatically with difficult situations.

One night I was with a student practicing GCA's, (ground controlled approach) when I was advised by the control tower to terminate after my next approach because each time I flew over a position near the main entrance to the base, tracers being fired at the plane could be seen. (GCA approaches are made with ground controller giving directional and altitude advisories under instrument conditions). A militant group, called the Huks, was attempting to overthrow the Philippine government and they were very active in the area surrounding Clark Field. Because of this, travel off base, was very limited and usually required an armed guard escort. The Huks disliked Americans because we sided with the present administration, even though it was well known to be corrupt. Needless to say we terminated our flight, but being shot at served a purpose for me. No one can claim I was on active duty during World War 11, Korea and Viet Nam without being shot at! War is hell!

About two o'clock one afternoon Frank Rowan, the General's Aide, called me at Base Operations instructing me to change into "a class A" uniform and take the General's C-47 to San Fernando Airport to pick up a passenger. I was instructed to take him anywhere he wanted to go and he gave no clue as to who the passenger was. I asked Frank Kelly, hoping he would go along on this "mysterious" mission and Frank consented out of curiosity, so we both went home to change uniforms. I had landed at San Fernando Airport several times before so knew there was no control tower, administration building, or communication facilities on the field.

We landed and parked in front of a dilapidated shack which was the only building on the field. After parking, we got out of the airplane and stood in the hot sun trying to look very military as we waited. and we waited and waited and waited and having no communications with Clark available, we felt very helpless. Finally, after well over an hour, we decided to take off, call Clark with the plane radio and ask for instructions. Just as we were about to board the plane, a caravan of vehicles appeared being led by a jeep with a 50 caliber gun mounted on the hood followed by five or six black limousines.

They parked alongside the plane and about twenty very well dressed men stepped out of the cars and boarded the plane without saying a word to us. I sincerely hoped these were our intended passengers, because Frank and I boarded right behind them and went straight to the cockpit. While I was starting the engines, a man came forward and instructed us to proceed to Manila. Up until this time I had no idea what our destination was going to be. We took off, climbed to altitude and after leveling off, a very distinguished looking man stepped into the cockpit and said, "my name is Magsysy," (I'm not sure that name is spelled correctly,) shook our hands and went back to the cabin. To our shock, we recognized the name as being the recently elected future President of the Philippines. We were taking him to Manila to attend his inauguration that very night. He had been hiding out in the mountains because his life was continuously threatened by the present crooked administration. I can't imagine what would have happened if we had taken off without him. The entire future of the Philippines may have been changed, to say nothing of the relationship between the USA and the Philippines and to take it further, the USAF and me! A couple of years later, President Magsysy was killed when a Philippine Air Force C-47 crashed. There were talks of possible sabotage.

I had the job of giving the head of the Philippine Air Force, instrument instruction and a check ride. He actually did pretty well and I was glad I did not have to flunk him! Not too much longer after that, he also was killed in an aircraft accident. I hoped it did not happen while flying on instruments!

The US gave the Philippine Air Force five surplus PBY amphibians. The PBY was used extensively during World War11 as a reconnaissance ship. It was twin engine and I was told it could remain airborne for 24 hours with out refueling. I know one of its missions was to patrol the Pacific Ocean in search of submarines. I'm sure it was a very stable plane and had earned a very good reputation. It seemed unbelievable, but within one year all five were destroyed while attempting water landings. The resulting fate of the crews was never revealed to us

The French Army and Air Force were actively supporting South Viet Nam against North Viet Nam. The US agreed to give the French our five C-45's which they intended to mount bombs under the wings and use as bombers. My job was to find crews to deliver the planes and lead the flight to Saigon, which is now called Ho Chi Minh City. I conducted a flight test on all five planes to determine the range at cruise power settings, using minimum fuel air mixture. The procedure was to lean the mixture out until the engine coughed or sputtered, then slightly advance the mixture control, in order to use the least amount of fuel possible. I took the pilot of each crew with me, told him this is the plane he will be flying making sure each pilot followed the same procedure, so our fuel consumption in each C-45 would be the same.

The C-45 was known to have a range of a little over five hours, which was about the time it took to make Nha-Trang, our only scheduled refueling stop. We were then to follow the coastline southward, to the tip of Viet Nam, continue to follow the coastline around the tip, until reaching a well defined river. Then turn right, descend to two hundred feet to avoid small arms fire and follow the river into Saigon. On the scheduled day we took off in trail, climbed to ten thousand feet, for the best fuel consumption conservation and headed west. The flight to Nha-Trang was entirely over water, so a C-119 Air Rescue plane accompanied us to provide navigation and communications capability. Upon arriving over Nha-Trang, I had a couple of hour's fuel remaining, so, after checking with the other four pilots, I made a "Command" decision. I asked the C 119 pilot to cancel our landing at Nha Trang and advise operations at Clark that we would continue to Saigon along the scheduled route. I found out later that upon hearing about my decision, Col Hendman, really got upset for not requesting his consent, before changing the flight plan. This had occurred to me at the time, but I knew in the interest of safety and for his own ease of mind, Col Hendman would not have approved the change. Besides that, he planned the flight and made all the arrangements. In planning the flight, we both agreed we could not make it non-stop! All five C-45's landed safely at Saigon and to our surprise, the French had set up a very elaborate banquet for us in the terminal building.

We spent two days in Saigon being entertained royally by the French and were flown home in the C-19. By the time we arrived back at Clark, Lt. Col. Hendman calmed down and he gave us a nice welcome instead of a court martial. I really think he finally admired my aggressiveness as a mere Lt. in making that decision.

Our son, Jeff, was born the month we were to rotate back to the States. At that time a number of new babies were contracting polio, so I was extremely nervous during his birth. This was a horrible experience for the parents, because the disease, also known as infantile paralysis, frequently caused the child to be crippled for life. About the same time our Son Jeff was born, our good friends across the street had a baby who came down with polio. When this happened, the parents and baby were immediately flown to Hot Springs Arkansas for treatment.

According to Air Force travel regulations a baby had to be three months old before traveling, so we were duly extended, which was fine with Barbara and me because we really wanted to start a family. During those three months I was sent to Manila to pick up Abby Lane and her husband Xavier Cugat, a very popular band leader. We sent both C-47's so I carried Abby, Xavier and the band members in the General's C-47 because it had the four plush seats. The other pilot whose C-47 carried all the band instruments did not think that was fair. But, since it was not my decision, I had no other choice. I'm mentioning this to divulge a well kept secrete. Abby Lane was known to be a very beautiful woman. She had been in many movies and always looked beautiful. Well, when she boarded the plane, I never would have recognized her! In fact, I would never have asked her out on a date. (Not that she would have gone) They were to put on a show at Clark for the troops entertainment. This was Part of a Far East tour, which many unemployed performers were making. After parking the planes at Clark, we hurried to the theater to watch the performance. I could not believe I was watching the same Abby Lane. She was actually beautiful, I thought, "How do they do it?" And pledged to myself that if I ever date a movie star, I want to see her "scrubbed down," first! I would not want to wake up next to the likes of Abby! Boarding the plane to return to Manila, she looked like the Abby I first picked up.

A couple of our T-6's were equipped with external tanks to provide mosquito control. I had to check out pilots I considered qualified to do the spraying. Clark Field was laid out on a slope starting at the flight line and ascending westward towards the housing area which was at the leading edge of foothills at the foot of a mountain range. We sprayed from about 50 feet above any obstructions and at daybreak, while the wind was normally calm. Our flight path was in an East/West direction which required continuously adding power when heading west. The incline, plus the additional weight of the spray and drag caused by the external tanks, required precise airspeed control. This was critical when making the 180 degree turn at the base of the mountains at the Western perimeter of the Base.

I must add here that I received many calls from residents in the housing area complaining about the noise which disturbed their sleep. I showed no sympathy because they expressed no appreciation toward the pilot who was always a volunteer. The Base commander advised me to be nice, but to ignore the calls. I very carefully made a list of pilots I considered qualified to be spray pilots. I'll explain how critical this was a little later.

I had become friends with an F-80 fighter instructor and explained that I really wanted to fly a jet fighter aircraft and be transferred into the fighter squadron. I had approached the Squadron Commander long before this but was turned down because of my lack of jet experience. The F-80 instructor needed an annual instrument check, so we arranged for me to give it to him in a T-33. (An F-80 with a back seat for an instructor.) He put me in the front seat after a very brief ground indoctrination. After showing me how to start the engine, he strapped himself in the back seat and I taxied out to take off position. After lining up on the active runway, to my surprise he put the instrument hood in place, which absolutely prevented him from having any visual reference outside of the cockpit, indicating he intended to make an instrument take off. He then immediately applied full power which sent us quickly accelerating down the runway. An instrument take off requires perfect directional control, solely using the directional gyro (compass) which, at this time, was not always perfectly accurate. He held pretty close to the centerline, not drifting off the side of the runway before we were airborne. After completing a standard instrument departure he leveled off at fifteen thousand feet and I then realized the whole concept of flying a jet was new to me. At 15,000 feet he asked if I would like to take control. I said yes and he suggested I make a few turns. In my first turn, I immediately started losing altitude before realizing the amount of back pressure it took on the control stick to hold the nose up. He saw my trouble and suggested I use the trim tab and I replied I would really like to if only I new where the actuating switch was. This was not covered in my five minute indoctrination. The trim tab is a small flap on the horizontal stabilizer controlled by the pilot and when adjusted properly, places the horizontal stabilizer in a position that relieves the pilot from having to manually apply pressure on the stick.

The instrument check went well and we returned to Clark Field with sufficient fuel to make a couple of touch and go landings. Except for the speed and control pressure required, the jet wasn't much different from a conventional prop driven aircraft. Somehow, that same instructor was able to schedule himself for several more flights in the T-33 and always took me along.

After about four flights he determined that I was ready to fly solo, and scheduled a solo flight for me. I was in operations picking up a parachute when I heard my name called. It was the Squadron Commander asking what I was doing. He did not know I had been flying the T-33 and made it clear that although he knew how bad I wanted to fly a jet, it was not possible for him to allow me to check out. He explained I had to attend a formal training course first, which was not available at Clark Field and that ended that!

A short time later Lt. Col. Hendman informed me that the fighter squadron was converting to F-86's, the latest, most modern fighter in operation. A team of instructors was coming to Clark Field to conduct ground classes to be followed by flight training and checkouts. He had arranged for him and me to attend the ground school and hopefully, the flight phase. Well, we completed ground school, but were told that we could not attend the flight phase until all the fighter squadron pilots had completed their check out.

I received my orders to depart Clark to my new assignment before my chance to check out came. The dual time in the T33 was to be my only experience in a single engine jet aircraft.

About the day after I received my assignment to Altus AFB in Oklahoma, General Sessems came to Base Operations looking for me. He said he had been told I received my new assignment and asked if I was happy with it. I frankly said "no" and explained that I was assigned to Altus Oklahoma to fly KC-97's equipped with booms to refuel Bombers. He asked what I would like to do. I replied that I had been reading some publications indicating the B-47 bomber program looked interesting. By that time I knew I wanted to make the Air Force my career and considering the B-47 was the first multi-engine jet aircraft to be manufactured, I thought B-47 training would be a good career enhancement. Without saying a word, he just nodded in agreement and departed. About two hours later, Frank Rowan, his aide, showed me an extract of Part of a letter General Sessems had just written. It started; "Dear Rosie" then went on to write, "I have in my Command a young First Lt. wishing to get into the B-47 program." He went on to explain that I had been flying him and other visiting dignitaries all over the area and recommended my present orders to Altus be rescinded and I be placed into the B-47 program. About a week later I had new orders assigning me to B-47's.

I later learned that General Sessems and General Rosie O'Donnell, Air Force Chief of Personal, were buddies from way back and it suddenly struck me that I probably could have received any assignment I wanted, even jet fighters! Instead, I volunteered to be assigned to "SAC," Strategic Air Command, an assignment I had gone to great lengths to avoid.

My orders indicated that I must attend "AOB" school (aircraft observer bombardier) in Waco, Texas, before being assigned to a B-47 Squadron.

A couple of weeks before I was to be relieved from my Base Flight Operations assignment I diligently made a list of all the pilots assigned to Clark and flying out of Base operations. I indicated which planes each pilot was qualified to fly and indicated my judgment as to their proficiency level in each plane.

My replacement, a Major, arrived about ten days before my scheduled departure date and I was relieved from duty immediately. I briefed him as to what his duties would be and went over my "qualification, proficiency list" with him, (that's what I called it).

For some reason, shortly after he took over, he was sent to Japan for a couple of days. I said I would look after his job for him while he was away. With five days remaining before departing Clark, Frank Kelly and I were driving to work about seven o'clock in the morning, when we saw the T-6 spray plane heading uphill over the Base housing area. We both agreed it seemed that his speed was slow, so we stopped and watched him. Instead of making a flat 180 degree turn at the foot of the hills, he did an abbreviated chandelle like a crop duster, which was an abrupt steep climbing turn followed by a rapid descent, lined up with the next intended track. He was "spraying," which is an entirely different procedure. Because of his steep climbing turn, at the peak of the climb, the T-6 did a half snap roll, slowly descending on its back behind a hill. We then heard a thud and saw a puff of smoke.

When I arrived at Base Operations, I immediately checked the spray pilot schedule my replacement had compiled. The pilot was a captain who I had emphatically emphasized on my qualification list as "not qualified as spray pilot!" I had checked him out in the T-6 and considered him marginally qualified, until receiving additional training. He had just arrived at Clark a few weeks earlier after being recalled to active duty and had not flown in several years. He definitely needed a lot of practice.

When the phone rang, it was Col Hendman wanting to know who the pilot was and indicated I would be held responsible for the accident. He hung up before I could explain that I had been relieved from duty and my replacement did the scheduling. Anytime an officer was responsible for an accident, that was the" kiss of doom" for his career in the Air Force. Everyone else on the Base thought the same as Lt. Col. Hendman, which was obvious by the looks and comments I was receiving. I tried to make an appointment with Col Hendman, but had to wait until noon the following day. As you might imagine, I spent a terrible day not knowing if having been relieved from duty, was an adequate excuse. I had volunteered to fill in during my replacement's absence, but hopefully, no one else knew this. In my own mind, I felt I should have checked the spray pilot's schedule. Then again, I reasoned to myself, my replacement did have my qualification list and either neglected to check it, or disregarded my recommendations. My other thought was I remembered how the spray pilot urged me to put him on the list of qualified spray pilots and I emphatically refused. I was told his wife and five children were on their way to join him at Clark Field and this was probably why I was being chastised by people on the base who did not have excess to all the circumstances involved.

I finally had my appointment with Lt. Col. Hendman and showed him a copy of my orders relieving me from duty and also the list of pilot's qualifications. He saw how detailed and comprehensive the list was and he grinned, shook my hand and congratulated me on my thoughtfulness and thoroughness. I guess today you would call it a "save your butt list" I then realized his deep concern. He was the one that assigned me to Base Operations and ultimately would be held responsible for making the assignment.

On the day of our departure a typhoon was headed for Manila Bay, so we boarded the ship and departed port early to avoid damage while in port. Every officer was assigned a duty and mine was as, "bay captain." The ship was transporting Philippine sailor recruits to the States for basic training. I had about sixty sailors in my bay and they were very cramped, sleeping on hammocks stacked four deep. As we pulled out of port, the typhoon struck bouncing the ship like a cork and within a few minutes almost all of the sailors became sick. (Don't try to eat while reading this). Most of them were in their hammocks trying not to throw up, but that made it worse. The ones in the upper bunks vomited on the ones below them and I have never seen such a slimy, slippery mess. The floor, being very slippery, caused many to fall down while attempting to make it to the head. (Bathroom) It was impossible to assign a cleanup detail because everyone was sick and it would not have done any good anyway.

Somehow I made it through my shift without throwing up. Barbara I and Jeff had been assigned a small stateroom and I was anxious to see how Jeff and Barbara were doing. Barbara was very sick, but made it to the bathroom before throwing up. Jeff was crying, but did not appear sick. Barbara said Jeff had to be fed and she could not get out of bed. I was still fine, so told her I would feed him. I mixed the pabulum and put a spoon full in his mouth. He pushed it out with his tongue and that was all I needed. I vomited and had to lie down. Jeff was crying again and Barbara and I felt helpless, but somehow I got on my feet and made it down the corridor to the infirmary and was given a large supply of Dramamine. I struggled back to the stateroom and we took the pills. I even gave Jeff a half tablet. Barbara and I went to sleep immediately and I guess Jeff did too, because he quit crying. I woke up a couple of hours later and felt fine. Barbara felt better and was well enough to feed Jeff. I guess that's why, to this day, I don't like to go on cruises!

Shortly after we boarded, the Captain requested all passengers with pets, join him in the dining hall. I believe there were eleven of us. Barbara and I had acquired our dog, Mickey, to be with her while I was away on trips. Mickey was a Cocker Spaniel and served his purpose very well. Base housing had frequent break-ins and we lived on a cul-de-sac with our back yard adjacent to the Base perimeter fence with nothing but open fields behind our house. Mickey barked at anyone approaching our yard and he particularly disliked the yard man, who threatened to quit if Mickey was not kept on a leash.

Anyway, back to the ship. With all pet owners present, the Captain informed us that I was the ranking pet owner, so assigned me head of the pet clean up detail. All pets had been put in a former gun turret on an upper deck which we were instructed to wash down every morning. I was responsible to make sure this was done. I split the pet owners into two man teams and assigned each team their duty days. I would be at the turret every day to supervise. Well, the day after the storm, almost all owners showed up to check their pet. The condition of the turret was comparable to the bay, except the turret was also the "head" for the pets. I almost got sick again and two women excused themselves. They probably would have added to the mess, so I had no argument against their leaving. All pets had cages or houses, all of which were very messy. The pets were all terrified and Mickey was shaking like a leaf. I really wasn't able to calm him down for several days. A hose had to be passed up from a lower deck and when the turret was washed down; all the waste fell to the deck below. From there we had to wash it overboard. I wonder how many fish we made ill! For the first week, everyone showed up at their scheduled time. After that, many days I had to clean up by myself. If I later ran into the scheduled persons, I would hear, "I forgot." What they meant was, "it's an awful messy job and I know you will clean up because you are the "big shot" in charge and will be blamed if it's not cleaned. Nothing more interesting happened for the remainder of the twenty one day trip; it wasn't pleasant enough to call a "voyage!"

We disembarked in San Francisco and I went to the Base Finance Office to collect my monthly pay. I was aboard ship pay day and needed money to travel. The Finance Officer gave me two months pay and I corrected him, explaining, that I only had one month's pay coming. He went back to his adding machine and upon returning, insisted I had two months coming. He added that if I didn't accept the full two months, it would mess up his payroll. I knew a First Lt. earned $478.00 dollars a month and was sure I would have to return it sometime later. Therefore, as soon as possible, I put it in a savings account and waited several years before spending it.

We had reserved a Pullman room for the train trip to St. Louis, where I had a new 1954 Chevrolet Bel Aire on order. The train trip was another different experience. Mickey was still hyper and kept us awake all night. Barbara had spread papers on the floor, but he would not cooperate. So every time the train stopped, I jumped off with Mickey, hoping he would relieve himself. He was very choosy about selecting the right spot and I would hear the "all aboard" call and whistle while Mickey was still searching. The conductor would be holding the boarding steps and frantically signaling me to get on board. It seemed every window on the train had a head looking in my direction, enjoying the suspense. Watching me at each stop apparently was the highlight of their trip. Barbara and I took turns going to the dining room and each car I passed through, I heard comments like, "Lt., has he done it yet?" I felt like a celebrity, the most popular person on the train.

We pulled into St. Louis around noon on Saturday and went directly to the Chevy dealer's lot. It was closed and I had planned to get on the road that afternoon, or at least get out of St. Louis. I called an emergency number posted on the door and explained my problem to the sales manager. The car was ready to be picked up so he came right down. I had paid a substantial down payment and intended to pay the balance by check. I started writing a personal check, but was told personal checks were not acceptable. I would have to wait until Monday and get a cashiers check or figure out some other form of payment. I tried desperately to persuade him that my check was good and I was an Air Force Officer certainly not about to pass off a bad check. He was adamant, not about to disrupt his system of payment, so I asked if I could talk to the dealership owner. He said that was highly unusual, but I insisted. After I explained my predicament he reluctantly agreed to accept the check. I'm sure having the baby and dog influenced his decision. They were getting very restless and Jeff would not stop crying. When we were finally on our way in our new Chevy, Mickey climbed up and laid down on the back seat window shelf. After about twenty minutes on the road, he threw up all over the shelf and back seat back rest. My new car no longer had that "new car" odor.

The Chevy had a turn signal which was entirely new to me. I used it for a long time before realizing it was wired backward. Pulling down indicated a turn to the right and visa versa. I drove the rest of the way to St. Petersburg trying to first remember to use the signal and then, which way to push or pull. Flying was not the only thing which had gotten more complicated.

I had not seen the family for two and one half years, so we had a lot to discuss. Mom and Dad and my uncle Ted and his wife had purchased a bar and restaurant in St. Petersburg named Tyrone Inn and were putting in very long hours.

Pete had sold Florida Aviation Corporation .shortly before I left for the Philippines and as a pay-off, gave my Dad and Ted each five thousand dollars, which is how they were able to purchase the bar. That was a far cry from the million they had been expecting, but Pete's "ploy" did get the entire Hubert family to Florida, for which I'll always be grateful.

My Dad and Ted enjoyed the business because they were able to drink draft beer all day, while the wives tended bar, cooked, waited on tables and cleaned. I knew I would never want to be in that business.

While I was home I was informed that I had been promoted to Captain. That came as a surprise because I had only been in grade as a 1st. Lt. for a little over three years. Maybe, finally I was in the promotion cycle I had read about in high school!

CHAPTER ELEVEN
"TRIPLE RATED"
COPILOT, (UGH)!

We stayed in St. Pete for about a week and then headed for Waco. I found a small two bedroom house not far from the base and began navigation bombardier training.

I thought I disliked weather school; this was worse, but essential. General LeMay, the SAC Commander, ordered that all B-47s have either the aircraft commander or copilot triple rated. That meant after completing the course I would be a rated pilot, rated navigator and rated bombardier. I understood that to mean I would be qualified to wear any of the three AF wings on my uniform. I had deliberately avoided wearing anything but pilot's wings by my persistence while a cadet during my pre-flight qualification phase!

The B-47 had a three man crew; pilot, copilot and radar navigator, who was also the bombardier. If he became incapacitated, the rated AOB would take his position (me). Our training was divided into three phases which were classroom, simulator and actual flight. Simulator time was practicing radar bombing and navigation and flight time was mostly celestial navigation. We had to identify all the stars used in celestial navigation and names of star formations in which they could be found. I still remember the "navigator's triangle," Vega, Deneb and Altair, which almost always provided a neat triangle which the navigator needed to plot a fix.

The only good thing about attending the course was maintaining flying proficiency. We flew B-25's which were target ships for officers attending EWO training. (Electronic Warfare Officer). We were to follow instructions provided by the instructor on board the plane conducting the EWO training. All we did was turn port or starboard to certain headings and I assumed the student had to determine our position by electronic signals. That's all I knew or ever wanted to know about the EWO program. Once I learned the difference between port and starboard, it was a simple, somewhat boring job. Because I had previous B-25 experience, I always flew as pilot for which I was grateful.

One hot summer day during take off, just as I became airborne', I lost oil pressure on the right engine. This called for a quick decision on my part. The procedure was to immediately retard the throttle on that engine to prevent it from freezing up. My landing gear was still down, but did I have sufficient runway ahead of me to abort? Should I raise the gear and safely abort, but "total" the B-25? Or do I attempt to climb out on one engine and attempt a single engine landing? The second option raising the gear and sliding to halt on the belly was definitely out, so I chose to leave the gear down and attempt to stop on the remaining runway. As I decelerated, rapidly using up runway, I began to have my doubts about this decision, but by the time I reached the end of runway, I was slowed down enough to hopefully turn off onto the taxiway without over stressing the landing gear. It worked and I received some rewarding compliments from the Squadron Commander. Was this decision a continuation of my good luck, or more evidence of a guardian angel? Oh, I forget to mention "pilot skill."

Just before completing training, our entire class received orders to report to Columbus Air Force Base in Ohio. A new B-47 Squadron was forming, so even though I was not "delighted" about living in Columbus, the idea of joining a new squadron seemed pretty good. About three days later, the Columbus orders were rescinded and we were given a list of SAC B-47 bases. We were instructed to select any three, indicating our preference in numerical order. Bases in Florida and California were to be excluded because their quotas had already been filled. It seemed everyone desired to be stationed in those two States. I reasoned, if I cannot be assigned to a base in Florida, it did not really matter where we lived. Therefore, I designated Florida one,

Florida two and Florida three, wondering what my punishment would be for not following instructions. A couple of days later, on the day our class planned a farewell party, our new orders arrived. I was assigned to Pinecastle Air Force Base, Orlando, Florida! That night at the class party, each of us in turn, announced our assignments. When I said Pinecastle Air Force Base, I heard sighs of disbelief and questions like, who do you know? Shortly after my announcement, Major Lee Curry sheepishly announced "Pinecastle." Now I had the same questions like, how did this happen? I assumed I was the only pilot daring enough to use my method of base selection. Lee and his wife Millie immediately joined Barbara and me to congratulate each other and started began planning our trip to Pinecastle. I asked Lee what bases he had indicated and he also marked Florida three times. I knew right then we would become good friends! The Curry's with their three children and Barbara, Jeff and I traveled caravan style to Orlando. We got along great, especially when deciding what type of booze to buy for a drink that first night out. Ancient Age was our unanimous decision.

We arrived in Orlando with about a week of leave remaining. This is where Lee and I goofed up! The first morning after arriving, we were anxious to have a look at Pinecastle and our Squadron headquarters, but did not intend to sign in. The building was vacant except for one officer and when we ourselves he had a bewildered look on his face. He said, "Why aren't both of you in Wichita, Kansas?" We gave him back the same bewildered look while explaining we were on leave and would sign in when our leave expired in one week. In the meantime we had to find a place to live. Then he explained that the entire Squadron had already started B-47 transition in Wichita and our Aircraft Commanders were waiting for us. Also he informed us that we were both assigned as copilots! This was very disheartening news to Lee, a Major and me, both having over two thousand hours of military pilot time and me with about the same amount of civilian pilot time.

We reluctantly went back to the motel, packed our cars and headed for Wichita. Both wives, being experienced Air Force wives, accepted the news without hesitation or complaint. We again traveled caravan style, making the trip in two days. After arriving in Wichita and finding a motel, Lee and I took one car and went to the base, while the wives used the other car to look for a place to live.

I will never forget my first look at a B-47. I already knew it was a tandem six jet engine aircraft, but the way the wings drooped, I felt sure that the drooping wings must have been the result of a very hard landing. Actually, that was the normal look on the ground, but while accelerating during take off, the wings gradually raised up to appear like a normal wing. Now I wondered how many times can a wing flex up and down before breaking off?

After signing in, Lee and I were introduced to our Aircraft Commanders and we joined the ground school classes which had started a couple of days earlier. Compared to what I had previously flown, this was an extremely complex airplane. It seemed like every system had a backup system and the backup system had a backup. I'm mostly referring to fuel, hydraulic, electrical and control systems. We had to learn why and how each system worked. We also received simulator time. The simulator's cockpit was designed exactly the same as a B-47's. I really did not like the tandem cockpit, which limited the forward vision of the copilot in the rear seat. I was used to being the eyes of the crew, with my head on a swivel. Also, it was the first time I ever used a written checklist. There was a "preflight" check list which included an examination of the aircraft's exterior, dip sticking the tanks and looking for fuel, hydraulic, oil leaks, etc. Then the "pre-starting" list, the "starting" list, "before take-off," ""climb," and "level off" check lists All the lists were critical because of the complexity and number of aircraft systems involved. What I really disliked was the copilot had to read every list to the pilot. Each step on a checklist required an exact response from the Aircraft Commander. I often thought a recording activated by the Commander, or a robot could read the checklist just as well as the copilot. The flight simulator is an amazing piece of equipment. An instructor or specialist, operating a control panel, is capable of duplicating almost any emergency that might occur in flight. It is an excellent training tool still used by all airlines and all complex military planes.

My aircraft commander was Charlie Rose, a Captain, recalled to active duty after many years completely away from flying. He was a very nice guy, but somewhat rusty, having been a school teacher, far removed from any flying activity. Six engines were a hand full of throttles and a lot of engine instrument gauges to watch while waiting for the simulator instructor to spring the next emergency. Procedures caused by emergencies requiring an instant reaction, had to be memorized and then followed by carefully going through the complete applicable checklist. There was a checklist for every conceivable emergency.

After completing simulator training we finally started the flight phase. Our first flight was called a "dollar ride." Actually it was an orientation flight with the instructor in the front seat and Charlie in the rear seat, (copilot) with me in the radar navigator position, which was below and forward of the pilot's seat. I was actually in the nose, which did not have a window looking forward. There was a small window on the left side, I assume, to prevent claustrophobia. The instructor took off, climbed out and after reaching twenty thousand feet, demonstrated a few maneuvers. Then he let Charlie try to duplicate them. From my position in the nose, I wasn't able to learn much. After about an hour, the instructor took the controls and explained he was going to demonstrate the let down, approach and landing procedures. In both the ground school and the simulator, two procedures were emphasized: Always advance the power slowly because the engines in the B-47 would stall at idle power if the power was advanced too rapidly. This was an inherent problem which did not have any known fix at the time; landing attitude was a maneuver equally critical. Having a tandem landing gear, a B-47, touching down nose wheel first, would result in a radical bounce and if power were applied, was very apt to hit nose wheel first again. This most likely would require a "go around" because of insufficient remaining runway. It was called a "kangaroo" landing. Approach speed in the B-47 was also very critical. The plane was so clean, (streamlined,) that if the speed was in excess of what the landing speed chart called for, it would cause the plane to float too far down the runway to make a safe landing. Speeds for every phase of a flight depended on gross weight, pressure altitude and temperature.

I assumed our instructor maintained the proper speed schedule prior to and during landing. He touched down nose wheel first resulting in a large bounce and then abruptly shoved the throttles full forward intending to go around. Engines one two and three on the left side immediately came up to full thrust, but engines four five and six on the right side, fully stalled at idle speed. We were landing to the north with parked B-47's and hangers on our right. The plane went into an abrupt right turn and as witnesses later testified, reached a ninety degree bank angle, while making a pivoted right turn with the right wing tip dug into the ground. I knew what was happening because I felt the bank angle and saw the hangers and parked B'47's through the small left side window. They were not supposed to be to my left! Charlie said both he and the instructor had full left rudder in and the control column turned fully left, but left the throttles fully advanced. I tightened my seat belt, but felt sure we were going all the way over, ending on our back. At what must have been the last critical second, engines four and five took hold and the instructor regained control. We climbed out paralleling the South East runway heading 135 degrees after having started the landing on a heading 0f 360 degrees. If we had not actually "pivoted" on our right wing causing a sharp right turn, we surely would have plowed into the parked planes.

The instructor climbed out on five engines to a safe altitude and by slowing down to stall speed, determined a safe approach and landing speed. I had no way of knowing, but found out later a section of our right wing, including number six engine, was gone. He decided that the minimum speed with which he could maintain control was too fast to affect a landing. The B-47 had a drag chute used on every full stop landing, so he planned to approach at the slowest possible speed, descend until the landing gear was just above the runway in landing attitude and then deploy the drag chute. I think it was a good plan, but he miscalculated our height above the runway when deploying the chute. I felt the plane dropping and shaking and again I thought, "This is it." We finally hit the ground, I guess in landing attitude and seemingly intact. We quickly got out and looked at the "sick plane." The wings were drooping excessively with all eight main tires "blown." We later were told that the plane had a lot of interior structural damage and was classed as "totaled."

During the accident investigation, witnesses, who were all experienced B-47 pilots, testified that we were in a vertical bank and everyone was sure we were going all the way over. More luck or what? In any case, I was reminded of the two critical items emphasized during ground school. However, I certainly did not expect them demonstrated on my first flight in the B-47!

After receiving a complete physical, including how the accident affected us psychologically, we were assigned a new instructor, Pete Torres, an Indian and we continued our flight training. I did learn that our first "instructor (?)" was a former fighter pilot with eighteen hundred hours total pilot time. This convinced me I should not have been the copilot and I resented the fact that all of my previous experience and total pilot hours to date were never considered before assigning me to a crew. The only criteria for qualifying as Aircraft Commander was four engine pilot time. At that time I had 65 hours of four engine time in General Sessem's B-17 and over 2,500 hours military pilot time, but that was completely ignored. When I volunteered for the B-47 program, it never occurred to me that I would not be an Aircraft commander.

After that first introduction ride in a B-47 nothing very exciting occurred during subsequent flights. I do, however, remember being diverted to an alternate base one night because of Wichita's poor weather conditions. As usual I was in the radar navigator's position down in the nose. En route to the alternate, I heard Pete Torres asking the ground control center for a change of flight plan because we were encountering severe thunderstorms. I informed him I had turned the radar set on and could help thread our way around them. He started asking for headings, and I was able to help him avoid the storms, without deviating too far from our intended flight path. After landing, Pete let me know how impressed he was but I never did mention that I had just completed AOB training, using the exact same equipment. A little later, as usual, I learned that I probably did mess up. Upon returning to Wichita, I noticed a new directive posted on the bulletin board. "Students will not operate radar sets under any conditions." It went on to explain that proper shut down procedures were not being followed which resulted in major repairs. No names were mentioned and no one approached me concerning the shut down, but reflecting back, I did "not" remember shutting down the radar set before aircraft power was cut. Pete never mentioned it, which was strange because the Aircraft Commander always got blamed for everything. In spite of that, I had difficulty convincing myself that I was not the guilty party.

Charlie did quite well flying the B-47, so on the scheduled tenth flight we were sent up solo. Finally I got out of the "hole" in the nose and into the copilot's seat. We spent the day before mission planning and Charlie explained one problem he had with the penetration for landing procedure. Normal procedure was to drop the landing gear over the station while at 20,000 feet and descend at 290 knots airspeed until turning back to the station after reaching an assigned altitude. He was uncomfortable with the descent angle at that speed, preferring to indicate 270 knots which provided a shallower descent angle.

After completing our scheduled flight without incident, we returned to Wichita passing over the start descent point at 40,000 feet. Charlie dropped the gear followed by establishing a 270 knot descent. Neither of us realized how far the excessive starting descent altitude and shallower descent angle would take us from the base. We finally made the one hundred eighty degree turn and homed, (followed a radio signal,) in on Wichita at about 2,000 feet. To add to the distance problem, we had a strong tailwind while descending and headwind heading back. We flew and flew and flew and still no base in sight. I heard a conversation from approach control to another plane while in his penetration, asking if they had seen a B-47 that started his descent long ago. The stationed explained they feared there may have been an accident and were alerting all aircraft to be on the lookout! Charlie did not interrupt and attempt to explain it probably was us, because by this time, he remembered that normal procedure was to start the penetration at 20,000 feet and descend at 290 knots. Finally after what seemed like an eternity, we finally sighted the field. For some strange reason, no one mentioned our stupid mess up. I think we were about one hundred miles from the base when we started back instead of what should have been about ten miles.

CHAPTER TWELVE

FINALLY SETTLED DOWN AT PINECASTLE AFB

That was our final flight at Wichita and we returned caravan style with the Curry's to Orlando. We rented both apartments in a very nice duplex near downtown Orlando. This worked well, because Lee and I could take turns driving to work with the wives always having a car.

When we arrived back at the base, we found that SAC had provided professional B-47 instructors to check the aircraft commanders out in air refueling techniques. The Wing Commander was anxious to have SAC announce our Wing, "combat ready," and to accomplish this, air refueling competency and a simulated deployment were the only remaining requirements. We flew practice missions every other day and did our mission planning the day in between. Mission planning was very detailed. The copilot computed the aircraft's weight and balance making sure the fuel was properly distributed and the total weight of the B-47 did not exceed limits after taking into consideration runway length, temperature and pressure altitude. (As best I can remember) He also prepared a performance chart indicating all the information pertinent to navigation, position reporting check points and fuel consumption. Fuel consumption was extremely critical. Training missions were scheduled for seven hours duration and fuel consumption was determined by aircraft weight, temperature, pressure altitude and phase of the mission, such as taxi, take-off, climb and cruise and we had fuel performance charts for each phase. Maybe now it can be understood why mission planning took all day.

Charlie was a good pilot as far as controlling the plane, but had difficulty following standard procedures and thinking ahead of the plane. When you are traveling over five hundred miles per hour, your next duty comes up fast and it's essential that you are ready for it. No daydreaming!

Training missions always consisted of high level simulated bomb runs, which were scored by ground control units equipped with instruments capable of determining exactly where a simulated released bomb would strike. This was accomplished by a tone initiated by the radar navigator and abruptly stopped at the simulated ground impact point. From this position "bomb plot" could measure the exact distance in feet between the target and impact point. These scores were forwarded to the bombers home base and evaluated by a team in the Wing's Bomb/ Nav section, which usually on the next day critiqued the applicable crew. A bomb scored outside of a defined "circle of error," resulted in severe criticism from the Wing Deputy Commander of Operations and Remedial Training. A black mark against the entire crew! Training missions also included a two hour celestial navigation leg. This is where I came in. The copilot selected three stars to shoot or the sun (hoping to form a triangle) and culminated on each star for two minutes with two minute intervals. This did not allow much time to record the information, locate the next star, adjust the sextant and prepare to shoot. Timing was critical, because at over five hundred miles per hour, we were traveling about seven miles per minute. The radar navigator was depending on plotting our position, in the center of a triangle formed as a result of the celestial shots. After considering wind direction, speed and time, from the last known position, he assumed our present position and plotted the celestial fix from that. The copilot, after completing the third shot as quickly as possible, completed computations on a specially designed form and gave "radar" a figure to plot. The copilot's seat was on a swivel and I had to unbuckle my chute to be in a position to culminate on some stars. In the beginning, we had hand held sextants and shot through a bubble canopy. How's that for a challenge? Later, we could hang the sextant from a hole in the canopy and subsequently, fixes were far more accurate.

Almost every mission had air refueling scheduled. We would rendezvous with a KC-97 tanker, at about sixteen thousand feet, because that was their ceiling due to their basic weight combined with JP-4 fuel to off-load to us. The rendezvous was a precision maneuver. SAC, in coordination with the FAA, had designated air refueling tracts. We entered the tract head on with the tanker, one thousand feet below his altitude. He would transmit a pre-arranged signal that our radar navigator could track on his scope and read off range separation to his pilot as the two aircraft approached each other. The tanker flight path was offset from ours just enough so as to allow the pilot to make a precise 180 degree turn from a pre-determined offset distance which placed him directly in front of us. We maintained a climb and speed schedule until "stable" in the "pre-contact" position. Then we closed with the tanker to a "ready" position and finally made contact with the tanker boom. The tanker pilot held a constant heading and altitude, while the bomber pilot flew formation slightly below and behind the tanker. Turbulence and maneuvering around thunder storms were the primary concerns of the bomber pilot. Both of these determined how difficult it would be for the bomber pilot to hold his position and avoid an automatic disconnect. The bomber copilot managed fuel distribution, opening and closing fuel tank valves, to maintain a center of gravity within limits. I have gone into detail describing these flight activities to show the importance of detailed mission planning and crew coordination. Later on I'll give an example of how a missed air refueling could jeopardize the Wing's standing in SAC's rating system.

Charlie and I were together at Pinecastle for just a short time when he received orders to report to MacDill Air Force Base. They had converted from B-29's to B-47's and I assume the MacDill Wing was short a qualified Aircraft Commander. I think everyone assumed that our Wing had to transfer one pilot and Charley was selected because of his indifference to some of the prescribed procedures. For example, he lived in a town quite a distance from Pinecastle and when we had a practice alert in the middle of the night; it took Charlie over an hour to report in. This frustrated the Squadron Commander because everyone was expected to report in less than thirty minutes and he was held accountable for crew adherence to prescribed procedures. Charlie refused to move closer to Pinecastle, displaying the same attitude as in making all penetrations at 270 knots instead of the normal 290 knots. In other words, Charlie was a "non-conformist," which was not condoned in SAC!

I was assigned to a new crew that had recently lost its copilot. The Aircraft Commander was Major Mike Spatz and the radar navigator was Captain Bill Elmore. Mike Spatz was a West Point Graduate that had been assigned to a mule Squadron in Panama prior to entering West Point. Much "unlike" an Academy Graduate, Mike Spatz still had the vocabulary of a mule skinner, unable to complete a sentence without using numerous expletives. One of his favorite stories was how amazing things are. He went from driving a mule at four miles per hour to flying a plane at over four hundred miles per hour. I personally think he was more at home in the mule squadron! He was also Assistant Squadron Operations Officer, so sat in the operations office trading war stories while Bill, "Radar" and I did the entire mission planning. Mike's absence during mission planning was obvious by the questions he asked during the mission. Frequently during two hour celestial navigation legs, I would see Mike's head fall forward indicating he had fallen asleep. He was on autopilot and probably bored, forgetting that he was supposed to be the eyes for Bill and me. This was in 1955, long before radar controlled air traffic gave "traffic advisories" such as advising a pilot when there is other traffic in his immediate vicinity. During VFR flight, when the expression "see and be seen," was popular, Mike Spatz saw nothing!

As I remember, the final evaluation by SAC to determine if our Wing could be declared "combat Ready," were were deployed to Sidi Slimane (?) in Morocco, North Africa. We took off about eight o'clock at night in three, five ship cells. Planes in cells took off at one minute intervals with a short time interval between each cell. The cell flew in SAC's standard "formation," five hundred feet vertical and one mile lateral separation. Our first scheduled air refueling was while coasting out over New Foundland. Each bomber in the cell had a specific tanker assigned, identified by the signal being transmitted on his transponder. The rendezvous went well and Mike pulled into the "ready for contact" position. Normal procedure was to lower the pilot's seat and Mike being so tall, this was almost essential. Lowering the seat made it easier for the pilot to look up at the tanker. This night Mike was not able to stabilize long enough for the boom operator to insert the boom. We were doing all kinds of gyrations behind the tanker, sometimes in extremely erratic positions. Mike was getting desperate with time passing by and he was not taking on fuel. He even asked me to hold the control column steady to prevent him from over-controlling. This made it worse because now he had to over come my pressure. The cell leader had requested each pilot to report when refueling was completed and all except Mike Spatz had reported. The leader informed Mike that the cell could not wait much longer which made Mike even more desperate. Finally the cell leader informed Mike that the cell could not delay any longer because at our refueling altitude of 16,000 feet, (KC-97 limit) they were quickly burning up the precious fuel just taken on. This of course made Mike even more desperate which was evident by the way he seemingly "attacked" the boom. The receptacle, in which the boom is inserted, is just in front of the pilot's windshield and I expected the boom to burst through at any time .Finally the cell leader instructed Mike to divert to Goose Bay Labrador. I was grateful for the order because I felt it had become a "do or die" challenge to Spike. Being rather unwilling to die with Spike, I was mentally prepared to pull the ejection seat handles at any time.

Bill gave us a heading to Goose and we landed without incident. The next day we were instructed to return to Pinecastle and the rest of the Wing returned a couple of days later. The Wing Commander had flown over with the Chief of Standardization and would return with him, so Mike spent some very anxious days waiting, not knowing what sort of reprimand to expect. Finally The Wing Commander requested that Mike and I report to his office At this time I might mention Mike was about six feet four and remember, I'm five six and one half. (When you're that short, every one half inch counts) We stood at attention in front of the Commander while he asked Mike for an explanation. I'll quote, "my G- - D- - Copilot set my G- - D- - lunch bucket under my G- - D- - seat so I could not lower my seat. He showed the crumpled lunch bucket as evidence. The Wing Commander grinned, probably trying to refrain from bursting out laughing, got up, put his arm around Spike and told us the rest of the Wing had a very successful mission, which gave the Wing a passing grade for the exercise and we were "combat ready." Mike had not said a word to me about the lunch bucket before this so I was not prepared to defend myself. I think Mike may have put the lunch bucket under the seat himself!

I often wonder how the interview would have gone if Mike had not been a West Point Graduate! He and another young 1st. Lt. were the only Academy graduates in the Wing. I might mention that the Lt. was Bennie were the who, years later, became SAC Commander in Chief, with four "stars" He and Mike used to needle each other, with Mike frequently making degrading, sarcastic remarks to him. I think Mike retired as a full Colonel before Bennie attained his four star position, probably lucky for Mike!

On a standardization evaluation flight, which was an annual requirement, Mike completed his requirements and then I completed mine from the rear seat, of course. It was customary to be critiqued after the flight and ours was very brief. The instructor said, "Mike, If you ever have to make an actual ILS(instrument landing system approach) let Bill make it." Mike gave me a dirty look as though I was trying to out-do him. Air Force pilots normally made GCA (ground controlled approach) approaches backed up by ILS if so equipped, whereas civilian pilots used the ILS system. The difference being when making a GCA, a ground controller, using radar, gives the pilot altitude and heading directions. ILS requires a system in the aircraft capable of receiving information transmitted from the ground to an instrument on the pilots' instrument panel, providing heading and glide slope information.

I was in squadron operations preparing to take off on a practice mission one afternoon when I got a call from Millie Curry. Barbara was in labor and Millie was leaving to take her to the base hospital. We had a seven hour flight planned, so I informed Mike about Barbara. Mike looked at me, like, "so what," and started walking out to the plane. I explained to Millie that she would have to take my place and she understood. In SAC, nothing took priority over a flight schedule! That was a long seven hours and I expected a message any minute, relayed through an FAA center, that I was a father. The message never came, so after landing, I called Millie. Barbara was still in labor so I changed clothes and rushed to the hospital. As it turned out, Marianne wasn't born until the next morning. I again was not able to be there because we had to "mission plan" for a flight the next day. I was sure Mike could not begin to compile the information required in the flight plan, however, he would never admit it he needed me!

A short time later our Wing was deployed to Sidi Slimane for a six month TDY (temporary duty) tour. This tour was rotated among all SAC Wings, so we were expecting it. My Mother came over from St. Pete to help Barbara, having her hands full with Jeff, who was just two years old.

At Sidi we flew routine training missions no different than at Pinecastle. Lee Curry was very much out of place being a Major, flying as copilot, so he was put in an upgrade program to become an A/C (aircraft commander,) while still flying as copilot on a crew, so he was pretty busy. We did not see much of each other. We slept in a Quonset hut we shared with two other three man crews. All meals were eaten at the Officer's Club, so after dinner with nothing else to do, we usually hung around the club for a while.

There was a fighter squadron also on temporary duty and they always seemed to be having a good time. Their normal training mission was one hour as apposed to our seven hours. This made a lot of difference in the amount of sleep needed and drinks to consume. The club had a piano bar and when the fighter pilots saw us they had a favorite song for us. I can remember the first Part of it. "There are no fighter pilots down in hell, there are no fighter pilots down in hell, the place is full of queers, navigators, bombardiers and there are no fighter pilots down in hell." I guess they knew better than to include bomber pilots!

Our radar navigator, Bill Elmore, frequently stayed at the club quite late and awakened everyone when he returned to the hut. He always put his slippers by the side of his cot because the latrine was about one half block away and always, at sometime during the night, Bill would have to "go." He would slip into his slippers while sitting on the side of the cot, before standing up. One night I nailed his slippers to the wooden floor. Later on, sure enough, he sat up, slipped into the slippers, started to take his first step and fell flat on his face. Boy, was he mad, but unable to put the blame on any one of the other eight of us. I think and hoped, he thought it was Mike, but anyway, from then on he was much quieter!

When returning from a mission late one afternoon, the landing gear would not extend using the normal procedure. There were short vertical bars behind the copilot's seat that could be used to manually ratchet the gear down. Sidi Slimane was under instruments conditions, (low ceiling) and Mike continued descending requesting a GCA approach. Normal procedure would have been to remain at altitude to conserve fuel until the gear was fully extended. I rotated my seat and began attempting to ratchet the gear down. Not having done this before, I had no idea how long it would take or how many strokes with the bars. Mike received his GCA pick up and I continued to ratchet. As we got lower, I warned Mike to be prepared for a go-around, but he ignored me. He was to engrossed in the GCA to listen to anything else and I felt he was determined to land no matter what! I did not like the idea of a crash landing with me sitting backward, unstrapped. Finally, just before he started his flare, (rounding out to assume landing attitude) I had indications the gear was fully extended. We landed with me still sitting backward which was not a comfortable feeling with Mike at the controls!

We finally returned to Pinecastle and received a warm welcome from our wives. Marianne was then six months old and cried when this "stranger" tried to hold her. It also took a while to achieve Jeff's recognition.

I mentioned Sam Castleberry at San Marcos. Sam was an aircraft commander in the squadron and was surprised to see me flying as copilot He remembered checking me out in one short flight in the B-25. Sam's copilot was a really great person, Captain Art Miller. Art and I had quickly become good friends and played a lot of golf together. He had a beautiful golf swing which I envied, but could not duplicate. One day we were making simulated bomb runs over Tampa and through a clearing in the clouds, saw heavy black smoke coming from the ground close MacDill. Mike commented on it and the sight gave me an eerie feeling. After returning to Pinecastle we were met by the squadron operations officer. He checked us off his roster and informed us that an aircraft had crashed in the MacDill area and as yet had not been identified. A short time later we were told that it was one of ours, piloted by our Chief of Standardization who was giving Sam Castleberry's crew their annual flight check. This had a horrible effect on Mike and me. Mike and Sam had become very good friends and of course, Art was my best friend in the Squadron. When the cause of the accident became known, everyone was astounded. The Chief of Standardization is normally the most proficient, knowledgeable and experienced pilot in the Wing. Our chief met all these prerequisites. It was determined that he was giving Sam an instrument check and because Pinecastle did not have an ILS system, we always went to MacDill for that Particular requirement. Instrument checks were given with the check pilot in the front seat and pilot in the rear seat with a hood up preventing him from having visual references. While in this conformity, a B-47 in the MacDill traffic pattern reported he was not sure of the position of his landing gear. He could not tell for sure that it was fully down and locked. Our Chief of Standardization check pilot offered to pull up behind and beneath the troubled B-47 to visually check the gear position. As he pulled in close, our Chief's B-47 was suddenly sucked into the bottom of the other aircraft. Both planes immediately exploded before anyone was able to eject.

Losing Art was a real shock to me. His wife requested that I escort his remains, if any, to his home for burial. I must tell you this was a very difficult thing to do. I spent the night at his parent's home and attempted to soothe the parents and relatives. It was easy to see that Art was a very well loved person. We later were briefed, that although we flew that same position with tankers, the extended B-47 gear caused a vacuum effect and apparently sucked the lower B-47 up into it. I don't believe this possibility was known before Sam's accident.

CHAPTER THIRTEEN
IN AGAIN AND OUT AGAIN!

Soon after returning home from the funeral I started receiving pleading calls from my Mother. The bar business was getting to my Dad who proved to be a much better customer than owner. She wanted me to get released from active duty and manage their bar and restaurant. At this time I had nine years of active duty and was finally in the Aircraft Commander upgrade program. More important than that, I really did not want to be in the bar and restaurant business. Also about this same time we were informed that our Wing, the 19th Bomb Wing, was being transferred to Homestead Florida.

After completing AOB training, I had a two year service commitment which would keep me on active duty several more months.

When my Mother called to tell me that the doctor had emphatically informed her that my Dad would "die" if he did not get away from the temptations available behind the bar, I decided I had no choice but to request release from active duty. When I informed her of my decision, I made it clear that I would purchase the business, including all the property presently included in their deed, rather than just manage the business. I already had enough of managing a business for a relative, remembering my situation with Pete.

The 19th Bomb Wing moved out and I was transferred to the 321st Bomb Wing which was also stationed at Pinecastle AFB. With such a short time remaining on active duty, I was not assigned to a crew, but instead was assigned to Base Operations, which suited me fine.

The Base Operations Officer was Major Lovell, a West Point Graduate, who also had a short time of active duty remaining as he had elected to retire after 20 years service. It was rumoured that he owned several orange groves in the Orlando area so was assumed independently wealthy. He liked to fly, so took all of the C-47 flights himself. I think he considered it his personal airplane. I immediately checked out in the Base C-45 and mostly flew with "behind the line" pilots while they practiced instruments. Eventually I did persuade Major Lovell to check me out in the C-47, which he did, but never had an opportunity to fly it again.

The 321ˢᵗ Bomb Wing had an Aircraft Commander that was a member of the Air Force swimming team. He was to attend a swimming meet in New York City and instead of going by commercial airline; I was scheduled to take him in the C-45. He had never been in a C-45 before, but because he was a "hot shot" B-47 Aircraft Commander, thought he was automatically the C-45 Aircraft Commander. I quickly straightened that out by informing him that his sole duty as "co pilot" was to make the position reports upon my instructions.

We landed at Newark and he headed for the swimming meet. It lasted two days and we had arranged for an early morning take off on the third day. I filed an instrument flight plan because the New York weather was terrible. Newark was closed for landings because of fog but allowed take offs for qualified pilots. My passenger was in a hurry to get back to Pinecastle, insisting that we take off. I refused, so he let me know he had a green Air Force instrument card which allowed him to take off at his discretion, with no minimum requirements. We had been briefed there were numerous thunderstorms in the area, and without radar I knew we had no way of avoiding them, because of zero visibility. He said, that if I wasn't capable, "he" would make the take off. Now he touched on a tender subject with me. I explained to him that even though he was a Major and thought himself far superior to me in rank, capability and qualifications, I was the pilot in Command of the C-45; he was the passenger and the decision as to when to take off was strictly up to me. In my mind I was thinking his poor judgment far out weighed his capabilities and really wanted to tell him so. Neither one of us said another word until taking off. When I was sure the thunderstorms had cleared the area, I took off, entering clouds immediately after breaking

ground. The flight home was uneventful with very few words spoken. I never ran into him again, but must admit it felt good being the pilot in "Command" again after be a copilot for so long.

Major Lovell arranged for me to take some passengers to MacDill AFB in order to attend a conference. He had a "behind the line" pilot needing instrument practice, so I was to drop off the passengers at MacDill, then take off, give a couple of hours instrument training, land, pick up the passengers and return to Pinecastle. I discharged the passengers and taxied out to continue our flight. I remained in the left (pilot) seat because the other pilot was not qualified in the C-45 and I was not an instructor. I went through the "before take off" check list, which included revving the engines up and then proceeded to take off. While accelerating down the runway, just as I broke ground and was reaching for the landing gear switch, I heard a loud explosion from the left engine. With plenty of runway remaining, I abruptly pulled both throttles back and with the landing gear still down, landed straight ahead. With the right engine still running, I called the tower to inform them I was shutting both engines down and requested a tow vehicle. It is almost impossible to taxi with one engine. After shutting down and getting out, I immediately saw my problem. The left propeller shaft had sheared between the engine nacelle and the prop. The propeller ripped the lower cowling off, struck the runway, bounced up and ripped a long gash in the bottom of the fuselage beneath the cabin. The twisted prop was lying on the runway a couple hundred feet behind the plane. At the time, this did not appear to be a "serious" accident. I was grateful that it happened while I could abort on the runway instead of during climb out.

If airborne, the damage to the engine nacelle would have created additional drag, making it difficult to maintain control on one engine. Later I read numerous C-45 fatal accident reports, where the propeller shaft sheared during climb out and the prop struck the nose fuel tank which exploded or caused sufficient structural damage to render the plane uncontrollable. Also, I was surprised at the number of fatal accidents caused by the propeller shaft shearing. I had a couple of hundred hours flying the C-45 and that was the only problem I ever had.

I had many misgivings about leaving the Air Force and later, when reflecting back, I realized what a big mistake it was. Two very significant reasons were, the effect it had on my "promotion list service" and the possibility of my being intra-grated intro the "regular" Air Force. I would like to expound on those two reasons because they played a very significant part in my future.

While being very active in the reserves between 1945 and 1950, you may recall, I never received a promotion. It just never occurred to me to be of any importance until I was recalled to active duty in 1950 and found I was 5 years in rank behind my contemporaries. My reserve time did not count toward promotion list service time. In the back of my mind I knew that if I got out, I would want to come back into active duty after I had resolved my parent's problem. After all, I already had almost 9 years active duty at that time and now I would lose more promotion list service time.

The second very important reason was the Air Force was about to begin a very extensive integration program. The majority of officers at that time were active duty reservists and most of the regular Air Force Officers were academy graduates. All reserve officers records were to be screened and a large number would become "regular officers." I felt my past record could possibly put me into the intergraded group. I was released from active duty Sept. 30, 1956 and later on you will realize how important this decision was to both my future career and subsequent retirement.

CHAPTER FOURTEEN

DISGRUNTLED BAR AND RESTAURANT OWNER

As requested, I was released from Active duty because of a "hardship," in order to retain my reserve commission. Upon arriving in St. Pete, my Dad and I worked out a manageable transfer of ownership. While in the Philippines my uncle Ted died and I had loaned my Dad $5000.00 to buy out Ted's wife, who wanted nothing to do with the business. (Can't blame her!) Therefore, the $5000.00 was my down payment. I paid a bank note of $300.00 per month on a first mortgage and paid my Dad $300.00 per month on a second mortgage. I think the interest on each loan was 6%. The total purchase price was $65,000, so I was carrying a $60,000 debt on "Tyrone Inn," as the business was called and $11,000.00 on a house I purchased a few blocks from the Inn. I was 31 years old, $70,000.00 in debt with absolutely no concept of my future income. In addition to that, I borrowed another $5,000.00 from the bank to remodel the Inn. I wanted to design the interior to look like a bar in Orlando Lee and I used to frequent.

Now for more bad news! (If that's possible) After signing all the paper work, my Dad informed me that Tyrone Boulevard was about to be torn up in order to tear out the present two lane asphalt road and improve it, by constructing a four lane concrete thoroughfare. It was one of the few roads to the Gulf beaches, which were becoming more populated daily. My Dad, later informed me that the State had already advanced him $11,000.00 for parking space he lost in front of the building which was to become part of the new road. After construction started, I cannot describe how torn up the area in front of the building was. There were many days it was extremely difficult to enter my parking area. Only the very regulars would attempt it.

This went on for the entire time I personally operated the business and as you might have surmised, I saw no part of the $11,000.00. I have gone into this much detail to emphasize what a mess I had gotten myself into. No wonder my Dad drank so much! I was ready to join him!

Shortly after I took over the Inn, I was informed of an Air Force Reserve Squadron being formed at the St. Petersburg/Clearwater Airport. I drove up there (30minutes,) to learn more about it and upon arriving, noticed several C-45's parked on the ramp in front of the Squadron Operations building, which made me feel right at home. I met the permanent party active duty Commander and when I explained my flying experience in the C-45, he appeared very anxious to have me join the Squadron. I signed the paper work that day and was scheduled to check out in the C-45 the next day. The check out flight also turned out to be an instructor qualification flight. At this time I was the only Reserve pilot in the Squadron with any significant amount of C-45 time. As a result, I flew several times a week and one weekend each month, the entire Squadron was on active duty. On those weekends I flew all day and sometimes at night. Although I was putting in many hours in the bar and restaurant, which I really hated, I put in a lot of time at the squadron which I really enjoyed. I participated in reserve activities as often as possible out of necessity, which I never really mentioned to any of the other Squadron members. Each four hours I spent on duty, I earned a full day of active duty pay. This normally equated to about $300.00 a month, which along with the left over food I brought home from Tyrone Inn, was what we lived on. That income probably paid some business expenses too.

With the road torn up, I was having a difficult time making expenses, but was extremely fortunate in having an excellent and honest bartender, Bob and chef, Ray. Other than that, it's difficult to describe how much I disliked the business. I must admit, on many nights, I joined the customers on their side of the bar and on those nights, Bob, the bartender would not let me help him on his side of the bar. I especially hated Wednesday night, Bob's night off because I tended bar from 5:00 pm until 2:00 am. I did have what I considered two excellent policies. Every evening at a random time between 5:00 and 7:00, I would set a free drink in front of every customer. It would be whatever they were drinking at the time. In those days there was no "happy hour," so this went over very well. Sometimes, the customer would buy me one back, which was difficult to refuse! My other policy was only used on Wednesday nights because I did not take time to learn how to mix many mixed drinks. If a customer asked for an "exotic" drink, I would invite him behind the bar to mix it himself. This would attract the attention of everyone sitting at the bar and frequently would result in several other patrons making the same request. It provided a great, inexpensive, entertainment feature!

One day the Reserve Squadron Operations Officer asked that I drop some passengers off at MacDill AFB. After landing, I went into Base Operations to file a flight plan for the return flight and noticed my name on their incoming flight board in two different places. After my name on the first one was the same arrival date and identification call sign, as the plane I lost the prop on during take-off many months ago. Most Base Operations posted the identification of the plane and pilot's name on an incoming chart and erased it when the pilot and plane departed. What struck me was that I had flown in from Orlando and left the C-45 on the runway so long ago and my name was still on the chart. Apparently it had not been repaired yet, but was not considered "totaled." Seeing this, gave me a strange feeling because now I was about to take off in another C-45! Finally I rationalized that it could never happen again on the same airport. (I hoped!)

One day I had fun with Uncle Pete. He had purchased some property on the East side of Boca Ciega Bay and set up a very short airstrip in the sand alongside the Bay. I was in a C-45 with a student flying over the area at a relatively low altitude and could see Pete with some friends standing near the airstrip. I circled around, dropped the gear and flaps and approached the strip as though I intended to land. If you will recall, this was the second time I saw Pete frantically waving at me because while on final approach I raised the landing gear but continued the approach as though I intended to land. Just before "touchdown," I applied power, raised the flaps and got out of there hopefully before anyone could get my identification number. I had forgotten about the student who was looking at me with a very puzzled expression on his face. I never did explain why I did this and he never asked, so I assumed he did not want any part of it in case we had been reported. I must add, that the next time I saw Pete he did not think my "flyby" was so funny and after some sensible reasoning, I had to agree with him. It appeared that I was making a mockery out of my "gear up" landing in the Cessna on Albert Whitted which certainly was not my intention. Think before you do something stupid, Bill.

The entire Squadron was sent to Miami for two weeks of active duty. We operated off of Miami International Airport while training to be a troop carrier Squadron, so flew daily practicing simulated troop parachute drops. It was really great being back on active duty again and I realized how much I missed it.

I had arranged for Bob, the night bartender, to manage the business while I was in Miami and to call me if absolutely necessary. I never received any calls, so assumed everything went well during my absence. That was not the case! I was informed that one afternoon about 3:00 several Beverage Inspectors came to the Inn from their Tampa Office and asked for steak dinners. It happened that the chef, Ray, an extremely hardworking person and great chef, was doing his shopping, as he usually did, about that time every afternoon. The girl daytime bartender explained the chef was doing his marketing and would be back shortly. If they could not wait, she would be happy to fix their choice of sandwiches. They rudely replied they could not wait and left. I think I had what is known as a 4X license. That designation required serving "full course meals regularly." I mistakenly interpreted that to mean full course meals at regular meal times. I knew that food must be served anytime the bar was open, but thought sandwiches would suffice at other than regular meal times. We also had to be able to seat 200 people at any one time and have flatware and dishes of every type in the same amount. I had only returned from Miami a short time when I was summoned to attend a hearing in Tampa regarding my violation. I went to Tampa thinking I could easily explain my misinterpretation of the operating manual and that would be the end of it. I had arranged for an attorney from the Reserve Squadron to meet me, but he did not show up, so I said I would represent myself. There was at least six beverage people and "lonely" me sitting around a conference table. They explained my violation and then I tried to give my prepared explanation, which definitely was scoffed at. I was emphatically told that if 200 people walked into my bar at 1: 30 in the morning, (we were open until 2:00) I must be prepared to serve all of them steaks, if that was what they ordered. This really triggered me off! I stood up and said "that was the G- - D- - - est, stupidest thing I ever heard. I was immediately told "better sit down Bill" by one of the beverage people, which implied to me I was only making matters worse. I left the room really upset, both at myself and the mentality level and lack of common sense of the people hired by the State to regulate and enforce the beverage laws. This convinced me I had to get out of the business! A few days after the hearing, (kangaroo court,) I received a registered letter from the Beverage Department stating that I must close on a certain date for eight days.

On the night before the closing I had a big closing party with half priced drinks. I had a tremendous night almost comparable to New Year's eve but without the expense of decorating. I hired a band and girl vocalist and gave the party a lot of publicity. As I saw how the night was going, I announced a reopening party in eight days. The morning after I closed, a Beverage Inspector came to measure and mark each opened bottle behind the bar. I had to be at his side for some reason, until he was finished. Then he inventoried every opened bottle in the bar and unopened bottle in the package store.

He really seemed to be taking his time and I angrily mentioned he was being paid for his time and I was not. I was again told I better watch what I said and I'm sure he noticed the large sign on the front door advertising the opening party which did not set well with him.

The opening party was also a great success and I considered having an "open and closing party about once a month instead of being open all the time. That way I would only be open two days a month and probably have about the same income. Bob did not agree!

I firmly believe Ken Conlin, owner of the Lighthouse, a well known bar, restaurant and package store nearby, heard I would be gone for two weeks and set the whole thing up with the Beverage Department.

Pete called me one day to let me know he needed my help. He had borrowed a bulldozer from the Commander of the Coast Guard in order to level off his air strip. After using it the first day, he left the bulldozer parked too close to the water line. During the night the tide came in, sinking the bulldozer in beach sand. He was calling everyone he knew, inviting them out to help pull the dozer out of the sand. He had not yet notified the Coast Guard Commander of his problem. At the given time, we all showed up with ropes and chains. Ropes snapped and chains broke loose, but the dozer did not budge. Bystanders stood well clear for fear of being decapitated and we were drawing a large audience. The next day, in desperation, Pete called the Chairman of the Pinellas County Commission and without explaining why, asked to borrow a County bulldozer. Being a good friend, the Chairman of the County Commission had a bulldozer delivered to Pete's airstrip. Like the man that delivered the Coast Guard dozer, he agreed to pick it up when Pete called saying he was finished. By this time the Coast Guard Commander called asking about his bulldozer and somehow Pete stalled him off. In attempting to pull the Coast Guard dozer out, Pete sank the County bulldozer at about the same high tide water level as the Coast Guard bulldozer. After both bulldozers spent several days in salt water, now even more desperate, Pete called his friend, the Commander of MacDill AFB. This time Pete explained his plight and the Commander agreed to send a bulldozer and a qualified operator. Pete was not to touch the bulldozer. During that time Pete was coming into the bar almost every afternoon and I have never seen a man more distraught. I don't think he had slept for a week! The Macdill bulldozer pulled both of the other bulldozers out and Pete made his calls to come pick them up. He did not say much about the response of the County Commissioner and Coast Guard Commander after the dozers were returned, other than, he was told to never again ask to borrow even a screw driver. I am sure both pieces of equipment were total losses.

Gratefully, Louis Pappas, who owned a famous family restaurant in Tarpon Springs, walked in one day and asked me if I would like to lease the business. I emphatically said "yes," and we immediately worked out a deal and drew up a 5 year lease at $600.00 per month. I was stupid because that did not cover taxes, licenses and insurance. As a result, I never had less than $100.00 each month out of pocket expenses to meet my obligations. I kept the same accountant in order to keep track of my expenses for income tax preparation. I wanted out of the business desperately but I made Louis Pappas agree to retain Bob and Ray as part of the deal.

A very good customer, Jim Perry, was head of Quality Control in a nearby factory that I believe was called Electronic Communications. It was contracted by the AF to manufacture Command radios for the F-86, a fighter aircraft presently being manufactured. Jim was aware that I had been an Air Force pilot so assumed I was knowledgeable in the operation and mechanics of aircraft radios. When he heard I had leased the bar out, he asked if I would like a job in Quality Control. I clearly informed him that my experience was strictly limited to turning one on, selecting a frequency and shutting it off. This satisfied him and I was hired. My Reserve pay was not quite enough to support the family now that I was not taking home left-over food, so I was glad to get the job.

My primary duty was to spot check modules coming off the assembly line for cold solder connections. Jim had to explain to me what a "cold solder connection" was. The women working on the assembly line were very professional and you can imagine how stupid and insecure I felt when I would boldly ask to inspect someone's work. This was done by trying to pry a solder joint loose from its terminal with a knitting needle. When I did find a "cold" solder joint, which was very seldom, I would discreetly give it back to the woman responsible and have it repaired without informing her supervisor. I, personally could never be capable of making a solder connection while working in such tiny spaces. I was not in a position to report someone that did it day after day, rarely making a cold connection. My other job, which soon became my primary job, was to be with an AF Captain while he inspected the finished radios for Air Force acceptance. I was to suggest an early and at least 3 martini lunch, to keep him away from the factory as long as possible. This part of the job, as you have probable reasoned, I liked very well.

As soon as the lease on the Inn became effective, I wrote a letter to AF Personnel, asking if there was any type of recall program in progress now or programmed in the future. A short time later, I received a letter back, stating there was not a recall program scheduled and in fact, a reduction in force was taking place.

The Reserve Squadron was being transferred to Miami with C-119's replacing the C-45's. That sounded exciting, but I would either have to move to Miami, or commute and I did not want to do either. The factory that I worked at was also letting people go, so my future looked very grim.

A very short time later I received a much unexpected letter from the Air Force, explaining there was a very limited recall program planned and asked if I would like to return to active duty. I immediately wrote back indicating I was available for recall at any time to any base. Several weeks passed without any further correspondence. Barbara and I had given up, when one day while I was at work; she received a phone call from the Air Force Personnel Office. She said a very nice Captain called, inquiring if I had received the letter concerning recall. He emphasized that the maximum age for recall of Captains was 33 years old, so this was undoubtedly my last opportunity as I would be 34 in December and this was September. He was indirectly telling her I had better decide at once. She replied yes, that I had answered immediately; giving an affirmative reply and the rest of the conversation was unbelievable. For some reason my letter was never received so he asked when we would like to report. Barbara said October, 1st. He then explained we had a choice of being assigned to any B-47 base in the country and asked if we had a preferred base. SAC had many B-47 bases throughout the country, but we liked Orlando and she informed him that was our unanimous choice. He said OK and finished the conversation after assuring her we would receive orders by telegram very soon. Sure enough, in a couple of days we received orders to report to Orlando and I submitted my resignation at the factory.

By coincidence, we rented our house out to the widow of a B-47 navigator stationed at Pinecastle AFB. He had been in an accident that happened immediately after taking off from Loring AFB in Maine.

CHAPTER FIFTEEN
ONCE AGAIN, HAPPY TO BE BACK IN THE MILITARY

Before going to Orlando I was assigned to Biloxi for a physical examination. Upon arrival I met the other former crew members that had been recalled. There were forty two of us, mostly radar navigators, with about seven pilots. We were told this was an experiment to determine if it was less expensive to recall former crew members than to train new ones. As far as I know this was the only recall program made at this time or anytime in the future.

After completing the physical I reported to the 321st Bomb Wing at "McCoy" Air Force Base. Pinecastle had been renamed after the Wing Commander, Col. McCoy, who had been killed in a B-47 accident. He had taken off in a B-47 with a British officer in the copilot seat and when attempting to fly over Orlando at a low altitude, lost control, did a half roll and dove into the ground. It was presumed he exceeded 425 knots and experienced aileron reversal, which we were told was a characteristic of the B-47. In view of the circumstances, no one could understand why Colonel McCoy deserved to have the base named after him. He had done a stupid, illegal maneuver and should have been chastised instead of being considered a "hero."

Barbara remained in St. Pete with the children while I looked for a house to rent in Orlando. Within a couple of days I found a three bedroom home and arranged to have our furniture shipped.

PILOT HERE OR PILE IT THERE

Without any refresher training, I was assigned as copilot to a crew and started flying training missions immediately. It was almost like I had never been out of the service because of flying so frequently in the reserves at St. Pete/Clearwater Airport. Crews were now pulling one week of alert every four weeks. A reminder that this was in the late 1950's during the cold war with the possibility of a Russian nuclear strike very real. Barracks had been remodeled to accommodate one Crew to a room and were confined to the barracks or immediate area for the entire week. Quite frequently we had practice alerts whereby engines were started and a message was broadcast from the Command Post with instructions as to what action to take. We had enemy targets assigned and never knew if it was a practice alert or the real thing until after receiving and decoding the message. Alert crews had to be fully prepared to launch at any time so always wore our flying suits and boots except while in bed, at which time they were easily available.

The cold war was getting into full swing, so each time you left home for a week of alert, you were not sure if or when you would see your family again. SAC crews displayed the height of optimism as to the successful completion of our mission if we were ordered to strike our "targets" and never complained about personal problems. No one ever made a big deal out of our always present "anxieties" or traumatic stress syndrome.

I was at McCoy a short time before it was discovered that I had never attended Survival School, which was a mandatory SAC requirement. I was scheduled to report to Stead Air Force Base, just outside of Reno Nevada, in the first part of January. After all the schools I attended in the military, I sarcastically thought, "how could they have missed this one?" I found I was really not in shape to attend survival training. Too many days of long hours, intermixed with a lot of beer drinking and absolutely no exercise.

The course was taught in two phases, the first of which was class room instruction. We were taught how to survive in hostile territory under extremely adverse conditions. The second week we were split up into groups of six and equipped with winter survival gear, including a parachute and snow shoes. How we were expected to bail out of an airplane holding or wearing a set of snow shoes, I'll never understand. Our leader was a young enlisted instructor and we were dropped off

somewhere along the Truckee River. For the entire trek we were only allowed to bring a couple of life saver rolls and were given a bar of jerky. The parachute was to provide us with some sort of shelter at night. We each had a chart of the area and took turns leading the six of us along a pre-arranged track that frequently crossed the Truckee. Mainly, I remember continuously going up hills and very seldom going down hill or trudging through valleys. It seemed to snow every day so wore snow shoes a good part of the time. For water we melted snow and had to trap food or spear fish if we wanted to eat. We trapped one rabbit and speared no fish during the five day trek. The six of us shared the little rabbit.

After about the third day I finished my life saver rolls and tried some jerky. It was too rich or something and I threw it up. Considering I was desperately hungry, I slowly ate the entire bar by the fourth day. This was a huge mistake. I started throwing up and could not stop. The pain in my stomach was getting progressively more severe and by that evening I could not even drink water without throwing up. The next day, Friday, was the final day and Friday night was to be our final test. After dark, each of us would be given a slightly different route to a final simulated escape destination, which was guarded by the "enemy" at various points along the route.

Occasionally throughout the trek, when crossing a road, a military truck would pass by and the driver would chat a few minutes with our instructor. About noon Friday, a truck had stopped and the instructor motioned to me to join him. I found he had been very concerned about me and called for transportation to take me back to Stead. With a little over half a day left to complete the course, I just I wanted to get it over with, no matter how miserable I felt. It seemed I had no choice and was taken to the Base Hospital at Stead. There I was immediately examined, had a needle stuck in me, was given some pain pills and told to stay in bed. The next day I was informed I was severely dehydrated and would have to remain in bed for a few days. The rest of the class had departed to return to their home bases and McCoy AFB was informed of my extended stay. Also, I was told I did not successfully complete the course and would remain at Stead until ready to try again. Two horrible thoughts crossed my mind. First I would probably be taken off a crew and considered unfit for crew duty. Second, I would have to go through that entire trek ordeal again and really dreaded it. Thankfully, on about the third day I was in the hospital, a Colonel came to my room and said they had reconsidered my situation and I would receive a certificate of completion. Thank goodness, I could forget this horrible experience!

After several months as copilot, because of my large number of pilot hours, I was selected ahead of all other copilots, to attend the Pilot Upgrade Program, (PUP) in Little Rock, Arkansas. Shortly after arriving, I was introduced to my crew, copilot Monroe Hatch and radar navigator, Jack Schuster. Because I had already attended ground training at Wichita as a copilot, we went directly into the flight phase. This consisted of 10 flights with an instructor pilot and instructor radar navigator.

Just after we had completed our fourth instructional flight, an evaluation team from SAC Headquarters arrived to randomly check the progress of one of the crews in training. Everyone always dreaded a flight check from SAC Headquarters because your career was really threatened. Guess whose crew was selected? With an evaluator in the copilot seat instead of our regular instructor and a radar navigator in the extra passenger seat to evaluate Jack, we flew a standard training mission. When we were debriefed after landing, I was told that I failed the check flight because I gave an erroneous position report during a celestial navigation leg. What happened was, Jack, by his celestial calculations, determined we were over a reporting station, when our actual position was 14 miles from it. Jack did not have access to the radar set, but the navigator evaluator did have access, so could tell our exact position. He, of course informed the evaluator pilot of my erroneous position report. During celestial navigation we never were able to accurately pin-point our position and as far as I knew, there was no other way. This was long before any of the modern navigational aids were available. I still do not know how our position could be determined while on a celestial navigation flight without a radio fix or with "radar" cheating by peeking into his scope. Celestial was mostly intended for over water navigation and small errors were expected as far as I was concerned! From 35,000 feet, 14 miles is just over the side of the airplane! Anyway, I felt I never would get over the embarrassment caused by failing the check ride but felt a little better when was later informed that our crew was selected by the Training Squadron Commander because of our excellent progress to-date. I felt I really let him down and I'm sure my failure was forwarded to McCoy.

About half way through the up-grading course, I was told a house was available for me on the Base if I desired to move. We had very little furniture, so the move would only require a few trips back and forth in our car. I carried Barbara and the kids to our new house on my first trip and left them to return to pick bicycles, toys and other boxes I had left in the driveway. When I arrived at the house for the next load, everything I left outside was gone. I checked with a neighbor and she said she had seen a suspicious looking, strange green truck in my driveway, so I called the police. They were asking me specific questions when Monroe drove up. He asked what was going on and I explained the missing items, the green truck and what the neighbor said. Monroe sheepishly replied that he had taken the load to our new house on the Base and had returned for another load. The cop gave us both a strange look and departed. Later I got to thinking. Hopefully, he did not know we were training to be a B-47 combat crew, because if we were that disorganized on the ground, how in the world did we operate as a crew. Well anyway, Jack and our wives got a laugh out of it and in fact, Monroe and I did too, after he accused me of attempting to have him arrested. I'll explain something a little later that makes this even more amusing.

Monroe had an uncle, a Lt. General, stationed at Little Rock in an important Command position. He invited Monroe and his family to dinner one evening, and Monroe, being a 1st Lt. was very nervous about visiting him which was understandable. It would make any junior officer nervous dining with a Lt. General, much less being his nephew. Monroe was sure he would be continuously evaluated during the entire visit, because his uncle knew he was a Naval Academy graduate career minded officer. Monroe was determined to make a good impression and that is when I think a person usually, accidentally messes up. I know, because I probably would have! This also will be more amusing when I mention Monroe further along.

We completed our training and returned to McCoy and gratefully, never heard the first word about failing the check ride. Being a student, I'm sure it was recorded on my flight training record, but I'm sure all SAC pilots at that time were guilty of the same or similar position reporting procedure.

Monroe, Jack and I quickly became well acquainted and I began learning more about their previous military experience. Monroe was an Annapolis Naval Academy graduate who voluntarily transferred into the Air Force. He spent some time in missiles before going through pilot training and joining our crew in Little Rock. Jack had been a navigator prior to attending radar navigation training, joining us shortly after completing the upgrade course. They were both First Lieutenants and we got along very well, professionally and socially. Before long we were called the "vaudeville team," Hubert, Hatch and Schuster" because it almost sounded like the names of a very popular vaudeville team at that time. We quickly began being recognized as a very capable crew and I was very grateful for the support of Monroe and Jack.

As soon as we were cleared for solo flight, I started alternating every other take off, air refueling and landing with Monroe. I was determined not to treat him the same as Mike treated me!

As an additional duty I was assigned as Squadron Ground Training Officer. Each crew member had certain ground training requirements to complete, either each quarter, semi-annual, or annually. My job was to make sure all ground training requirements were met in a timely manner. Some of them were ridiculous, but having been instigated by General LeMay, were mandatory. As an example, one of these was judo and several of the tactics taught, my being 5 ft 61/2, would insure my certain death! Anyway, I designed some charts indicating training requirements, attendance and completion dates which the Wing Ground Training Officer liked and that very much pleased me. He made some of them standard throughout the Wing, making sure I got the recognition for creating them. These accomplishments were reflected in my next Effectiveness Report, so were well worth the effort.

Each quarter, SAC combat crews were required to complete certain flight training requirements which consisted of tactics and procedures we would expect to encounter on an actual combat mission. At McCoy, the Wing Commander's staff conducted a contest to determine which crew accomplished the highest training score for the quarter. This was determined by simulated bomb scores, air refueling ability, celestial navigation legs and electronic warfare procedures, all of which were somehow scored. The second quarter in which we participated in the contest, while still in the lowest phase of crew experience, (an "R" Crew which stood for Ready) we attained the highest overall scores in the Wing. Monroe, Jack and I received an engraved plaque with each of our names and crew position inscribed on it. I still have mine hanging on the wall in my home office and am very proud of it. I wholeheartedly believed then and still do now; any Aircraft Commander could win with Jack and Monroe on their crew.

Not long after receiving the award, we were elevated to "Lead Crew" status. I might explain. As established by SAC Headquarters, there were three crew status ratings. The first being, "Combat Ready," which was designated after being considered capable of flying combat missions. After proving that you can handle any situation that may occur, having gained enough experience to lead a flight into combat and maintaining an acceptable training accomplishment record, the designation of "Lead Crew" (L) is placed before your crew number wherever it is listed. The final and most prestigious crew status was "Select." Select was normally only awarded to standardization Crews and possibly one other highly qualified crew. Each Squadron was limited to three crews whose duty was to evaluate all other crews in the Squadron. The Chief of Standardization and his crew normally evaluated the other two standardization crews. Then a SAC team came on Base and evaluated the Chief of Standardization and his crew. It was a clearly defined chain of Command with all crews having to pass an annual evaluation with no exceptions. I will get more into "select status" later.

Now that I have confused you (and quire possible bored you,) with the inner workings of a SAC Squadron and Wing, I'll attempt to relate a few of my experiences, while assigned as a B-47 Aircraft Commander.

One night while making simulated high altitude bomb runs over Birmingham, Alabama, I noticed a very bright light that appeared to be about our altitude and growing in intensity. I brought it to Monroe's attention and he agreed that it seemed to be heading directly toward us. It was too bright to be another aircraft's landing lights and although neither of us came out and said it, "UFO" was our immediate thought, because of the attention UFO's were getting at that time. Then, as suddenly as it appeared, it seemed to reverse direction and began very rapidly to fade in intensity. When we no longer could see it, I "dutifully" called the control center and reported what we had seen. They acknowledged my call and agreed to check into it. Upon returning to Orlando, I received a call from Jacksonville Center. I believe I can quote the controller's transmission which unmistakably sounded like a combination of amusement and sarcasm. "For your information that strange object you reported, while over Birmingham, was a missile being launched from Cape Canaveral." I felt like replying, boy, am I relieved! I'm sure that would have bewildered him. Instead, all I said very unconcerned like was, "roger," as though my reporting this was routine business.

This reminds me of another time while we were on our way to Sidi Slimane Air Base in Morocco. We were probably about 35,000 ft. and while Monroe was selecting stars to shoot for a celestial fix, he told me to look up to my right. There was a satellite with about the same light intensity as many of the stars in view and as we were traveling over 500 miles per hour, it was passing us as if we were standing still. We agreed it was a very eerie feeling.

That was our first flight to Sidi and it was unusual from the beginning. We were to take off in a three ship cell and I, being the most recently qualified Air Craft Commander, was number three. We were to take off at night, so as to arrive at Sidi the next morning after sun up. After starting engines, I had no indication of oil pressure on number six engine. The ground crew immediately began looking for the problem, but was having trouble finding the cause. The other two planes were rapidly burning up precious fuel, so they were instructed to go ahead and launch and hopefully, I would follow shortly. I knew that normally an instructor pilot would accompany a crew on their first trip to Sidi, but for some reason, we were to go without one, which was fine with us. Finally after sitting in the cockpit about two hours, the problem was resolved and we took off. I still did not trust number six engine, so watched it closely throughout the flight. Our flight plan called for us to descend to about 16,000 feet in order to refuel with a KC-97 over Bermuda where SAC always had tankers stationed. More than hour to go before we were to start receiving a specified signal from our assigned tanker, Jack began receiving the exact signal on his radar scope that he was expecting. Monroe had been taking celestial fixes and Jack was reasonably sure of our position. We had not received word we would be met early by our tanker and to prematurely descend to refueling altitude would have very possibly left us insufficient fuel to make it to Sidi. Jack was positive it was the correct signal, but I decided to remain at altitude and stick to the scheduled flight plan. Finally after a very anxious "long" time, Jack again received the correct signal and we refueled as originally scheduled. After that I was a believer in the "Bermuda Triangle," an area in which both aircraft and ships mysteriously disappeared during World War II.

Several hours later we were to pass over a check point called Ocean Station Bravo. Up to that time, position reports were made by using a high frequency radio which was often garbled and sometimes we had difficulty making contact. Ocean Station Bravo had UHF (ultra high frequency) communications facilities with homing devices capable of informing aircraft of their actual position. Our flight time since passing Bermuda should have placed us within radio contact of Bravo, but I did not receive a response to my many attempted calls. I must confess, I was getting very nervous, but continued following Jack's directions. I began to think of Amelia Earhart and what a helpless feeling she must have had. We were about an hour behind schedule when I finally made contact. What a great feeling! Bravo informed us we were experiencing a very rare, strong, direct headwind from the East. We had flight planned for a tailwind from the West because at our altitude the wind was always planned coming from the West and I assumed there was no way of forecasting such a strange occurrence. Monroe was recalculating our fuel remaining versus time to go and informed me we would not have a lot of fuel to spare. Along with every thing else that went wrong on this flight, this bit of information was no surprise. Now all we needed was bad weather at Sidi to complete our problem cycle!

We finally arrived at Sidi and cleared to penetrate after setting some sort of record for length of time en route. I was making a GCA when instructed to make a low approach prior to a full stop landing. This was the normal procedure for a first time landing at Sidi. I explained that I had landed at Sidi as copilot before, but was informed that did not matter. From the very beginning this had been a very tedious flight, so I guess this was just a part of it. By this time I had been in the pilot's seat over 10 hours, most of which were quite stressful.

Before radar was available at high altitudes, we flew at "quadrantal" altitudes as determined by the direction you were heading. The sky was divided into quadrants, which if adhered to by pilots, provided adequate separation between aircraft.

We had just completed air refueling late one night, putting us close to maximum gross weight for our altitude and resumed our scheduled activities. After completing the first simulated bomb run over the Atlanta bomb plot, I returned to the "IP" (initiation point) to attempt another run. While making the 180 degree turn back toward the target, I climbed or descended as required to the proper altitude when heading North West. As soon as I resumed straight and level flight, I asked Jack to pour me a cup of coffee and had to lean forward and reach down to take it out of his extended hand. This only took a couple of seconds, but when I looked up, what looked like a Christmas tree, was directly ahead at the same altitude. I truly believed a crash was inevitable. My immediate impulse was to abruptly apply back pressure thinking my best chance was to pass above it. My sudden "jerk" on the control column at that altitude and heavy gross weight caused the B-47 to "high speed stall," resulting in an immediate descent. The "Christmas tree" was actually another plane. It roared directly over our cockpit, so close, I do not know how he missed our vertical stabilizer. I recovered from the stall and when able to regain my composure, called Atlanta Center to report the near mid-air collision. I inquired about other reported aircraft in the area and the reply was that I was the only aircraft they were aware of in my immediate vicinity. I reasoned it must have been another B-47, because scheduled multi-engine airlines were not yet flying at that altitude. I hope the other pilot suffered the same terror I felt. I was at the proper quadrantal altitude but he, like many other pilots before radar was installed in control centers must have been too complacent to bother changing altitude for short distances. I also checked with the bomb plot and was informed we were the only bomber working the plot.

In another experience that we frequently encountered at night when returning to Orlando, was having to thread our way through a line of thunder storms running from Jacksonville in the shape of an arc, down toward Cross City. The same as the squall line I tried to circumnavigate in a Bonanza while en-route to Atlanta, on that night charter out of Tampa, I had described earlier.

Late one night, when returning to Orlando and attempting to make our away around a line of storms, a bolt of lightening suddenly struck the left lower side of the fuselage, just forward of the cockpit. It sounded and felt like being slammed by a sledgehammer. We immediately lost all electrical equipment, except for the auto pilot. It was a horribly isolated, helpless, feeling. Every flight instrument failed, so I never did understand why the auto pilot continued to operate, but thank goodness it did. After what seemed like an eternity, one by one, lights came back on, flight instruments and radios slowly came to life and we were back in business. There was one final problem. The air speed indicator had gone to zero and remained there. We were approaching McCoy, returning with limited fuel as usual, so I decided to request a chase plane. As I mentioned earlier, maintaining the B-47's speed schedule is critical, particularly during approach and landing and I did not have enough fuel to chance having to make go-around at traffic pattern altitude. A chase fighter plane could lead me in at the proper speeds. I was about to call the Command Post to make the request, when slowly the airspeed indicator in sort of a ticking motion, began showing it was trying to come to life. I assumed the pitot tube had iced up because it had not been heated during the loss of electrical power. When the airspeed finally appeared to be indicating properly, we penetrated and landed. I was fully expecting to see aircraft skin damage, but could not even find a scorched area. I was grateful for having Monroe and Jack with me to verify my story.

Another time, Jack, Monroe and I had completed our three week tour at Sidi and were scheduled to be number three in a three ship cell to return home. It was a hot summer day and we had a full fuel load for the long flight. I accelerated as normal down the runway and passed the safe abort line just before number 4 engine failed. As a result we used almost every foot of available runway before lifting off, but being an "inboard" engine this caused very little directional control problem. After raising the landing gear and flaps, I called the Command Post to inform them of my engine problem. From the cockpit, I could see no signs of physical damage to the engine, so assumed it was just a "flame out," so I informed the Command Post that I would attempt a "re-light." As I brought the engine up to cruise power, I noticed the fuel flow indicator "pegged" at the max position. I immediately shut it down, assuming I had a fuel leak in the fuel line, but still saw no sign of damage or indication of a fire. I found out later, the procedure for engine failure or any other emergency immediately after take-off from Sidi was to burn fuel off until down to landing weight and land back at Sidi. After informing the Command Post I was going to attempt a " re-light," I neglected to tell the controller the results. So having received no further instructions, I proceeded on with the flight home. Climbing out on five engines with a full fuel load was slower then normal. Al York was flight leader and he and Bob Stanley, who was in number two position, slowed their rate of climb in order for me to keep up. After reaching cruise altitude and in level flight, I had no problem keeping up with them.

I did have several decisions to make before heading out. Number four engine provided one of the two hydraulic pumps and if I remember correctly, also operated one of the two alternators. If for some reason I lost the other hydraulic pump or alternator, I would be in very serious trouble, possibly causing me to have to ditch, or bail out. I elected to take my chances and continued on rather than abort. We had two air refuelings scheduled because of the anticipated headwinds encountered while flying in a westerly direction. Monroe reported that our fuel consumption was considerably greater than planned and according to his five engine operating charts, even after two refuelings, reaching McCoy non-stop, was highly improbable. I relayed this information to Al York and he and Bob conferred. They determined each could spare me an extra 25,000 lbs. of fuel at both refuelings, which Monroe computed would allow us to continue non-stop. Now I would have six critical air refuelings instead of two! I found air refueling with five engines, behind a KC-97, was a strange experience. Being prop driven, the KC-97 was limited in airspeed, so in the B-47, as we became heavier while taking on fuel, I found it more and more difficult to stay in contact position. Toward the end of the third refueling I could feel the plane shutter like it was in a semi stalled condition. This was caused by combination of the additional 50,000 lbs., slow airspeed and operating on only five engines. I felt this reaction during each of the three air refuelings, and fortunately did not have any accidental disconnects from the boom. And thanks to Al's good judgment and "generosity," we made it home non stop

Al decided to make a formation low altitude "fly-over" the runway before landing at McCoy. He cancelled our instrument flight plan and motioned Bob and I to close in. We were cleared by the control tower to make the pass over the runway and then to separate for spacing prior to landing. Landing was to the North, with a strong crosswind from the West. Al approached first, but had a little difficulty in attempting to land, so made a go-around. Bob and I successfully landed and it was then that I remembered I was on five engines and supposed to call in an emergency before landing. This in turn, would automatically require fire trucks and emergency vehicles positioned along the side of the runway before I could land. I had been flying with one engine shut down for so long, I completely forgot the procedure. Al landed on his next attempt and we taxied to the designated parking ramp. We had been airborne 11 hour s and 25 minutes instead of the normal 9-10 hours. That's a long time to sit in one position!

As we parked on the ramp, a crowd started gathering around my number four engine and when I got out, I saw the reason. The entire lower section of the engine, which could not be seen from the cockpit, was severely damaged with part of it totally gone. It was apparent I had an explosion that was not felt in the cockpit and the extremely high fuel flow, was caused by a broken fuel line which was pumping fuel directly over the hot engine. I finally realized at that time how much more serious this could have been. We were burning fuel in excess of the five engine performance charts because of the additional drag caused by the damaged engine nacelle.

Al was called on the carpet for making the runway fly over because he was not aware that it was prohibited by the "reflex" operations manual. "Reflex" was the designation of the Sidi Slimane tour of duty. Not a word was said about my continuing home after losing the engine and I never mentioned it because I would have exposed the fact that I had not read the manual. I assumed everyone believed the problem had occurred much later during the flight because I did not abort and return to Sidi.

Soon after we returned, Al York was assigned Squadron Commander, so I assumed the admonishment he received was strictly for "show."

A "mass gas" was a SAC training requirement to be accomplished by each crew at certain times throughout the year. The procedure was for five B-47's to take off with a very short interval of time between each plane and join up at a prescribed altitude in the standard SAC formation. This was having one mile lateral and 500 feet vertical separation between aircraft. Then the five B-47's would join five KC-97 tankers for a "mass gas." I'm quite sure the exercise was always performed at night.

One night on a mass gas flight, after we leveled off and formed our standard formation positions, we headed west out over the Gulf of Mexico intending to meet five KC-97 tankers. Junior Hendricks, a standardization instructor pilot, led the formation. At the scheduled time and place, I could hear Junior attempting to contact the tankers but never receiving a reply. Suddenly the tankers appeared a little below us and slightly to our left. It was too late to attempt a normal rendezvous and I can still hear Junior say, "every man for himself!" Instead of a "mass gas," we had "mass confusion." The sky was full of B-47's and K-C 97's, all with lights flashing. The B-47's were all making a 180 degree left turn, crossing in front of each other, hoping to line up behind their assigned tanker. Somehow, all five B-47's found their respective tankers, took on the prescribed fuel load and continued on their individual missions. Visions, like the sky full of flashing lights, stay with you forever. I am not criticizing Junior, because his quick decision probably saved the exercise. It took guts on his part to depart from standard procedures in order to complete the mission. I always anticipated, if we were ordered to fly our assigned combat mission, which entailed several air-refuelings, low level navigation legs over very rugged terrain and flight through no telling what debris, we would have to do plenty of improvising.

The concept of a "mass gas" was an excellent training tool, but after two B-47's out of Homestead AFB collided while performing the maneuver and losing both crews, SAC discontinued the requirement as far as I know. I only remember participating in the exercise the one time that I described.

Another rather exciting annual requirement was called an "ATO," assisted take off. Eighteen ATO bottles were strapped to a heavy metal belt which was wrapped around the aft section of the B-47 fuselage. B-47's on alert needed this assistance to expedite acceleration to attain take-off speed because of the excessive weight of the weapons and full fuel load. Without this boost, the runway length at McCoy was insufficient in length, especially on a hot summer day. With ATO assist, as the plane accelerated down the runway and attained a certain speed, the pilot actuated a switch which ignited the bottles, giving the plane a sudden burst of speed. Very quickly take off speed was reached and the B-47 lunged into the air. The initial climb out was very steep to stay below flap and landing gear airspeed limits. Unlike present day jets, the normal procedure after take off in a B-47, was to hold the nose down while retracting landing gear and flaps, until normal climb speed was attained. To come think of it, modern jets take about the same climb attitude we did with ATO bottles and we had six engines! That's the difference in engine performance between then and now. When the ATO bottles ran out, the nosed was lowered and we proceeded to climb out as normal. We would proceed directly to designated drop area over the Atlantic Ocean, make sure it was clear of boats and drop the ATO belt. The ocean surface was cleared both by radar and visually before releasing the belt.

Very late one night, when we returned to McCoy, the runway was closed for landing because of ground fog. With no chance of the fog lifting, we were diverted to MacDill, which was the only base in the Southeast still open, capable of accommodating a B-47. Fortunately, flight time from McCoy to Macdill was about 12 minutes and as usual our fuel was low, so I was anxious to get on the ground. Upon arriving at MacDill, we were told to enter the holding pattern, (no sky hooks!) and we were about number four or five in the stack. I slowed down to conserve fuel, as I nervously watched the fuel gauges, which were on my right side, just below the canopy. If I remember right, there were twelve lights that turned bright red when the tanks fell below a certain level. All twelve of my red lights had been glowing for some time and the needles were bobbing close to the empty line, when it finally came our turn to penetrate. Just as I was about to drop the landing gear and retard the throttles to start down, another B-47 called in declaring an emergency because of low fuel. By the pilots tone of voice he sounded desperate, so I advised approach control to let him in ahead of me which of course he immediately agreed to do. Finally I was cleared to start my penetration with Monroe and I agreeing that the first attempt to land was probably our only "chance to land" because we would not make it around the traffic pattern a second time. We penetrated from 20,000 feet toward the Southwest, then made a 180 degree turn to line up with the runway heading Northeast As we broke through the overcast, the visibility was good, however as we approached the field I could see a fog bank moving in from the East, covering about a quarter of the far end of the runway. Now we were sure there would be no second chance! After landing, by the time I slowed down enough to turn off the runway, we were in the fog with just a couple feet of visibility, so I had to request a ground vehicle to lead us in.

It would have been interesting to dip stick our fuel tanks; to actually see how much fuel we had remaining. When we arrived at the debriefing room, several other crews were still there. Monroe, Jack and I could not believe what we heard when an aircraft commander, sitting at the table next to us, brag about how "slick" he was in declaring a low fuel emergency resulting in being cleared for an immediate penetration. I'll never forget what I said, "Captain, we were the crew that allowed you to come down before us and we had an "actual" low fuel emergency. I have a good mind to have your fuel tanks dipped and you better have very little fuel!" He started apologizing saying he just wasn't considering anyone else and claimed it would never happen again. I cut the conversation by telling him I'm going to really give this a lot of thought and he might be hearing further about it. I just hope he had a few very sleepless nights.

At about the same time, late 1960, that I was informed I was to become an instructor, the Wing was notified that the base was being converted to B-52's and crews would be re-assigned to other B-47 bases, or selected to transition into B-52's. Things looked very promising for our crew if we remained in B-47's, so we were hoping to be re-assigned to another B-47 base. A personnel team from SAC Headquarters had arrived on the Base to review each crew member's records and make assignments accordingly. We were still the latest crew to join the Wing, so did not expect much recognition. When the list of assignments was posted, our crew was selected to go into B-52's intact. Select Crews, with spot promotions, remained in B-47's to retain their spots. Select crew members were normally given temporary promotions to their next rank, until receiving a normal promotion, goofing up, or taken off a select crew. As it turned out, as far as I know, we were the only crew left intact, to go into B-52's. All other crews were split up, with some members assigned to B-52's and others remaining in B47's. This was supposed to be a prestigious advancement, but confidentially, I later decided it had to be some form of punishment. I'll explain that later.

A list was posted of all B-52 bases allotting just enough assignments to accommodate the number of aircraft commanders designated for B-52's. Aircraft commanders were listed by rank and date of rank, the highest ranking one getting first selection and so on down the list. I was the lowest ranking aircraft commander, so actually did not get a choice. Naturally the better located bases were selected first, so needless to say, the least desirable one was left for Monroe, Jack and me. I must say that both of them accepted being assigned to Loring AFB" in northern Maine much better than I did. I loved Florida for many reasons other than the tropical climate and I decided right then and there, Loring would be a short assignment. But of course I kept that to myself.

CHAPTER SIXTEEN

A "HAND FULL" OF THROTTLES! (8)

We were first sent to Merced, California for three months of ground instruction. Like in the B-47, we had to learn all the many complex systems involved. I recall one part of the trip out to the West Coast that my children will never let me forget.

Our car was not air conditioned, so to prepare for the trip across the desert between Phoenix and Los Angeles, I bought a case of beer and two cokes to put in the cooler. It never occurred to me to bring some water or more cokes! The trip was hot, dry and long, so Barbara and I made it as pleasant as possible by consuming a lot of beer. The kids drank their one bottle of coke and let me know what a thoughtless, greedy, cheep person I was. In fact, when that trip is brought up, even to this day, they still let me know! I tried to make up for it by taking them to Disneyland the night we arrived in Anaheim, but apparently what I had done was unforgivable.

After arriving in Merced, Luther Norton, a Navigator, John Duncan, an Electronics Warfare Officer and a young Sergeant a Gunner, joined our crew. We were now a six man crew which placed a few additional responsibilities on me as Aircraft Commander. Monroe and Jack required little or no supervision so I had to get used to not having that luxury.

While in Merced we visited Yosemite National Park and the Monterey, Carmel Area. Why couldn't we have been assigned in that area instead of Maine, I longingly asked myself?

After completing ground training we were sent to Roswell, New Mexico for flight training. I quickly learned the B-52 had a couple of unique features that took a little time getting used to. The landing gear had a function called, "cross wind crab." This enabled the pilot to face the fuselage of the plane into the cross wind (called crab) and align the landing gear with the runway. With cross wind crab set in, the pilot actually had to look to his right or left, depending on the wind velocity and direction, just before landing, in order to adjust his line of sight up with the runway. After breaking through a low ceiling, it required a quick adjustment to the pilot's line of vision. In the past, I had always compensated for a cross wind by lowering the windward wing and cross controlling with the opposite rudder pedal to remain aligned with the runway. The other new feature was having spoilers instead of ailerons. When making a turn, to establish a "bank" angle, a spoiler on top of the wing in the direction intending to turn rose up, disrupting the air-flow on top of that wing. This caused loss of lift, which in turn, allowed the wing to lower and establish the desired amount of bank. The spoiler reacted a little slower than an aileron, which until getting used too, could cause slight over-controlling. This was especially noticeable during air-refueling, where control corrections to maintain the proper position behind the tanker, had to be very slight.

Things went well and we started functioning as a six man crew. The Squadron Commander flew with us one night and the next day I was called into his office. He explained that the Wing was forming a new Squadron and unlike the present training one, it would be a combat ready squadron. He was quite sure there was a vacancy for one more crew and asked if my crew would like to have our orders changed and remain at Roswell. It was unanimously agreed upon, that we would like to remain at Roswell! The next day I reported to the Squadron Commander giving him our decision. He regretted to inform me that the Wing Commander had just filled the last opening without consulting him. I informed the crew and as usual, they accepted the disappointment without any disgruntling words.

We finished B-52 transition and left Roswell for Loring AFB. I very well remember the day we left Roswell. There had been a severe ice storm the night before and the streets were solid sheets of ice. Our car, a little Mercury Comet was stuck in the driveway and I had to get it going by rocking back and forth between drive and reverse gears to back out. We spent most of the day driving in the storm so made very poor time. By the time we stopped that night, we were a little ahead of the storm. Like almost all fronts, it was moving from West to East, so by the time we were on the road the next morning, it had passed over us, but we quickly caught up and again we were in it most of the day. I thought things were bad until we got to St. Louis.

About the time we entered the city; the Comet would not change gears and was stuck in drive position. We made it to the Ford garage and explained the problem. I was told it was caused by reversing gears while still in motion as I tried to get out of my driveway. I apparently damaged a part of the transmission. The repair estimate was $25.00 to $35.00. This was Saturday morning and I was assured it would be ready before closing time at noon. Well before noon it was repaired and taken for a test drive. The problem had not been corrected so the transmission was again taken apart. A small cylinder in the transmission was not sliding between components because of slivers of metal jamming it. After the second attempt to repair it, it still was not working so they took it apart for the third time and I watched them rinse off the parts hoping this time it will surely work. By then it was getting well past noon, so we went to lunch. The kids were really getting restless after sitting in the waiting room all morning and I was anxious to get back on the road because by this time we were slightly ahead of the ice storm and I definitely wanted to remain in front of it. I wasn't concerned about the time it was taking as far as cost was concerned because we had agreed on a price. I expected it would be the full $35.00. After the fourth attempt it finally worked and I was given a bill for $150.00. I reminded him that we had agreed on $25.00-$35.00 and handed the bill back to him. He refused to take it and explained that he had no idea it would take that long and they were on overtime since noon. I had no choice but to pay the full $150.00 before the keys would be released to me. As I gave him the cash, I emphasized that customers should not have to pay full price for "on the job" mechanic training. Credit cards and ATM's were not in use then, so after paying the bill, I was practically out of cash. I have never been back to St. Louis since and will avoid it forever!

Still driving in the ice storm, we finally made it to Elmhurst, where we intended to spend a few days. A good family friend, Leo Potvin, cashed a check for me and on the third day we proceeded on our way to Loring AFB, again catching up with the storm. Up to this time, it was mostly freezing rain, but as the temperatures grew colder, we were encountering sleet and snow. Every night for the duration of the trip, while we slept, it would overtake us, almost as though we were playing some sort of game, only I was not having any fun.

I planned on arriving at Loring late in the afternoon, but with just a little over 100 miles to go, the snow storm became very intense and after seeing many cars off the highway in snow banks, I pulled into a small town to have snow tires installed. By the time the tires were installed, it was too late to continue to Loring that day so we found a hotel and called it a day. By the time we departed the next morning, the weather had completely cleared, roads were plowed and finally, for the first time during the trip, I enjoyed the ride. Of course by this time all we had to look at was potato fields. I have given a detailed account of the trip from Roswell, because I compare that miserable trip, to what I faced at Loring the entire "miserable" 5 ½ years stationed there! I fully compensated the family for the horrible trip, by taking us to the Officers club that first night for a famous Maine lobster dinner and I tried to convince them they were "paid in full."

After a couple of flights with an instructor, we went on our first solo mission. All missions were scheduled for twelve hours from take off until landing. We met at Base Operations 3 hours before take- off for a weather briefing and to synchronize our watches. We were then taken by bus, with all our flight gear, to the B-52 and started the pre-flight. At exactly 30 minutes before take off time we started engines (all eight of them) and at exactly 20 minutes before take off we started taxing. Unless during pre-flight a problem was encountered, believe me, timing was always precise. Brakes were released to begin the take off roll on the navigators hack (count down) and during all this time before take-off, the copilot is reading check lists.

Our first solo flight went well until arriving back at Loring. The weather ceiling minimums for a crew on their first solo mission was 500 feet and Loring was below that, so were diverted to Goose Bay Labrador. The weather at Goose was fair when we landed, but by the next morning when we were to return to Loring, Goose was below minimums for landings. It was snowing very hard causing very limited visibility. SAC, having no weather minimums for take-off at that time for qualified pilots, left us no reason to not take off. Heavy snow had been falling all night and the ramp, taxi-ways and runway looked like one thick heavy blanket. Snow removal equipment could not keep up with just keeping the runway clear much less the taxiways. Now that we had completed our first solo flight, we had the same weather landings minimums as all other crews, those being, 150 feet altitude and 1/4 mile visibility. Believe me, considering the wing span of a B-52 is 187 feet and landing speed is over 150 miles per hour, there is not a lot of room for error.

A Lt Colonel Air Craft Commander from Loring had also been diverted to Goose the night before, so in deference to his rank, we agreed that he would take off first. I lost sight of him shortly after he departed the ramp but just as we were getting ready to board our plane, we heard the sound of his engines as he started his take-off roll. We could not see the B-52 and only could hear the roar of his engines and see the thick flurry of snow the blast of his engines was making. Suddenly the noise from the engines abruptly stopped and we had no idea what happened.

While we were performing our starting engines check list we saw him pull up beside us on the ramp so at least we knew the crew was OK, but did not know why he aborted take- off. I started to taxi and my only ground reference was to distinguish the ramp and taxiways lights on each side, so I tried to go down the center. Determining the runway location was the same because it was outlined by the lights on each side spaced at 1000 foot intervals. In both B-47's and B-52"s, you always straddled a centerline on the runway during take-off and landing. This time I did not have one visible. Immediately after take off, I was on instruments and remained on instruments almost until level off. Now I began questioning the logic in diverting me to Goose, at night, a strange field to me and then having me launch in such miserable conditions. Did I become a highly seasoned, unconditionally qualified pilot between the time I shut down the engines last night and starting engines this morning? But then I remembered many other strange procedures in SAC, so accepted this as just one more.

After arriving back at Loring, I was informed that the other B-52, while taking off from Goose, aborted on the runway, after the pilot heard what sounded like a loud explosion from his right side. He assumed it was an engine problem so did the proper thing. Back on the ramp, none of the four engines showed any physical damage and they were not able to determine the cause. A short time later they made a successful take-off and after landing back at Loring the pilot admitted to being very apprehensive about attempting another take-off in the existing weather conditions and in an airplane he did not fully trust.

A few missions later, for some reason, our KC-97 tanker did not show up at the scheduled time and place. Upon returning to Loring late that night, I informed the Command Post of this and was directed to remain at altitude until receiving further instructions. I reminded them, that without the fuel from the tanker, I could not hang around very long as there were no sky hooks! Finally they came back with a solution. A KC-97 was being launched out of Bangor, which is in the Southern part of Maine and would meet me over a designated re-fueling track that headed East- bound from the Atlantic Coast line. I calculated by the time I flew down there, descended to around 16,000 feet and remained at that altitude for any length of time, that tanker must be there. Otherwise, SAC would have a B-52 in the Atlantic. Fortunately the tanker was at our scheduled rendezvous point and although the weather was clear, I remember how black it was down below. I had an eerie feeling, while remembering a B-52 had descended and splashed into the Atlantic during a refueling mission, not long before this. We took on our fuel and made it home as though this was routine.

In SAC, full emphasis was put on completing each part of a scheduled mission, because the SAC grading system put everyone's career on the line every time an aircraft was airborne. Also verything that took place on or off the Base was evaluated. The expression "the buck stops here" applied to every Wing Commander. This put tremendous pressure on them. For example, if a B-52 made a late take off for no apparent reason, even if only for a few minutes, the Wing would lose points in the SAC grading system. Completing each training requirement as scheduled and within certain parameters, was critical to both the crew involved and also to their superiors.

Before SAC came out with very strict restrictions on landing or taking off on icy runway conditions, we landed one day on a solid sheet of ice. When I deployed the drag chute, which was normal procedure on a full stop landing, a cross wind from the right started sliding the plane to the left and I had positively no control. The B-52 had a steerable nose wheel but the nose wheel tires just kept sliding with absolutely no traction. It had anti-lock brakes, but they were ineffective on solid ice. I did not want to slide off the side of the runway into a snow banks built up from plows clearing the runway, so I asked Monroe to "cut" numbers (engines) 1,2,3,6,7 and 8, This would greatly reduce the thrust from the idling engines but by allowing 4 and 5 to continue to operate, I would still have hydraulic pressure for brakes and steering and electrical power for the radio. Monroe misunderstood me and cut all eight engines. We stopped short of the snow bank still fully on the runway, but had no way of notifying the control tower of our predicament. Monroe and I got out of the airplane and started frantically waving at the tower. Someone finally spotted us and sent help out. Surprisingly, nothing was ever said to me concerning the incident. Several B-52's had gone into snow banks in the past and I guess by comparison I had done pretty well. Shortly after this incident, SAC came out with new guidelines, putting limitations when operating with ice or snow on the runway. A vehicle with some kind of deceleration meter installed would be sent out to check the runway condition reading (RCR) and that figure (number) would be transmitted to pilots intending to land. Pilots had a chart listing other landing considerations and by entering the RCR number, could then determine if a landing was feasible.

The pilot's chart required some interpolations which seemed difficult to read so I designed one, whereby following two lines to a point where they intersected, the pilot would arrive at the exact figure to use. I sent my chart to Eighth Air Force for approval and I understood it was recommended for use throughout SAC. That is my one and only achievement of that sort!

One training requirement was to fly low level night weather routes, one of which terminated with a simulated bomb run over Watertown, New York. The route ran from East to West, which necessitated climbing and descending over very rugged mountainous terrain. It was our navigator's job (Luther) to keep us on track and to direct climbs and descents as required by the height of the terrain we were flying over. This was extremely critical over mountainous terrain. Luther had been having some difficulty performing his navigational duties, so Jack, sitting alongside of him, always monitored whatever task Luther was performing. This always doubled Jack's workload and he wasn't too pleased, because it detracted from his own performance.

While flying this route one night during instrument weather conditions, we were getting close to the IP (start of the bomb run,) with Jack concentrating on his bomb run, he suddenly yelled, "pilot, climb, climb, climb!" Luther had descended us too early and there was a mountain range between our position and the target. Visibility was zero from the cockpit, so Monroe and I had no way of realizing this. Fortunately, Jack had glimpsed at his radar set, probably out of habit working while with Luther and shouted the warning. Without hesitation, I shoved the throttles full forward and established a very steep climb angle until Jack said to level off. Somehow, Jack was able to recover his bearings and make another one of his very successful simulated bomb runs. Nothing was said about the incident until while de-briefing after landing. Jack laid a map on the table and plotted our exact position where the incident occurred. After arriving at the same conclusion several times, he estimated that we had to have been going through a very narrow valley when he gave warning. After that, Jack, Monroe and I frequently discussed Luther's limitations and I started putting 2 minute tick marks on my low level charts, so I would always know our position. I might mention, low level navigation routes were always entered at a precise time and every check point along the route was met at the exact flight time planned. SAC had bombers entering the routes at 15 minute intervals, so perfect timing was essential.

SAC B-52 Wings were rotated taking turns flying airborne alert missions which were scheduled to be 24 hours in duration. We had two different routes which either orbited over the Mediterranean or Thule, Greenland. Our flights at this time originated at Loring and terminated at Loring. A third pilot would be placed on board to give the pilots rest time. But as Aircraft Commander responsible for the conduct of the flight, I had difficulty trying to "rest" during my break. Events on three of these missions are still fresh on my mind.

On one of these missions, after crossing the Atlantic, our first refueling was over a mountain range just after coasting in over Spain. By this time our tankers were KC-135's, which had replaced the KC-97's. KC-135's were 4 engine jets, a great improvement over KC-97's. Normally we could top the storms and turbulence, but on this one night, the refueling track had numerous thunderstorms that towered far above our refueling altitude. As I hooked up to the tanker, I discovered my control boost, was not working. This was by far the most difficult air refueling I had ever attempted. My problems were a combination of having to manually control the plane in an unusual amount of turbulence, making numerous turns to avoid thunderstorms and being distracted by frequent lightning caught in my peripheral vision. By sheer determination (and pride,) I managed not to get a "disconnect," while taking on 100,000 pounds of fuel (over 16,000 gallons) from the first tanker and 25,000 pounds from the second. When refueling was complete, I was soaking wet from perspiration and completely exhausted. The radar navigator who had an altimeter in his station, informed me that several times I had pushed the tanker up as much as 1,500 feet, followed by a descent of the same amount. After refueling was completed, the tanker pilot informed me that his auto pilot also was not working. This accounts for the climbs and descents, but it also let me know what a great pilot he was! He was able to sense my pressures on his tanker and played along with me preventing a "disconnect." It wasn't too long after this that a tanker and B-52 collided off the coast of Spain while attempting to refuel! This created quite an international cause for alarm and a lot of people angry, when it was revealed that the bomber, which now lay on the bottom of the Atlantic, had nuclear weapons on board.

The second airborne alert mission I'll never forget was the day of the "Cuban Crisis" This was the time our Navy boarded Russian vessels carrying nuclear weapons en route to Cuba and that day our crew was patrolling the Mediterranean. We were glued to the high frequency radio waiting to receive a coded message which would direct us to proceed to our Russian targets. Those were tense moments mostly because we had no other way of knowing what was transpiring which of course, also made it all the more intriguing. You can imagine our relief when we finally completed our scheduled orbit time and headed back to Loring.

Another mission which was so memorable took place on another night. We were between the IP and target, making a low level simulated bomb run over Watertown, New York, when Jack announced there was a severe thunderstorm a short distance just past the target. He advised me to make a sharp right turn immediately after "bombs away." Monroe and I were on instruments, in clouds, so could see nothing. After making the simulated release, I had just started the right turn, when lightning struck the base of the windshield, directly in front of us. Fortunately I was again on auto-pilot, because both Monroe and I were temporarily blinded and like last time, we lost all electrical equipment including the airspeed indicator. This time, however, I felt sure that very shortly, everything would come back on line, which it did. I climbed back up to about 10,000 feet and headed straight for Loring feeling certain we must have sustained structural damage and did not want to press my luck any further. After landing, I anxiously got out and checked the point of impact to again find absolutely no damage. The B-52 was painted black, so not even a stain was visible. I could not believe I could be so fortunate!

The Bomb Wing had a contest of some sort and our crew took first place. The reward was a week- end cross country to any B-52 base in the U.S. We decided to go to McCoy, as it had completed it's conversion to B-52's. The flight down and back wasn't all that easy. We took off very early on Friday morning, flew a normal 12 hour mission and landed at McCoy about 6:00 in the evening. The next morning my Dad picked up Monroe, Jack and me and took us back to St. Pete, where we spent Saturday night at my Folk's home. I had picked up a box of smoked mullet from Ted Peter's in South Pasadena and packed it in dry ice before my Dad drove us back to McCoy Sunday afternoon. Monday, we had another 12 hour mission planned, the first part being a low level navigation flight taking us over Lake Okeechobee. I was looking forward to this because the last time we flew that route, I descended to about 50 feet over the lake and I'm sure I scared the wits out a couple of fisherman and the occupants of a sailboat. I had throttled back coming in from their rear as quietly as possible and then, when directly abeam, shoved the throttles forward, making a heck of a roar. Later on when I gave it some thought, it did not seem amusing at all, just stupid! (Back to our flight home) We were to start our descent over St. Pete, which was 12 minutes from Orlando but were advised by special bulletin that tornadoes were forming in the Tampa area. While we were listening, severe damage was occurring at MacDill AFB, directly beneath us. Much to my chagrin, we had to cancel the low level part of our flight, but I believe everything happens for a reason, because I may have been tempted to do the same stupid thing over Lake Okeechobee.

We arrived back at Loring late Monday afternoon and as soon as I arrived home began calling friends to come over for some smoked mullet. Most of them had never eaten mullet before and fortunately I had plenty of beer to help them rinse it down. I still get a kick out of telling people that the Air Force let me borrow a B-52 one weekend to fly down to St. Pete to pick up some mullet for a cocktail party. After they disgustedly complain how much that cocktail party must have cost the taxpayers, I just nod my head in agreement, never letting on that two training missions were involved.

We had made Lead Crew quite quickly and Jack and Monroe were being eyed by Standardization Aircraft Commanders, who could select any crew member they wanted to fill a vacancy on their crew. They were both doing exceptionally well, making me look pretty good.

After being stationed at Loring about three years we were scheduled for our annual standardization check ride with Lt. Col. Jake Kaplan and his radar navigator, Capt. Wayne Lockwood. They were both known to be very critical evaluators so we were not looking forward to the flight. I used to really dread evaluations to the extent that I never could sleep the night before. I would lay in bed all night going over and over every phase of the scheduled mission. On the scheduled day we flew a normal training mission, each of us being evaluated and graded on both our individual procedures and coordinated crew activities. Then as always, the Aircraft Commander received an instrument check after returning to the home base. The mission went well and then after arriving back at Loring, I completed the standard instrument check maneuvers, which took well over an hour. Jake called the Command Post and requested our scheduled mission landing time be extended, which had already taken over twelve hours. Much to my disappointment, the extension was granted and Jake had me demonstrate several additional approaches, such as loss of communications, two engines out go around and other abnormal procedures. I was really tired of him seemingly playing games with me, just waiting for me to goof up and I was about ready to tell him so, when he finally said "let's terminate." I had no idea why the extra maneuvers, but thought the overall flight went quite well.

The next day I was called into the Squadron Commander's office and found Jake also sitting there. To my utter amazement, the Squadron Commander said Jake was looking for a replacement to take over his "select" crew, because he was to become the Squadron Operations Officer and he had selected me over several other Aircraft Commanders. It was offered to me as an option, but the commander explained I would be losing Jack and Monroe before long and Luther and the EWO Officer, John, were really not much of an asset with their limited experience. A very experienced instructor pilot, Bernie Zimmerman, was to take over my crew to prepare Monroe to qualify as Aircraft Commander. Jake's crew was to be replaced in Standardization, but would retain its "select status." The Squadron had four select crews, three of which were in Standardization, so it would be a prestigious advancement for me. Considering all this, I accepted the position which took place immediately.

I think Jack and Monroe at first felt I was just looking out for myself, but after relating the Squadron Commander's reasoning to them, they completely understood. We had been together for almost five years and this move was also to their benefit. As it turned out, immediately after Monroe was qualified as an Aircraft Commander, but before being assigned a crew, he was transferred to a highly classified assignment, which he never did reveal to anyone. Sometime earlier, Monroe had complained about being a 1st. Lt. for an extra long time and I tried counseling him, explaining, being an Academy Graduate, he had a great future ahead of him. I did not tell him that he and Frank Borman, were in my mind, by far, superior to any junior officer I had ever worked with. Monroe could handle the B-52, including air refueling, as well as the best of Aircraft Commanders and he thoroughly understood SAC directives and procedures which were sometimes difficult to make sense of. I intend to clarify the last part of that statement. I was absolutely right about Monroe, because he eventually became Vice SAC Commander and impressively ended his career having attained the rank of Full General (4 stars) and assigned to one of the highest positions in the Air Force.

While I'm on this recognition of outstanding officer's subject, I want to mention that Frank Borman was the first astronaut to leave the earths orbit and orbit the moon. Later on, after leaving the service, he became President and CEO of Eastern Airlines. Do I know how to judge men or what?

Now I'll return to "my" feeble achievements and "boners" which brings to mind the expression "compared to what?"

A short time after taking over Jake's crew, the Squadron Commander informed me that I had been selected to become an Instructor Pilot. SAC had a program designed to standardize upgrading pilots to instructor status, by attending a course at Castle AFB in California. The course actually lacked teaching instructor techniques, but I did not attempt to enlighten them! Mostly it was to see if we could handle all phases of a mission from the right (copilot) seat which is where instructors normally sat. I flew several flights from the right seat, including air refueling, touch- and-go take-offs and landings and that was all there was to it. I would have thought they would evaluate us on out ability to recover from a "bad" landing and erratic gyrations behind a tanker. What we did do could easily have been accomplished back at Loring by a Squadron instructor pilot. Instructors were the only pilots permitted to make touch- and-go landings because there were several critical controls to re-position after landing and before taking off in a minimum amount of time on the runway.

My first assignment as an instructor was to give an instrument recheck to an Aircraft Commander. I received no specific instructions, so had him do the normal required procedures. He did an excellent job and of course I passed him. When I informed Jake, the Squadron Operations Officer, of the great job the pilot did, he exclaimed, "you were supposed to fail him!" This was the first I knew about it and I tried to explain I would not have failed him even if directly ordered to do so. He absolutely deserved to pass. Then I found out this had been a "set up." Someone deliberately failed him on his first check. If he failed the recheck, he would be taken off a crew, grounded, passed over for his next promotion and eventually put out of the Air Force. He was black and I immediately thought this could cause a huge problem if he claimed prejudice and I could be caught in the middle of it. Finally I was told the reasoning behind this strategy. He had rented a motel just outside the Base and operated a house of prostitution. In addition to this, he was accused of several other illegal activities, so someone apparently thought having him grounded would be the easiest method of putting him out of the service rather than go through all the legal hassle. Anyway, before long, he was taken off crew duty and I lost track of him. If I had failed him and word got out why I "failed" him, I would probably be in more trouble than he!

I quickly realized the Radar Navigator, Wayne Lockwood, thought he ran our crew. This was compounded when he received a spot promotion to major a few weeks after I came on board. As I mentioned earlier, most Select Crew members held a spot promotion which was one rank above the regular rank the person held. This brought an immediate pay raise and counted as time already in grade when receiving the next normal promotion. A normal promotion always required a minimum time in grade before becoming eligible so some SAC crew members advanced in rank very rapidly under the spot system. I felt certain that my spot promotion would be coming shortly but just when I became eligible, the spot promotion system was terminated. Crew members presently holding spots, kept them, but no additional spots were awarded. It was rumored that other branches of the Air Force were complaining about the inequities in the SAC spot promotion system, so I guess a stroke of the pen by someone not involved solved that!

I was scheduled to give Captain Charlie Luse an instrument check. Charlie was extremely well liked in the squadron and also a pretty good friend of mine. He was sort of a happy-go-lucky person but a very conscientious Aircraft Commander. By this I mean he knew when to "play" and when to do his job, which I might add, he was very good at. Charlie ran a good crew and everyone knew it. One of the requirements during an instrument check was to demonstrate a steep turn. With Charlie under the hood, when the time came, I asked him to make a steep turn. A normal turn was about 25 degrees of bank if I remember correctly and a steep turn about 40 or 45 degrees. Believe me, that doesn't sound too difficult, but in a B-52 it seemed quite steep. If a fighter pilot read or heard this I'm sure he would have something sarcastic to say. Well, Charlie did not hold the nose up, which takes considerable back trim and some manual back pressure on the control column. It appeared to me the plane was about to get away from him so I made the recovery. This was a critical part of the check and a cause for failing, so that's the way I wrote it up. Charlie's pride must have really been hurt, as I know mine would have been, but he was very understanding of the situation and did not show any outward resentment towards me, for which I was grateful.

But the incident made me recall when I had about 9 years as a Captain, a promotion to Major list came out and not being eligible, I was not on it. The Wing Commander asked when I was going to be promoted and I assumed he knew more about that than I, so I responded, "probably never." I was hoping he would say he would do something about that, but he only grinned. The next year after having been commissioned for 20 years with 10 of it as a captain, I finally made Major. What happened to the rapid promotion schedule of every three years that I read about in high school? Of course, the two breaks in service of five and two years respectively lost me a lot of promotion list service time. I had gone from being one of the youngest Second Lt's. to one of the oldest Captains. This was becoming embarrassing.

Charlie Luse was eligible for promotion to Major at the same time I was but his name was not on the list. He was passed over and would not be eligible until one year later. Charlie was really hurt and I felt terrible about it. One more pass-over would put him out of the Air Force and I would be to blame because of the instrument check. When someone informed me that Charlie had been divorced; I hoped this was the reason for the pass-over because up until that time the services really frowned on divorce, which normally attached a stigma to the individual's service record. The last I heard of Charlie, he made Full Colonel and was Base Commander at Eglin Air Force Base in Florida. I was extremely pleased to hear this.

Fortunately, after a short time of "Wayne" trying to run the crew, I was put in Standardization with an entirely different crew. I was really getting tired of Wayne saying, "This is the way Jake did it." A few times, "the way Jake did it," was contrary to regulations or exceeded B-52 flight limitations. Wayne failed to recognize the fact that the Aircraft Commander, regardless of rank, was in charge and responsible for all crew activities.

One advantage of being in Standardization was that we pulled fewer weeks of alert. Instead of one week out every three, it was more like one out of every four. This was because instead of pulling alert, we flew more missions. Standardization crew members gave annual and spot evaluations to all of the other crew members in the Squadron, in addition to having to accomplishing their own normal training requirements.

My new crew was a pleasure to work with. For the third time I had an excellent Radar Navigator, Mac Wilson. Discounting Wayne's domineering personality, I must say at this time and ever since being in bombers, I firmly believe the crew Radar Navigator held the key to a crew's success. Almost everything pertaining to grading the success of a mission was centered on, "Radar." He could make a pilot look good or bad, depending how he performed. The pilot just tried to be a good chauffeur.

After leaving Monroe and becoming an instructor, I changed copilots quite often. Copilots would be assigned to me when close to having enough pilot time, (I think 2000 hours) to become an Aircraft Commander. Once a Copilot became qualified to be an Aircraft commander and to recommend him to be assigned his own crew, pretty much depended on how much I liked him personally. I distinctly remember one copilot who was a pretty good pilot, but chewed gum all during each flight and the way he worked at it was very annoying. Also pilot and copilot shared a room on alert and he made strange noises in his sleep, so as you guessed, I got him his own crew in a hurry. To this day, gum chewing really annoys me. Ask my son and daughter.

CHAPTER SEVENTEEN
AT LAST! MY TRANSFER
TO THE "SOUTH"

After being at Loring for 5 ½ years one of the two Bomb Squadrons was transferred to Plattsburg, New York. Volunteer crews from each Squadron were to be accepted first and when too many crews volunteered, crews were selected by time spent at Loring. My entire crew had volunteered and with the length of time we had spent at Loring, we were among the first accepted.

I would like to mention at this time, the AF had what was called, a "North/ South rotation policy." I assume this was considered our "South" assignment, but I did not complain because I was really happy to leave Loring. Just before leaving I was assigned a new copilot, Len Svitinko, who was in the Aircraft Commander upgrade program. Len's twin brother, Lou, was also based at Loring. They had gone through the Air Force academy together, were extremely close and both were in the upgrade program. Their careers had paralleled ever since entering the Academy, an arrangement which I understood, was very unusual in the Air Force. More about Len later.

Plattsburg is on Lake Champlain, almost across from Burlington Vermont. We frequently used Burlington Airport to practice ILS approaches because Loring did not have the capability. One night while with a student practicing ILS approaches to Burlington airport, I was reported flying excessively low over the city of Burlington. It happened that while on our second practice approach the student and I heard the following transmission from the tower. Our call sign followed by, "Turn right to 270 degrees and climb to 2000 feet." At this time we were at about 200 feet ready to start our go-around for another approach which would have been to climb straight ahead. Because it sounded like an urgent traffic advisory, I immediately motioned the student to apply climb power and start turning. Nothing more was said by the tower and we continued making approaches. While in debriefing at Loring, I received a call from the Command Post. The 8th Air Force Director of Safety urgently wanted to speak to me, so I was phone patched in to him. I was told a Vermont U.S. Senator had been called by a doctor in Burlington, concerning a low flying B-52 that passed directly over his house in a steep turn, rattling dishes, shaking the whole house and scaring his family. The Director asked why I made a steep turn at such a low altitude over the city of Burlington and implied that I was probably in deep trouble. I quickly explained that I received a "traffic advisory" from the tower and assumed there was conflicting traffic, so immediately followed the controller's instructions. Then I repeated what the controller said, adding he should have first said; "after completing your approach, turn etc." The Director of Safety, being a former B-52 pilot, told me I was right and to forget about it.

When the tower controllers at Burlington heard we were moving to Plattsburg, they requested Loring to schedule a B-52 to make a low pass over the field so they could get a good close up look at one. I was selected to make the pass at the end of a routine training mission, which pleased me a lot, as this was my kind of flying! By the time we got over Burlington, our fuel weight was down and I could make the B-52 look like a high performance aircraft, which, in my mind, it certainly was not! As I was approaching the field, I asked the tower operator if he was familiar with the incident concerning the low flying B-52 reported to a U.S. Senator. He answered he "sure was," having been the controller that gave the instructions to turn and climb. He said a tape confirmed what he said, which he admitted was misleading and that was the end of it. I've gone into detail on this to demonstrate how precise pilots and Air Traffic Controllers must be in their phraseology.

Before starting my approach to Burlington I had lowered the landing gear and flaps, so over mid-field, I applied full power, raised the gear and flaps and started an exceptionally steep climb. I wanted people to think this was normal performance and the B-52 was "quite a machine." My crew got a big kick out of it.

Lt. Colonel Bill Winsor, the Squadron Operations Officer, was to be Squadron Commander at Plattsburg. Paul Maul, was made Chief of Standardization and my crew and I would remain in Standardization. Because of a busy schedule our crew was the last to leave Loring,

Immediately after arriving at Plattsburg, each crew had to brief our new Wing Commander, Col. Radell, on our particular assigned mission in the event of an actual alert. This was all part of the overall war plan in which all branches of the services participated, each having their own specific mission. I assume this was coordinated in the Pentagon. We had very little time to prepare for the briefing and were the last ones to brief the Commander. Each member of the crew gave a briefing on his own individual responsibilities. Mac Wilson, our Radar Navigator, did an outstanding job. After we completed briefing the Wing Commander, he acknowledged that he was told how rushed our schedule had been with little time for preparation, he paid the crew a very nice compliment by saying, "they saved the best till last." Believe me, this is a great way to start on a new Base with a new Commander. Bill Winsor, the new Squadron Commander, also heard the remark, which I hoped would show up on my next annual effectiveness report.

What a change from Loring! We were now living in a great house, on a great Base bordering between Lake Champlain and the City of Plattsburg. The surrounding countryside was beautiful, being only thirty five miles from Lake Placid, which boasted some of the best ski areas in the States. Even the temperature in the winter was almost pleasant.(compared to Loring)

Everything went routine, until one afternoon while our crew was on alert, Mac received an emergency call to come home as soon as possible. The entire crew was replaced on alert very hastily and Mac was escorted home by a pair of MP's. When he entered the door, he saw his wife lying on the floor with the front of her face partially blown off. She apparently had committed suicide and this is what his kids encountered after returning home from school. My wife was immediately called and brought the kids back to our home. This was an awful shock to all the crew member's wives, because between mission planning, flying and alert, husbands were gone much of the time and wives were left with all the responsibilities concerning the household and children. Every wife could not help but be under a lot of strain and finally Mac's wife "broke down." I'm sure many wives were thinking, who is going to be next? I accompanied Mac for the next few days while he made all the funeral arrangements, which was something no one ever expects to have to do. Mac was taken off crew duty and given a job in the Bomb/Nav Department so he could keep regular hours and look after his kids. I don't recall who replaced him on the crew.

I was preparing my copilot, Len Svtinko, for his flight check to up-grade to Aircraft Commander, so let him ride in the pilot's seat (left) for an entire mission. When we returned to Plattsburg the weather was reported to be 150 foot ceiling and 1/4 mile visibility, which was Sac's minimums for landing. I heard the Command Post direct other aircraft to an alternate field, so assumed we also would be diverted. When I reported to the Command Post, I was told the weather was holding at minimums, with no lifting forecast, but they needed a B-52 to fly a scheduled mission the next day. We were cleared to attempt to land so I assumed they considered me, being a standardization pilot, was more apt to get the "bird" safely on the ground. (Only birds would fly in that kind of weather and they weren't traveling over 150 mph and have a 187 foot wingspan) We requested a GCA and would use the ILS for a back-up. Len, being in the left seat, made the penetration and approach. He did a perfect job following the controller's instructions and according to instrument approach procedures, I was to announce when I had the "runway in sight." Again, according to procedures, if I did not make the call before reaching minimum altitude (150 feet,) he was to initiate a missed approach procedure (go around). Just as he announced he was starting a go-around, I caught a glimpse of light from the strobe lights. They are a string of extremely high intensity blinking lights which start a short distance in front of the runway boundary lights and are aligned with the centerline of the runway. I could not see the actual runway lights, but knew we were lined up with the centerline and on the glide slope. I instinctively put my left hand over Len's right hand on the throttles to prevent him from applying climb power. That gesture, reflecting back, was not a very smart thing to do. Fortunately I spotted the runway lights immediately after that and informed Len I had the field in sight, "take over visually" and land. When firmly on the ground, I could sense a sigh of relief from the crew and we all congratulated Len on his terrific performance. As we taxied past the control tower, Len and I could not see lights on the top of the tower because they were in the clouds. I vowed to myself right then, I would never again put myself in that predicament. At debriefing, I announced to the crew, that Len just completed his check ride qualifying him as an Aircraft Commander.

I failed an Aircraft Commander, John Haug, on a recheck and recommended he be taken off crew duty. I realized this was the "kiss of death" for any pilot, but felt I had no choice. During the check ride, he had difficulty remaining within the altitude, airspeed and heading parameters allowed in the flight manual. In my mind, he exercised poor judgment at times and his approach and landing finalized my decision. John was assigned to Base Operations to await his fate.

Shortly after this, Colonel Reddell, the Wing Commander, was transferred to SAC Personnel. Before he left the Base, John Haug pleaded with him to be returned to crew duty and the Squadron Commander received an order to give John a crew as soon as possible. A crew was quickly formed with members quite capable, but considered difficult to get along with. Knowing John's limitations, I recommended Len Svtinko as copilot, which would provide support I felt John needed and would be temporary while Len was waiting for his own crew.

Sometime along here I received my promotion to Lt. Colonel. This was about 3 years after making Major, so I was slowly catching up! Paul Maul, Chief of Standardization, left for SAC Headquarters shortly after Col. Reddell left and I became Chief of Standardization, which dramatically expanded my responsibilities and also my authority in recommending Squadron crew assignments pertaining to crew performance. I still had my own crew, but our quarterly training requirements and alert schedule were reduced to offset the time spent directing standardization activities. It was a very prestigious position, supposedly held by the most experienced and proficient pilot in the Wing. I had mixed emotions about both of these perquisites, often alternating between thinking, "who am I kidding?" and "I deserve to be here" Anyway; I tried my best to prove my worth.

The Wing was taking its turn in performing Chrome Dome duty. This required a B-52 crew to fly airborne alert, a mission that orbited over Thule AFB, Greenland, for twelve hours, remaining airborne a total of 24 hours, including the time in flight to and from Plattsburg. A third pilot was carried to give the pilot and copilot a rest period.

On a Chrome Dome mission my crew flew, things went routine until after being airborne about 12 hours we were unable to obtain sufficient cabin heat to remain comfortable. This was in January and it was extremely cold at our altitude, so I suggested we use the alternate heat system. As best as I can recall, this required a procedure called "select emergency right- hand inboard." Hot air was directed into the cabin from, I believe, number three engine and it bypassed the heat exchange unit which prevented excessive heat from entering the cabin. Prior to setting the control valve, the number three throttle was retarded and the copilot monitored a temperature gauge in a panel to his right as the valve was turned on. Then the throttle could be slowly advanced until the gauge indicated the maxim allowable temperature. It was critical to continuously monitor the gauge until returning to normal heat.

A few minutes after switching to the alternate system, we sensed a strong odor, like that caused by hot or burning rubber or oil. We immediately switched back to the normal heating system and the odor disappeared. After landing at Plattsburg, I described the problem to the crew chief and followed up by writing a comprehensive description of the problem in the flight log (I think it was called the form 1). I knew the same plane was scheduled for the same flight the next day, so was interested in making sure the discrepancy was corrected. Everyone feared a fire in flight! The next morning the same B-52 again departed for the Thule orbit. That night I received an emergency phone call informing me that the B-52 had crashed just outside of Thule AFB and nothing further was known other than the other aircraft commander was John Haug.

The Eighth Air Force Safety Office notified Plattsburg Command Post that I was to be picked up very shortly in a Lear Jet and flown to Thule, as part of the Accident Investigation team assigned to the Operations Group. Enroute to Thule we were told the crew had declared an emergency to Thule tower, relating that they had a fire in the crew compartment and the smoke and fumes were so intense it was unbearable and they were going to "bail out." Although it was pitch black out and the temperature was far below zero, by the time we arrived, somehow, they had miraculously already found the six crew members that were in ejection seats. Len Sventiko who was not in an ejection seat was still missing.

Just before the emergency, Len had been relieved from his copilot seat by Joe DeMario, the extra pilot on board, so Len was in the crew rest position, which was a bunk behind the pilot's seat. Joe was the Wing Director of Safety and an instructor pilot. We were told the pilot gave the "bail out" command as they approached Thule AFB at 5,000 feet and Joe's landing in his chute was uncanny. He landed on Thule AFB next to a lighted, heated hanger, with a truck parked in front with the engine running. Joe had gone into the hanger, found a phone, called the Command Post and reported his location. According to Joe, they offered to come pick him up, but I understand he said, "Don't bother, I'll just use the truck parked outside." The other six crew members did not fare as well. Even though none of them were exposed to the cold very long, they suffered serious freezing of the toes. Everyone had parkas and thermal boots on, which is why they were able to survive at all. Len was not found until the next day with part of his head scraped off after having been dragged along the bottom of the fuselage. This was the result of the excessive air speed the plane had accelerated to during the descent and his attempt to bail out through the open escape hatch left by the navigator after he ejected downward. This really affected me, because I was so involved in placing him on this crew.

I immediately realized how ironic the entire situation was. This was the scenario as I saw it! I had failed John Haug on his last standardization check, recommending he be relieved from crew duty. 2, I was the last one to pilot the B-52 prior the flight that crashed. 3, I had experienced smoke and fumes in the crew compartment and recorded it in the flight log. 4, I was Chief of Standardization responsible for the performance of every crew member in the Squadron. 5, I am now on the accident investigation team investigating an accident that I attempted to prevent by my earlier decisions. It was amazing the six crew members were found so quickly considering the chill factor was far below zero and it was a very black night. How I wished Len had been one of the survivors!

A full Colonel, Col. Felecias, very well known in the Air Force, headed the accident investigation board. I was on the operations team, headed by another Lt. Colonel and we also had four or five additional team members. Our responsibility was to determine if the accident was caused by or could have been prevented by crew procedures.

Other teams from Boeing, who were power plant (engines) experts and airframe engineers along with FAA inspectors quickly arrived to start their part of the investigation. SAC, as usual, expected a quick evaluation and cause of the accident in order to prevent future accidents caused by having the same problem. The control tower, by radar had pinpointed exactly where the B-52 impacted the earth. If I remember correctly, it was about 9 miles west of Thule AFB. A dog sled team was organized with experts from the power plant and airframe teams to physically examine the impact area and aircraft wreckage. I was thankful the operations team was not considered as needed, to evaluate the scene.

As soon as word got out that the B-52 had nuclear weapons on board, dignitaries and newspaper reporters from all over the world started arriving at Thule. Our team had to be put in an isolated room to avoid questions.

The dog sled team returned unexpectedly early from their trip with the "strangest" report. While searching a wide area, they found no trace of the B-52. After some deliberation, we determined the severe intensity of the heat generated by the exploding fuel, melted the ice, allowing the entire wreckage to slip through the ice cap. The extreme cold temperature at the impact area immediately re-froze the surface, resulting in the complete disappearance of the B-52. Quickly after word got out that a B-52 with nuclear weapons on board went through the ice cap and was present presumably laying on the bottom of Baffin Bay in Davis Strait, which is connected to the Arctic Ocean. This alarmed the entire world because it became known to the general population, that Air Force aircraft flying overhead were possibly carrying nuclear weapons. Now the general public knew what only heads of state knew before. I am quite sure the U.S. had agreements with countries permitting this kind of mission with certain air corridors being provided. This then limited nuclear traffic to certain approved routes which ordinary citizens were not aware of

Col. Felecias selected me, because of my previous involvement with this crew, to interview each crew member and make a recording of his recollection of everything leading to, during and after the accident. I had already been informed that smoke and fumes encountered during my flight were caused by an oil soaked rag accidentally left in the heat duct by a careless mechanic, so my first solution was discounted.

To be brief, Joe, the Wing Safety Officer, unknowingly stacked a pile of flammable cushions over a heat duct shortly after take-off and then, when relieving Len in the copilot's position, did not follow the proper procedure when switching to alternate heat. The intense heat, which should have been monitored on the temperature gauge, caught the cushions Joe had stacked over the heat duct on fire. It also had positioned them directly under the aircraft's primary electrical control panel, which flames from the cushions had engulfed. The wires burning in the panel caused the intense smoke and fumes to become unbearable and necessitated the bail out Command. In addition to Joe De Mario's "major" mistakes, the radar operator and navigator, instead of getting out of their seats, attempted to extinguish the fire from their crew positions with the two available fire extinguishers. The fire was 12-15 feet behind them, well out of effective range of the extinguishers. The Pilot, in attempting to return quickly to Thule, exceeded air speed limitations and shed secondary aircraft structure. Parts were found strewn along his flight path leading up to the impact point. The excessive airspeed killed Len when he attempted to leave through the navigators open hatch. The maximum speed for a safe exit through the hatch was part of the published emergency procedures, supposedly memorized by all B-52 pilots.

Joe, in addition to having been an Aircraft Commander for many years, was an instructor pilot so he certainly should have known the procedure for using the alternate heat system. As far as I know, Joe was never reprimanded for his part in this combination of errors, but I can imagine he became a better "Wing Safety Officer" as a result of it all.

One thing I heard from each crew member during the interviews, was the last words everyone heard on the interphone after receiving the bailout order. They were from Len, who said, "what about me?" I'm sure the question was ignored everyone only thinking of himself!

I don't know what happened after the accident to any of the crew members except John Haug, whom I understand, was released from active duty. Len's wife and brother, Lou, took it very hard. I really did not have an opportunity to see his wife because I spent 10 days at Thule and then a short time at Loring AFB before we finalized our report. By the time I arrived back at Plattsburg she had been moved off base.

A short time after my return, Lou applied for test pilot school and was very appreciative of my flattering endorsement when he was accepted. I never heard from him after he left Plattsburg but I assume he had a rewarding career.

Col. Felecias gave me the difficult task of writing up the entire operational part of the accident report, including who or what to place the blame on. I was told he was a grammar expert, so I spent a lot of time making sure the sequence of events, phraseology, punctuation and wording were correct. He was to sign the report before it went to SAC Headquarters and I was elated when he complimented me on the report.

When the report came out, Col. McClain, Plattsburg Wing Commander, had a furnace constructed and with bellows, somehow duplicated the cause of the fire putting emphasis on the flammability of the cushions. He required each crew member to witness the intense heat generated by the alternate system and the flammable cushions were replaced in all B-52's.

SAC required that whenever a Wing experienced an accident, the Wing Commander had to report to the SAC Commander and give a detailed account of the cause and corrective action taken, Our Wing Commander, Col. McClain, intended to fully prepare himself for this briefing, so had me spend many hours in his office while he rehearsed his presentation. I was to make sure he was familiar with every little detail. The briefing was extremely important in determining a Wing Commander's future assignments and promotions. Col. McClain came back from SAC Headquarters smiling, so I assumed he did well.

Not long after this, the Squadron Commander retired and Col. McClain assigned me to replace him. I was finally relieved from crew duty, but assumed other duties, some of which were quite critical. For example, I now made up the alert schedule, leave schedule and most importantly, determined crew position assignments. I quickly learned that the Squadron Commander was responsible for the conduct, performance and training of everyone in the Squadron. Most important of all, after attending several staff meetings, I realized that the sole purpose of the entire AF Wing at Plattsburg, was to support the Bomb Squadron. This also included the Tanker Squadron whose mission was to provide in-flight refueling to the Bomber Squadron. Of course, this held true for all other SAC Wings. Until becoming one, I honestly never realized the responsibilities of being a Bomb Squadron Commander. Suddenly, I understood that the capability of the Bomb Squadron to perform its mission in accordance with standards established by SAC was closely monitored by almost every organization in the Wing. The Bomb Squadron's performance level, when evaluated by Division or SAC Headquarters, pretty much determined the ratings received throughout the Wing. None of us wanted supervisors or monitors hanging around the Base watching every move we made in order to improve our performance level. This happened when a Base fails a Higher Headquarters evaluation which I observed at Loring AFB after the Bomb Squadron failed a routine SAC Headquarters evaluation.

Once each month, on Saturday morning, we had a Combat Crew Capabilities Meeting. This is when I attempted to justify crew changes to the Wing Commander. Col. McClain did not like crew changes, so I always attended the meeting well prepared. Before making a change, there were four basic considerations I studied. First, the individual's level of experience. Second, his ability to perform his job in a professional, efficient manner. Third, in the case of pilot positions or radar and navigator positions, how well they would support each other. Fourth, crew members personality to determine how well the new member would blend in with the five other crew members. I had been on a crew and flown with every member of the Squadron enough times to pretty accurately make these evaluations. My primary concern was making sure a new Aircraft Commander had the support of an experienced copilot and a new radar navigator, had the support of an experienced navigator. This also was true, vise/versa, in each position. Examples I have explained earlier were Jack Schuster, radar and Luther Norton, navigator, also John Haug aircraft commander and Len Svtinko copilot. Because of a third pilot on board, this theory did not work with John Haug. Col. McClain's career was dependent on crew performance, which was continuously evaluated by SAC Headquarters. If a crew performed poorly, the Squadron Commander would initially be blamed. But if a certain portion of the Wing did poorly, the Wing Commander took the blame. Anyway, I always eventually made my point and received approval for the changes I requested.

I had not been Squadron Commander long, when a new Aircraft Commander reported in. He was an Air Force Academy graduate, now a Captain, having recently returned from overseas. His family had not yet joined him and about the third night he was on the base, he came alone to a party at the Officers Club. In the course of the evening he got noticeably drunk and was observed by Col. McClain. The next day I received a phone call from the Col. telling me to keep my eye on the Captain. It was easy to tell Col. Mclain already did not like him. Then a couple of days later, Col. McClain received word that the Captain was presently under investigation for not properly safeguarding highly classified information while at his overseas station. This really stirred Col. McClain up and I was told to assign the Captain in a copilot position even though he was Aircraft Commander qualified. I was impressed with how well the Captain accepted this "come-down." I was also impressed with his appearance and overall military bearing. This certainly was not the Officer I saw at the party and fortunately I was able to place him on a relatively inexperienced crew knowing that he would provide the added support the new crew needed.

Unfortunately the Captain became due for his annual Effectiveness Report at this time. Writing the report was the Squadron Commander's responsibility, but it was endorsed by the Deputy Commander for Operations and finally by the Wing Commander.

Col. McClain was told of the pending Effectiveness Report and directed me, in a very discreet way, to rate the Captain an overall "six." This was also the kiss of death career wise, even for an Academy Graduate. There was no possibility of him ever being promoted to Major and after two "pass over's" would be released from active duty. I reluctantly gave him a six and he again accepted the comedown very well. I will get back to the Captain a little later.

I guess because I owned a bar and restaurant, I was made a member of the Officers Club Advisory Council. A Master Sergeant managed the club but the council approved the restaurant menu, prices, etc. We had a monthly meeting and it very pleasant having a say in club management, but "not responsible" for paying bills. After a year, I became Chairman of the Council, so now I was sure I could keep the price of martinis during happy hour on Fridays at 25 cents!

I was at the Officer's Club on a Friday talking to Col. McClain, while downing my usual quota of martinis and the Division Commander, a Brigadier General, came in. I had met him numerous times and he had endorsed my Effectiveness Report several times, always recommending I be promoted to Col. ahead of my contemporaries. Col. McClain asked him to join us for a drink which he promptly did. The General mentioned he wanted my opinion concerning a new alert procedure he intended to present to SAC Headquarters. Our normal response time for an alert, after hearing the klaxon to landing gear up (take-off,) was programmed to be less than 15 minutes. We had to really scramble to make that time and this was with the B-52's parked on the ramp in front of the alert facility with the crews within a few minutes of the planes. Now the General wanted to implement a three minute response time by having the planes parked at the end of the active runway with the crews in them. When I explained this was totally impractical, he became adamant, insisting it could be done. I asked how much experience he had in B-52's and replied none, but he had flown in a KC-135 tanker. I tried to explain how long it took to start 8 engines and complete extensive checklists before take off, but he still insisted it could be done. Then my martinis responded! Being tactful, I said, "General, I've never said this to a General before, but you're full of "sh—t." Our little meeting broke up right after that without giving me a chance to apologize. I fully expected Col. McClain to call for me the next day, but it did not happen.

A very uneasy week went by for me and when I went to the Club the next Friday, the General was standing at the other end of the bar. I was thinking "there is only one reason he is back here so soon." He caught my eye and invited me to join him. I thought, "Here it comes!" Instead, to my complete surprise, he shook my hand, acted extremely congenial and never mentioned the previous Friday night. I was greatly relieved and swore never again to let martinis take over my tongue! Anyway, I never heard another word about a three minute response time. Reflecting back, I probably saved the General from revealing what little he knew about the B-52.

The Base had 12 Squadrons, ten of which were there to support the Bomb and Tanker Squadrons. The council decided each month a different Squadron should sponsor a party at the Officers Club. A buffet dinner with a certain "motif" would be served, followed by entertainment of some sort. This worked out very well because it gave the wives a challenge and it was determined that the Bomb Squadron would be first to stage a party.

I conducted a Squadron meeting and asked for volunteers to organize the party and provide the entertainment. Charlie Luse suggested we have a clambake. This was to be in November and everyone agreed it was a good idea. Considering Charlie suggested it, I assumed he knew all about clambakes, so I asked if he would like to be in charge. He said he had never been to one, knew nothing about them, so asked if anyone else had been to one. No one responded, so Charlie offered to go to the Base Library and read a book on the subject. We all agreed that was an excellent idea and it was unanimous that Charlie was in charge. Barbara had experience in dance choreography so she offered to come up with some dance routines.

My job was to obtain the lobsters and clams. The Wing Commander thought we had a good idea, so agreed to let us send a C-47 from Base Operations to pick up the lobsters and clams at a seafood port along the Coast of Maine. As a backup, because the weather along the coast in November was very unpredictable, I arranged for a truck from the motor pool to make the trip if necessary. Including husbands and wives, we had sold over 400 tickets, so I wanted to make sure every possible problem was covered.

Early, on the morning of the Saturday night "dinner dance," Charlie had a crew dig a deep hole alongside the Officer's Club. Then built a big fire at the bottom and loaded the lobsters and clams in layers on white sheets. I observed part of the start of the operation and made several visits throughout the day, each time being assured everything was going well. I did not interfere with the operation because I had no idea of how this was done.

Dinner was to be served at 7:00 PM so I got to the club about 6:00 PM. Fortunately, I had a couple of martinis, when at about 5 minutes to 7:00 PM, Charley came into the bar. A line already had formed that extended from the buffet table, which was on the far side of the club, into the bar. Charlie informed me, that as they were bringing the first load of lobsters into the kitchen, the lobsters were jumping off the sheets. They hadn't even begun to cook! We went to the kitchen and explained the predicament to the head chef. He had three or four steam cookers that could hold 5 or 6 lobsters each and would it take about 3 minutes to cook each load. I went back into the bar and very quietly recruited several Squadron members and their wives to assist Charley in the kitchen. Charley established an assembly line and in just a few minutes the dinner line was moving. It was an unbelievably smooth running operation.

The men did a box dance routine which went over very well. With trouser legs rolled up and the rest of their bodies covered by a large box, they performed a crazy dance step made up and directed by Barbara. The women did a costumed dance routine also created by Barbara.

The next week I kept hearing what a great party it was and they were already looking forward to a repeat clambake next year. I do not think anyone outside of the Squadron was aware that the lobsters were actually cooked in the kitchen.

I would like to mention here, Charlie Luse was promoted to Major and no one was more pleased than I. He had been made an instructor pilot and eventually assigned to Standardization.

At a Commanders staff meeting Col. McClain mentioned he intended to have a "dining- in" and he asked what we thought about the idea and if anyone could suggest a guest speaker. A "dining in" is a mandatory dinner that all officers on the base must attend wearing their mess dress. "Mess dress" is the military designation for formal wear, cummerbund, pants with stripes etc. Officers were seated by rank and date of rank; a very formal occasion.

Shortly after the staff meeting Col. McClain left for 8th Air Force Headquarters to attend a senior staff conference. I thought Frank Borman would be a perfect guest speaker for the dinner. This was a short time after his famous flight in which he was the first person to depart orbiting the earth, proceed to the moon, circumnavigate it and return to earth. He was a genuine celebrity and would be an excellent guest speaker. I called Astronaut Headquarters and immediately got through to Frank. He accepted the invitation and I asked if he wanted to stay in the Visiting Officers Quarters or in our home. I was very excited when he said our home! I did not mention this to anyone until Col. McClain returned. I fully expected him to jump with joy, but instead he informed me he already invited the 8th Air Force Commander, a three star General, who was his boss, to be guest speaker. This almost put me in a state of shock. Col. McClain made it clear that he absolutely could not cancel the General so I suggested we invite them both, but Col. McClain was afraid Frank would draw all the attention, which is true.

Now, I had the horrible job of calling Frank and canceling him. I rehearsed for a day what I would say before finally mustering up enough nerve to make the call. As I expected, Frank was very gracious and fully understood my predicament. My family was really disappointed, but not as much as I.

Col. McClain was transferred and I immediately researched the Air Force Regulation concerning deleting Effectiveness Reports from an officer's records. The Captain I mentioned earlier was completely exonerated from the "not safeguarding classified material accusation," and finally got his own crew. I stated in my request that I was the Reporting Officer on the report and was coerced by the Wing Commander into giving the low rating. I went into detail describing the Captain's attitude and performance. I did not tell the Captain about the letter because I did not have much faith in the system and did not want to further disappoint him. When he received word a couple of weeks later that the Effectiveness Report had been deleted from his file, he was totally surprised. Then when he heard I was the one who initiated the request, showed his appreciation. Even the new Wing Commander was surprised, because this so seldom happens. I often wondered if Col. McClain was informed and if so, what his reaction was.

Col. Multhrop, Wing Deputy Commander for Operations was promoted to full Col. and transferred to Loring AFB as Wing Commander. It was customary to have a party at the Officers Club for departing senior officers. Air Force regulations prohibited giving expensive gifts to officers, so I tried to come up with something he would keep as a remembrance. Everyone knew he was an ardent golfer and his game would be somewhat curtailed because of the Loring weather, so I wanted to present him with something relevant to golf. I remembered the wooden shafted clubs my Dad used and figured "wood" would not be as affected by the severe cold as much as metal. Also I thought grips wrapped in fur would help keep a player's hands warm. An old canvas golf bag would also be appropriate.

I had a very energetic copilot in the squadron not presently assigned to a crew, so I sent him out to go door to door if he had to, in search of clubs, fur and a bag. Within a few days he reported with exactly what I had in mind. He had already wrapped the grips and I knew everyone at the party would get a big kick out of this

After the party was well under way, I announced that the Bomb Squadron had a presentation to make. The copilot and I had kept the clubs a secret, so when I told Col. Multhrop that we wished him well in his new assignment and having been at Loring myself, the Bomb Squadron had something he would really get a lot of use out of. He would be the envy of everyone on Loring Air Force Base! No one could imagine what we had, until I called the copilot to join us and he walked up with the clubs. Everyone roared and I made sure Col. Multhrop knew the copilot was responsible for locating the clubs. He was dumbfounded and the expression on his face emphasized his appreciation.

The Wing Commander, Col. Pendergast, who replaced Col. McClain was not at Plattsburg very long, but was quickly well liked and respected by the crews. However after being at Plattsburg a relatively short time, he was transferred to a more responsible position in SAC. I will always remember his favorite expression which he frequently used to focus crew members on the "big picture." It went like this. "Don't get stomped by an elephant while swatting fleas."

We planned a party for his departure, so again I had to come up with a meaningful but trivial gift. I had another copilot in the squadron with a power saw mounted in his garage for his wood working hobby. I asked if he could make a gun about 6-8 feet long, we would call an elephant gun. He came to my office a few days later with a beautifully crafted wooden gun. It was an amazing replica of exactly what I had in mind.

The night of the party, I again announced I wished to make a presentation. After going into a dissertation, elaborating on the Col's favorite expression, which everyone was very familiar with, I called the copilot to join us. We then presented Col. Pendergast with his elephant gun, and it was a great hit, especially with the Col's wife. Then, as we had pre-arranged, the Tanker Squadron Commander walked up with a fly swatter, explaining the Tanker Squadron wanted to provide him defense on all fronts. It's difficult to describe the enjoyment I and everyone else got out of these presentations. Senior staff officers in a Bomb Wing were always under severe pressure and to observe the pleasure they showed during and after these presentations, was pure joy.

During an evaluation of the Wing's effectiveness by SAC Headquarters, A B-52, the lead aircraft, crashed shortly after take off from Loring AFB. It was a night take-off; the plane had a full fuel load and was piloted by the Chief of Standardization. Eye witnesses saw the plane climb to about 1000 feet and then appeared to gradually descend straight ahead, with wings level, into the tree tops. I was again selected to be on the Accident Investigation Board and this time as Chief of the Operations Group. I assumed the 8th Air Force Chief of Safety had decided I was the B-52G expert in 8th Air Force and I was pleased to hear Col. Felecias would again be the accident board commander. He seemed very satisfied that I would be part of the operations team and this time, as head of the team. I hoped I was capable of achieving the results expected of me because unfortunately, this time, there were no survivors to interrogate. This would make a huge difference because I could only surmise what transpired in the cockpit before the crash because we did not have "black boxes" or recorders. To make matters worse, there were no communications between the aircraft and a ground facility. I knew my conception may differ from other experienced pilots, so I would have to back up my theory with proven, uncontested facts. My first sight of what was left of the B-52 made me realize how difficult this investigation was going to be.

Shortly after I arrived at Loring, Col. Multhrop gave me a nice greeting and I was invited for dinner in his home. Upon entering his home he immediately directed my attention to the golf clubs which were hanging over his mantle and it was easy to tell he was very proud of them.

The newly appointed Chief of Standardization and his crew were assigned to my team to assist me. Studying the wreckage at the crash site was particularly eerie, mainly because I knew most of the crew members from when I was stationed at Loring. The radar navigator and navigator had attempted to eject but their seats ejected downward and the parachutes did not have time to fully open before hitting the trees. Their bodies were found hanging from the trees along the flight path. The electronics warfare officer ejected upward, but his trajectory landed him in the exploding wreckage, so his remains could barely be identified. The pilot, copilot and gunner "went in" with the plane so the same goes for their remains.

The throttle quadrant was enough intact to determine the position of most of the controls on impact. The condition of the engines was the only positive clue we had for the cause of the crash. The engine experts from Boeing could not see any symptoms of mechanical failure. Five engines appeared to be operating normally, but the tail cones of three engines on one side had the exact indications of a "flame out." As I recall, a flame out during or shortly after take-off, could be caused by an improper fuel/ water ratio during a "water injection" take-off. Under certain weight, temperature and pressure altitude conditions, water was injected into the engine to add additional thrust. Standard procedure was, if certain engine instruments indicated a higher reading than allowed during or immediately after take off, the copilot was to retard the applicable throttle or throttles until they read below the maximum limits. This procedure would not have caused a control problem for the pilot, but there was a warning not to retard the throttles too far on a water injection take-off because of the possibility of a flame out.

The entire investigation was too comprehensive and extensive for me to go into detail in this story. So to be brief, I conducted evaluations in the flight simulator and in an actual B-52 in attempts to duplicate the problems the pilots may have experienced on or immediately after take-off. If engines had flamed out, I assumed that the pilot, in order to maintain lateral control, retarded throttles on the operating side, which would explain the shallow descent. He had to sacrifice altitude for airspeed.

Ground maintenance ran tests on all B-52 G's and found most engines were considerable out of "trim." As I understood it, this meant that the indication on the applicable gauge in the instrument panel gave a higher reading than it actually was, quite possibly resulting in the throttle to be unnecessarily retarded.

With this finding, the cause of the accident was divided between crew error and maintenance; so that's the way I wrote up the investigation report which seemed to satisfy SAC Headquarters.

While I was in the middle of this investigation at Loring, I received a telegram stating that all Reserve Officers with over 20 years of active duty were to be retired. This came as a huge disappointment because I had about one year and a half to go before becoming eligible for full Colonel. I already had just a little over 20 years active duty, so I was on the list to be put out. A promotion to Colonel would have given me a big increase in retirement pay, in addition to the prestige that went with it. I went to the Officer's Club the evening of the day I received the notification and was sitting at the bar when Col. Felecias came in and sat next to me. I mentioned the telegram to him and I remember so well what his response was. "Bill, don't worry, they won't do that to you." Boy, was he wrong!

I returned to Plattsburg and resumed my position as Squadron Commander. My original retirement orders were to be effective in April, but were extended to July 1st in order to allow my son and daughter to complete the school year.

For some reason I was not relieved from my job until the day I retired, which of course was also the day we had to move out of our house. To this day I cannot understand why this happened because anytime I brought the subject to someone's attention, I was ignored or met with a grin. For some reason, I know it was deliberate and somehow thought to be humorous. There were seven of us being retired on the same day and I was the only one not relieved at least a week early because of all the preparations involved.

I assumed that because there were so many of us, the Wing Commander decided to have a Saturday parade in our honor. None of us really planned on retiring at this time, so it was a very thoughtful gesture.

The Friday before the parade the Squadron sponsored a golf tournament in my honor, followed by a dinner and presentations to me at the golf course clubhouse. To my surprise and bewilderment, all flying for that day was cancelled in order for everyone to participate. I had never seen this done before. The tournament was called the "Bill Hubert Open," and a huge sign with that on it was placed over the clubhouse entrance. The men played in the tournament and the wives all brought covered dishes for dinner, after the tournament. Trophies were handed out to the tournament winners and I, not winning one, was given a trophy with "Bill Hubert Open, longest without a trophy," engraved on it. I have it displayed in my home office. I distinctly remember one gift I received. It was well known that I was not able to keep my head down after swinging a club. It's called "looking up." One of the wives made a jock strap with extended straps attached to a golf cap. The cup had some ominous looking long tacks sticking straight up. Of course, this was to prevent me from "looking up," which I'm sure it would have done if I had the courage to wear it. Also, Elmer Bradford, "Brad" who at one time had been my copilot, presented me with a caricature which I really treasure. He was the most versatile, talented; individual I have ever known and was a Lt Col. standardization Aircraft Commander when I retired. . The caption on the caricature reads, "I'm known as wild Bill and I fly for the thrill. But in trouble my ass is, when I forget all my glasses." I had been accused of using separate glasses for take-off, air refueling and landing. He has me sitting on the upper wing of a bi-plane, labeled "Matel." The golf tournament and party were a tremendous tribute for a reserve Lt. Col. to receive and I hope I deserved this flattering recognition.

I retired July 1, 1970, at the age of 45 and really had mixed emotions about leaving the Air Force. Now I would be relieved of the constant pressure faced daily, mainly, from the many responsibilities involved in being a Squadron Commander. This was a big difference to get used too. I was proud of my achievements and career advancement in the Air Force, but also was ready for a change.

CHAPTER EIGHTEEN
STARTING OVER AND TRYING TO "ADAPT"

I had absolutely no idea what career, if any, I would pursue as a civilian. I was too old to be hired by an airline and did not want the irregular hours of a corporate or charter pilot. Anyway, after having primarily made my living as a pilot, I was not sure I wanted to continue flying. Unlike most pilots, I had participated in many different types of flying and had flown a large variety of planes, from very small to the largest and heaviest at that time. Maybe it was time to quit while I was ahead!

While I was Squadron Commander, I was still an instructor and flew at least twice a month with a different crew each flight. I felt it was important to remain current and observe the performance of all Squadron crew members in order to write a realistic annual "effectiveness report" on them. I did not want to admit it, but I think I was glad to get out of aviation for a while. Especially instructing and evaluations.

I had made up my mind long before retiring, the three occupations I wanted nothing to do with were; insurance, real estate and used car salesman. In fact, I did not want any part of being any kind of salesman!

I arranged for an interview with an employment agency. While waiting for my turn to be interviewed I accidentally overheard the types of jobs being offered to a couple of persons ahead of me and was going to "walk out," when I decided to challenge the interviewer. When asked my background experience, I said I was a former bomber pilot, capable of dropping bombs anywhere in the world. She laughed and informed me it would take some time to find me a position and suggested I go to a vocational school and consider a different occupation. In a way, I accepted her suggestion and enrolled full time in a local college. I took courses that would lead to a degree in middle management and realized that I could be a pretty good student if I tried.

I had attended the college for less than a year when I was offered a job with "Difini," a golf clothing manufacturer. For the next two years I was a golf clothing manufacturer sales representative and called on Golf Pros running "pro shops" all over the Southeast. I quit after realizing I drove 50 thousand miles my second year and barely earned enough for gas! My cousin, Eddie Greenleaf got the job for me and I had accepted, after he informed me he was making over $100,000 per year. I must admit I was no "salesman!"

After being retired for several years, I decided to check out in a light plane, strictly flying for pleasure. I went down to the Albert Whitted airport and spotted an Aeronca Champion sitting in front of a flight school building. I went in and asked about checking out in it. One of the instructors seriously emphasized it was a "tail dragger" and very tricky to fly. I had to ask what he meant by "tail dragger?" When he explained, and added that it took a minimum of five hours dual instruction with a certified instructor to check out in the Aeronca, I replied, without trying to sound boastful, that I had instructed in them myself and had a lot of time in Aeroncas. Also I mentioned that the first airplane I checked out in was a Stearman, (tail dragger,) far more difficult to handle on the ground than an Aeronca. He totally ignored this and reiterated it was a tricky plane and required 5 hours of instruction. That was the end of checking out in a "tail dragger"

I went to the St. Pete/Clearwater Airport and in one hour checked out in a piper, "something." It had a tricycle landing gear, was four place, and I enjoyed taking friends for sight seeing flights around the Bay area. This was the type of flying I enjoyed, but I sure hated having to pay to fly. I was always "paid" to fly!

I met a young pilot that who owned a Cessna 150. He offered to let me fly his Cessna anytime I desired at a very minimum charge. It was two place, side by side and great for just "tooling" around the local area. Now I was able to get as much flying time as I desired, when I wanted and not have to please anyone other than myself.

My aunt Ruth, Pete's wife, suggested I join the Civil Air Patrol. (CAP) She had been a member since its inception, or shortly thereafter in the 1940's and was still very active. I joined and again was flying under someone's direction but the difference being this was voluntary. The CAP Pinellas Senior Squadron operated out of the Albert Whitted Airport which was my favorite airport. They had a Cessna 172 assigned, which was four place, so I seldom went up alone. I participated in search missions, cadet orientation flights and sundown patrol. Every Sunday just before sundown, the Squadron launched the Cessna to patrol a given route along the gulf beaches. The purpose was to report to the Coast Guard any boat or person in distress. It was a well coordinated mission.

I would like to add this concerning the CAP. It consists of extremely dedicated, professional volunteers, but unfortunately does not receive the recognition or support it deserves. One thing for sure, non members do not know that members pay for most of their activities. This includes travel, uniforms, conferences and some training in civil activities such as hurricane evacuation, from which all of us may benefit one day.

At the time, the National Commander of the entire CAP program was General Bill Cass. Lt. Col. Joe Lill, a member of our Pinellas Senior Squadron, had been working with General Cass in creating a CAP drug program under the sponsorship and in cooperation with the United States Customs Service.

Under Joe's supervision and with the encouragement and approval of General Cass, the first CAP drug program was established in the Pinellas Senior Squadron, Florida Wing. Joe divided the State into five equally sized sections and appointed a CAP pilot member to head each section. He selected me to take over the section I was in. This covered from Ceder Key, to the North, down to Fort Meyers, the South boundary.

Joe invited me to accompany him and General Cass to several meetings with Customs Service, during which we formulated an operating procedure. They also asked me to design application forms for pilots and other forms they deemed necessary. That was an interesting and meaningful assignment because these forms were eventually recommended for use not only in Florida, but through-out the States, as they entered the drug program.

The intent of the program was to locate boats which Customs determined may be smuggling drugs into the country by way of the Gulf of Mexico. Joe and the General devised a procedure to check and then record the name or number of suspect boats. The CAP pilot was to, retard the throttle so as to reduce the engine noise, drop down to 10 or 12 feet above the water and approach the boat from directly behind. This was to get close enough to read the name or number on the stern of the boat before the persons in the boat realized what was happening. Then after reading the name or number perform an S turn to the right or left and start climbing back to 800 feet flying parallel to the boat's direction. It was a heck of a fun maneuver to do, because normally, the passengers on the boat did not see or hear the plane coming and when power was applied to start climbing, while directly abeam the boat, everyone looked startled because of the sudden roar of the engine. This was my kind of flying and I personally, had to check out every pilot in my section that volunteered for the program, which included the Florida Wing Commander.

Joe Lill invited me to visit the section heads in the other Florida Sections to explain the forms and flight procedure. My section had already started coordinating with Customs and I had flown a number of flights, so I was prepared to speak with some confidence. I guess I was the "voice of experience."

Eventually the CAP Drug program received Cessna 182's paid for by the U.S. Air Force. I should mention, the CAP is an Arm of the Air Force. The Cessna 182 had a retractable landing gear which made the practicability of surviving after ditching in the Gulf much more feasible. Our search tracks usually took us 60 miles out from the coast line, so there was always was that possibility.

The CAP held a National Conference each year in various parts of the country. And each year I was asked to attend and present a briefing on the drug program. I always enjoyed the conferences.

General Cass completed his tour as CAP Commander, so Joe no longer had the full support of CAP Headquarters. Joe was not the most tactful person in the world and on occasion, provoked the Florida Wing

CAP Commander. The program was really operating very smoothly when suddenly; Joe was fired from the job. The reason was never fully exposed, but I suspected a personality conflict had taken place.

Joe had put his heart into the program and his hurt was obvious. I, being his closest deputy, tried to console him, but when I was named as his replacement, he became very aloof. At least he had the satisfaction of knowing he created and put into operation, a program that had now spread to all the Border States.

One problem I encountered at the onset, was recruiting qualified pilots. Quite often I heard discussions about the possibility of getting shot at, or the aircraft being sabotaged while parked on the ramp. Sugar in the fuel tank was the most usual sabotage worry. Because of these considerations and the fact that most pilots had full day time jobs, added to the recruitment problem. As a result of this, I frequently flew 4 hour flights, two or three times a week, and for some reason was never too concerned about sabotage.

Operating the program for the entire Wing entailed a lot of paper work. I processed every application and all other applicable forms prior to giving them to the Wing Commander for his approval. I also had forms to send to CAP National Headquarters so pilots, who were required to pay for fuel they used, would receive reimbursement. The process required a lot of record keeping and sometimes the Government was very slow in repayment.

The Wing Commander was a bottleneck in the application process. For some reason, he was slow in approving new pilot applicants, which caused undue difficulty for the Section Leaders, including myself. By this time, it seemed to me, that I was getting instructions from ranking CAP members that knew nothing about the drug operation. The Wing Commander seemed to have lost interest in the program and was probably fearful something might happen to blemish his record. I think he had aspirations of becoming National Commander that would make him a Brigadier General! While all this was going on, I was working full time in Real Estate. (One of the things I vowed never to do) I was one busy person!

The program had been in operation for several years and I felt my paper work requirements needed some streamlining. The Wing Commander was not responding to any of my problems, so I wrote a detailed letter to the National Commander of the Civil Air Patrol. Of course, I knew after having been in the service all those years, abiding by the "chain of Command" policy, was essential, but I bypassed that nonsense. I did not receive a response from Headquarters, but very quickly heard from the Florida Wing Commander. My letter was not very flattering toward him, in fact, much the opposite. He was really irate and I was immediately fired for insubordination. My job was given to the Section Leader in Fort Meyers and I was actually grateful because Joe Lill and I became good friends again. I also think he was proud of me. The Wing Commander did allow me to continue flying drug missions, probably because there were so few qualified pilots available.

A very intelligent, likeable person, Harry Brugman, took my job as Section Leader. He had helped me immensely in the past, so he fit right in.

I had one interesting, challenging and different type of drug mission. Harry asked me to pickup a Customs agent at Clearwater Airport, carry him to Sarasota and follow a drug suspect's car, while he supposedly delivered drugs along a busy highway. We were to spot his car, which thankfully was yellow, parked at the restaurant where he ate lunch every day. The restaurant and proposed route he would travel were within the immediate control of the Sarasota control tower so I obviously was going to be a menace to local air traffic. Sarasota is a very busy airport. Without revealing our actual mission, I explained to the tower, as best I could, where I would be maneuvering. The tower operator was very cooperative and requested I keep him advised as to my proposed route, but I had no idea what that would be!

We spotted the car parked at the restaurant and began orbiting. In a short time we saw the car pull out of the restaurant parking lot and enter the busy highway. I was asked not to lose sight of him, but also remain at a distance that would not cause suspicion. In the meantime, I had to keep the control tower advised. I realized this was not going to be easy so I instructed the copilot to watch for other air traffic in order that I could concentrate on flying the plane and keeping the car in sight. The yellow car made several stops and we orbited, while attempting to remain inconspicuous. Several times our orbit took us directly through the airport landing flight path and this gave me a very uncomfortable feeling, even after being cleared by the tower. This went on for a couple of hours and I was getting very tired, when the yellow car headed over a causeway leading to the Gulf Beaches. Just then the Customs Agent recognized an unmarked Customs car trailing behind the suspect car and our part of this was over. I landed at Sarasota for fuel, carried the Customs Agent back to Clearwater and finally headed back to Albert Whitted Airport. That was a brand new experience for me. I would not care to do it again.

When I turned 65, I began having serious medical problems. In one year I was in the hospital five times requiring surgery four of the times. I was either laid up or recovering so did not attempt to do any flying. When I finally completely recovered the last time, I pretty much decided to put that part of my life behind me. My hearing had deteriorated to the point I had trouble complying with the many in-flight communications modern aviation required and I was having cataracts forming on both eyes. I probably could not pass the physical.

By this time I had accumulated almost 10,000 hrs of much diversified flight experiences starting when I was 18 years old and until I was 65. In those years I had gone from single engine, to twin engines, to 4 engines to six engines and finally 8 engines and then back to a single engine. I consider myself fortunate to have learned to fly in prop driven planes and eventually go into jets. I personally think there is a very significant difference between props and jets that starts when first planning a flight. I have met former Air Force pilots that have never sat in a prop driven aircraft. I believe these pilots have missed part of the experience and challenge prop planes have to offer. One might say I have run the "gamut." I must admit, I never have really "missed" flying. Some pilots express themselves about flying by saying, "I just want to be up there," but I never really had that feeling. I think maybe just the many diversified challenges and uncertainties, were my primary driving force, along with pride in some of my achievements. I certainly had to "swallow" my pride on occasions which probably intensified my challenge to show "I could do it." Many, many pilots far exceeded my accomplishments, but as I mentioned several times, I was always aware of my limitations, so therefore "limited" myself accordingly!

For the past thirty years I have been a licensed Real Estate Associate. If you will recall that is one profession I definitely did want to get into! For many years I was very active, specializing in condominium sales and rentals. For the past few years I have limited my activities to rentals, inter-mixed with an occasional sale. I work out of my home which I find very convenient.

I have lost track of all but five of the friends I have mentioned in my story and one other, Bill Nichols, who was the Tanker Squadron Commander at Plattsburg at the same time I was the Bomber Squadron Commander. Bill and his wife Jan, came to St. Petersburg after retiring from the Air Force, a full Colonel, about three years after me. We occasionally have lunch together which I really enjoy.

Over the years I have kept track of Monroe Hatch who had been my copilot for almost five years both in B-47's and B-52's. Monroe had an extremely successful career and as I mentioned earlier retired with the rank of Four Star General. Monroe and his wife Delores, recently purchased a home in Sun City Florida and I had the pleasure and honor of having lunch with them a short time ago. You can't imagine how much I enjoyed that. I must confess I was quite nervous about being with a Four Star General and I had to keep reminding myself that at one time I was his boss. When he came to my door to pick me up, he immediately put me at ease by sincerely showing me how happy he was to see me.

We agreed to do it again the following year.

I have always kept track of Jim Cronin my mentor and neighborhood friend that I've known since I was five years old. He had not been to Florida since leaving in 1947, so a few years ago I tried to convince him that he should come down for a visit. About the same time a friend of mine, Gwen Lightsey, located Craig Anneberg as a result of her expertise on the computer. I had not seen or heard from him since we parted at Rapid City, South Dakota in October, 1945. This was in the year 2000, 55 years later. Shortly after I called him, he arranged to come down to Florida from the State of Washington where he lived. We had a great time, even though "he" was much older and I had not aged! Craig has been visiting every year since then. When I informed Jim Cronin about what a great time us "old" guys had, he agreed to join us the following year. We have made this into an annual affair we really look forward to. Jim spent his life as a court recorder in the Chicago area and Craig was quite successful in the lumber business. Fortunately, they both like beer, so it can't be said that we have nothing in common! One other friend Craig and I were with during World War 11 was John Barber. We call him while Craig is here and invite him to join us, but his wife will not allow him to leave. (?)

The fifth person I am in touch with is Bill Winsor. He moved to St. Petersburg after retiring from the Air Force, but shortly after I retired, he moved to Tennessee. Bill was Chief of Standardization at Loring AFB and then, Squadron Commander at Plattsburg. He has visited me a number of times and makes it a point to tell my friends what a "screw up" I was when he was my Squadron Commander. I remind him how terrified I was of him, especially as Chief of Standization and how strict he was when he was my Squadron Commander.

I still have ties with the military presently being a member of an American Legion Post on Treasure Island, Florida, close to my home. It is an extremely active Post so I drop in quite often. I think there are close to 300 members and we have determined that only three of us were World War 11 veterans. What does that tell me? I am fortunate enough to receive excellent medical treatment at the Bay Pines Veteran's Hospital in St. Petersburg, FL and on occasion frequent the MacDill AFB Commissary, Base Exchange and Liquor Store.

I would like to end my story by stating that I have had a pretty interesting life and I am particularly grateful to the military for allowing me to achieve a somewhat rewarding career. I have had the privilege of competing with and working side by side, many very special people. This, in addition to the many benefits available to veterans is all that anyone could hope for in this life.